Monsters and Monstrosity from
the Fin de Siècle to the Millennium

Monsters and Monstrosity from the Fin de Siècle to the Millennium

New Essays

Edited by SHARLA HUTCHISON *and* REBECCA A. BROWN

McFarland & Company, Inc., Publishers
Jefferson, North Carolina

LIBRARY OF CONGRESS CATALOGUING-IN-PUBLICATION DATA

Monsters and monstrosity from the fin de siècle to the millennium : new essays / edited by Sharla Hutchison and Rebecca A. Brown.
    p.   cm.
Includes bibliographical references and index.

ISBN 978-0-7864-9506-1 (softcover : acid free paper) ∞
ISBN 978-1-4766-2271-2 (ebook)

1. Monsters in mass media.   2. Monsters in literature.
3. Monsters in motion pictures.   4. Zombies in popular culture.
5. Zombies in literature.   6. Zombies in motion pictures.
7. Vampires in popular culture.   8. Vampires in literature.
9. Vampires in motion pictures.   I. Hutchison, Sharla, 1970– editor.   II. Brown, Rebecca A., 1976– editor.

P96.M6M66 2015
809'.9337—dc23   2015025559

BRITISH LIBRARY CATALOGUING DATA ARE AVAILABLE

© 2015 Sharla Hutchison and Rebecca A. Brown. All rights reserved

No part of this book may be reproduced or transmitted in any form or by any means, electronic or mechanical, including photocopying or recording, or by any information storage and retrieval system, without permission in writing from the publisher.

Front cover image © 2015 iStock/Thinkstock

Printed in the United States of America

McFarland & Company, Inc., Publishers
  Box 611, Jefferson, North Carolina 28640
  www.mcfarlandpub.com

Acknowledgments

The editors would like to acknowledge the contributors for their hard work and patience throughout the drafting and editing process. They would also like to thank family and friends for their ongoing support.

Rebecca would like to specifically thank her husband for his ever-present love and patience as well as the baristas at Uptown Coffee, Chocolati, Fremont Coffee, and Muddy Cup for keeping her caffeinated while working on this project.

Sharla would like to specifically thank her partner, family, and close colleagues, all of whom offered the quiet comfort and support needed to complete this project.

Table of Contents

Acknowledgments — v

Introduction
    Sharla Hutchison *and* Rebecca A. Brown — 1

Part I: Forgotten Monsters and Social Unrest

"She has a parasite soul!" The Pathologization of the Gothic Monster as Parasitic Hybrid in Bram Stoker's *Dracula*, Richard Marsh's *The Beetle* and Arthur Conan Doyle's *The Parasite*
    Emilie Taylor-Brown — 12

Marie Corelli's *Ziska*: A Gothic Egyptian Ghost Story
    Sharla Hutchison — 29

The Queer God Pan: Terror and Apocalypse, Reimagined
    Mark De Cicco — 49

Attack of the Mushroom People: Ishirô Honda's *Matango* and William Hope Hodgson's "The Voice in the Night"
    Anthony Camara — 69

Part II: Monstrous Violations of Private Life

Through the Eyes of the Monster: Angela Carter's "The Lady of the House of Love"
    Jameela F. Dallis — 92

Re-Vamping the Early 1960s: Freakish Vampires and Monstrous Teens in Richard Laymon's *The Traveling Vampire Show*
    Rebecca A. Brown — 111

Gothic Commodification of the Body and the Modern Literary Serial Killer in *Child of God* and *American Psycho*
    Christopher Coughlin — 129

Rocking and Reeling through the Doors of Miscreation:
  Disequilibrium in Shirley Jackson's *The Haunting of Hill House*
    SUSAN POZNAR   144

Part III: Millennial Monsters

"I think I am a monster": Helen Oyeyemi's *White Is for Witching*
  and the Postmodern Gothic
    BIANCA TREDENNICK   168

"Madness and monstrosity": Notions of the Gothic and Sublime in
  Comics Adaptations of H. P. Lovecraft
    REBECCA JANICKER   187

The Monster of Massification: *A Serbian Film*
    L. ANDREW COOPER   206

"Bears that dance, bears that don't": Aggression, Civilization and
  the Gothic Bear
    JULIE WILHELM *and* STEVEN J. ZANI   228

About the Contributors   245

Index   247

Introduction

SHARLA HUTCHISON *and*
REBECCA A. BROWN

It is no longer a truth universally acknowledged by Gothic, horror, and fairy tale critics that a single monster in possession of immense hunger must solely represent repressed transhistorical fears. The word *monster*, which derives from *monstrum*, meaning "'that which reveals,' 'that which warns'" (Cohen 4), is a harbinger of change, a signifier of futurity, and fifteen years into the twenty-first century, we are unlikely, as our Renaissance predecessors were, to read a limbless child as a symbol of God's displeasure at our licentious behavior (Burnett 26). In short, we have redefined what monsters are, and in tangent with that project, we understand that contemporary monsters—human killers, animalistic hybrids, fictional beasties—possess more meanings than ever and are consistently subject to metamorphosis. Consequently, monsters' bodies and behaviors are read as unbounded signifiers and symptoms of various socio-historical, socio-political, and socio-cultural anxieties, including, but not limited to, gender roles, the marginalization of racially, ethnically, and sexually othered peoples, geographical transformations, postcolonial woes, and the vagaries of capitalism (Halberstam 21–22).

It is, however, a truth universally acknowledged that inserting a myriad of monsters into a Jane Austen novel—*Mansfield Park and Mummies: Monster Mayhem, Matrimony, Ancient Curses, True Love, and Other Dire Delights* (2009), *Sense and Sensibility and Sea Monsters* (2009)—results in stupendous sales and infinite offshoots (*Jane Slayre* [2010]), reminding us that monsters are, in fact, commodities. Catherine Spooner addresses this issue by declaring that the Gothic mode, of which monsters are often part and parcel, is "profoundly concerned with its own past, self-referentially dependent on traces of other stories, familiar images and narrative structures, intertextual allusions. If this could be said to be true of a great many kinds of literature or film, then Gothic has a greater degree of self-consciousness about its nature, cannibalistically consuming the dead body of its own tradition" (10). Less symbols of millennial Gothic anxiety, the inclusion of monsters in a variety of media and products in the late twentieth and early twenty-first century—from breakfast cereals (Count Chocula) to television shows (Cookie Monster), from car commercials (Frankenstein's creature) to narrative picture books (*Zombie in Love* [2011]), from Barbie Doll variants (*Monster High*) to crocheted cuties (Cthulhu)—ensures that we buy the product and the monster attached to it, endowing us with a sense of control fictional and cinematic characters rarely experience when threatened with or by the monstrous. Of course, Renaissance cartographer Olaus Magnus, first-wave Gothic fiction writer Mrs. Carver, Victorian bestseller Bram Stoker, and twentieth-century occultist author Dennis Wheatley were all aware that the inclusion of monsters helped sell maps, books, and other cultural ephemera and that their audiences enjoyed being shocked, titillated, and scared to death by/of aquatic animals, grave robbers, transformative parasites, and Satanic nightmares. So it seems that monsters may (simultaneously) represent the Freudian and Jungian repressed, socio-cultural transformations and anxieties as well as commodity culture. We, in turn, remain obsessed by their sometimes destructive, sometimes domesticated, always unpredictable presence, consistently seduced by the possibility of learning from them or about them so as to understand our selves, our societies, our nations, and even our increasing globalization.

Capitalizing on monsters' burgeoning socio-cultural presence and the escalating popularity of all things Gothic, academic monster studies, in the wake of such 1990s luminaries as Noël Carroll (*The Philosophy of Horror* [1990]), Judith/Jack Halberstam (*Skin Shows: Gothic Horror and the Technology of Monsters* [1995]), Nina Auerbach (*Our Vampires, Ourselves* [1995]), Kelly Hurley (*The Gothic Body: Sexuality, Materialism, and Degeneration at the Fin de Siècle* [1996]), Jeffrey Jerome Cohen (ed., *Monster Theory* [1997]), and Marina Warner (*No Go, the Boogeyman: Scaring, Lulling, and Making Mock* [1999]), have become, like monsters themselves, such a prolific niche market that the publication of the *Ashgate Research Companion to Monsters and the Monstrous* (2012) seems only apropos. Currently, we can glean ideas about the place and significance of monsters and monstrosity in several eras of British literature and culture: *Constructing "Monsters" in Shakespearean Drama and Early Modern Culture* (2002), *Monstrosities: Bodies and British Romanticism* (2003), *Medieval Monstrosity and the Female Body* (2010), and *Monstrous Motherhood: Eighteenth-Century Culture and the Ideology of Domesticity* (2012). Similarly, creature-based studies—*American Zombie Gothic: The Rise and Fall (and Rise) of the Walking Dead in Popular Culture* (2010), *Werewolves and Other Shapeshifters in Popular Gothic: A Thematic Analysis of Recent*

Depictions (2012)—as well as medium-based monographs—*The Vampire Film: From Nosferatu to True Blood* (2011, 4th ed.), *Gothic in Comics and Graphic Novels: A Critical Approach* (2014)—and works that explore the vital overlap amongst the monstrous, race, and nation—*Black Frankenstein: The Making of an American Metaphor* (2008), *Writing Monsters: Essays on Iberian and Latin American Cultures* (*Hispanic Issues* Vol. 15, 2014)—can all be readily obtained through academic and non-academic presses. And what is remarkable about most of these works is that, whether they emphasize Gothic, horror, or popular culture in their titles, they demonstrate the ways that monsters cannot be contained by mediums or eras or modes, and that the centrality of the body, particularly the non-normative one (female body, queer body, black body), remains essential to studies of monstrosity, even as we hurtle ever and anon towards cyberspace disembodiment in our daily lives.[1]

A simple, yet significant question arises then from these long-winded prefatory remarks: aside from capitalizing upon current trends and attempting to inveigle money from the public, why publish yet another study on monsters? What does our little book offer discerning academic and non-academic reading audiences that others do not?

Our study seeks to accomplish several tasks. First, our contributors focus on two kinds of monsters and images of monstrosity within American, European, Japanese, and Serbian contexts: those that have escaped the general confines of criticism, such as the deity Pan, the Gothic Bear, mushroom people, and Lovecraftian monstrosities as well as these familiar works whose monsters and images of monstrosity are read anew, including the titular edifice in *The Haunting of Hill House* (1959), Patrick Bateman in *American Psycho* (1991), the vampire in "The Lady of the House of Love" (1979), and Dracula and his late–Victorian progeny. This is to say, our study juxtaposes the familiar with the unfamiliar, seeking to create an uncanny effect where what seems new to academic criticism—Richard Laymon's ultra-sexy female vampire in *The Traveling Vampire Show* (2001)—is read, nonetheless, within the context of established monster theory and what is not new—Lester Ballard in Cormac McCarthy's *Child of God* (1973)—is read through the lens of monstrosity to make it different. In doing so, we hope to extend ongoing academic conversations about monsters and monstrosity as well as to push the proverbial envelope towards an increasing awareness of what these monsters or familiar texts might teach us differently.

However, there is more that we offer. We focus on monstrosity in its threatening, violent, corporeally transgressive, abhuman, all-consuming forms that provoke effects such as shock and horror rather than domesticated or humanized monsters in popular culture and fiction who would like to be our friends and neighbors. To this end, while we showcase a variety of bodies in this study and consequently allow each contributor to define monster or monstrosity based on the nuances of his or her text, there are patterns several contributors adhere to throughout these essays. Kelley Hurley argues that the monster is ultimately one of the most important features of Gothic fiction, referring to "monsters" as "liminal bodies," each one an abject spectacle in which a disturbing portrait of abhuman identity is envisioned as "that [which] occup[ies] the threshold between the two terms of an opposition, like human/beast, male/female, or civilized/primitive" ("British Gothic Fiction" 190). Noël Carroll refers to such "liminal bodies" as "categorically interstitial, categorically contradictory, incomplete, or formless" (32). According to Julia Kristeva, an abject body produces disgust and revulsion because such a body trespasses into what is seemingly unthinkable, and in doing so, "disturbs identity, system, order" (4). Our contributors largely examine living-dead bodies in a state of decay, the half-human, half-other hybrid, animalistic, or the indescribable, oozing, gelatinous organisms—in short, repugnant visions of bodily corruption. The monstrous bodies we explore, then, represent contamination and threaten an orderly vision of human existence; they break down cultural categories and signify social taboos. Our monsters disturb our sense of safety and order, and yet with that certain distance allowed by fiction and film, the arousal of emotional agitation caused by imagining a monster enables audiences to safely experience the unimaginable in small shocks. As Carroll astutely observes, the origins of the term "emotion" are particularly instructive: "The word 'emotion' comes from the Latin 'emovere' which combines the notion 'to move' with the prefix for 'out.' An *emotion* originally was a *moving* out" (24). That is to say, it is the transitory quality of the emotions experienced, the small shocks of fear and disgust that momentarily *move* or disturb audiences upon viewing the monstrous that enables audiences to imagine the unthinkable. In sum, and not to put too fine a point in the matter, our contributors analyze a range of monsters that would frighten Charlaine Harris' Bill Compton and would undoubtedly eat the Cullen family for dinner, without the requisite side of fava beans and a nice Chianti.

    Finally, and no less importantly, by limiting our focus in this study from the late–Victorian period to the present, we accomplish another task. We highlight the sheer range of horrid, fearsome creatures that emerged in a short span of time—serial killers, "freaks," vampires, parasites, Egyptian ghost femme fatales, deities, bears, mushroom people—from roughly the 1890s to the 2010s. Consequently, we chart an exciting transition, from texts featuring bodies/creatures/beasties that are monstrous to entities/concepts (such as novels, films, and graphic novels) that are monstrous. As contributor L. Andrew Cooper declares, the outrage created by *A Serbian Film* (2010) "suggests that the movie is a monster to be contained; like many monsters, the movie hurts people, leading them into legal danger, self-harm, and troubled psyches." Cooper goes on to say, "I use *A Serbian Film* to interrogate how a film text can transition from being *about* (representing) monstrosity to *becoming* monstrosity and to address the social and political significance of the mediated object's apparent transformative agency." In a similar vein, Bianca Tredennick's essay about the novel *White Is for Witching* (2009) and Rebecca Janicker's essay concerning Lovecraftian graphic novel adaptations shows us a similar transition—that novels and comics consume monsters as well as depict consuming monsters. Ultimately, the texts become monstrous themselves.[2] Unlike *A Serbian Film*, *White Is for Witching* and graphic novels do not emotionally harm audiences, and their social and political significance is notably different for reasons which the respective authors address.

Why is it that the late–Victorian period to the present allows us to survey these particular concerns? What is uniquely interesting about the horrors that migrated into numerous nineteenth and twentieth-century texts is the variation and availability of monsters made possible through increased literacy and mass production. In England, mass literacy, made possible through Forsters Education Act (1870), combined with improved mechanical technology for book production and the advent of lending libraries to usher in an era in which debates about the evils of reading novels actually masked what Patrick Brantlinger outlines as Victorian social fears about national progress rather than any truly "pathological" fictions (18). As Brantlinger attests, a long history exists regarding the vilification of the popular novel in its various nineteenth-century genres—Gothic romance, penny dreadfuls, shilling shockers, sensational fiction, crime fiction and any number of recombined popular forms—all of which were objected to on the moral grounds that, when read for pure entertainment, fiction could lead to social vice and personal disease in the form of sexual licentiousness, the promotion of criminal activity, and personal laziness. With the late Victorians, for the first time in history, reading actually becomes an avenue to mass entertainment; fiction becomes an "extraordinary shock or thrill" to excite the reader (Brantlinger 143). Reading audiences were not disappointed, but the public debates registered anxious questions about the purpose and function of mass entertainment. (To some degree, such debates continue today, but obviously the terms of the debate have shifted to focus on new mediums, primarily digital media.) Fin de siècle entertainment novelties created mass access to unspeakable monsters, making what were once not so easily imagined by individuals far more imaginable in a collective literacy.

Late-Victorian fiction trafficked in strange proliferations of monsters that emerged in popular fiction, offering readers a parade of horrifying entities: demon-possessed sexual sirens, vampires, werewolves, mummies, shape-shifting human hybrids, zombies, ghosts, and various other undeads. Gothic fiction, previously characterized by encounters with the sublime, power-hungry aristocrats, and haunted castles, became re-harnessed for mass culture during the late-Victorian era, and its villain, the monster, morphed into strange subhuman forms. Simultaneously frightening and entertaining, these monsters expressed a variety of cultural anxieties and fears familiar to readers: female power, sexual transgression, disease, foreign wars, imperial policies, and criminal violence.

Not unlike the wild ride of fin de siècle popular fiction, the twentieth century monster reveals historically relevant ideological motifs, even as writers adapt and reinvent the monstrous body while drawing on past visions of terror: bioterror, torture, sexual transgression, murder, mental illness, and cannibalizing consumerism. As Jack Morgan notes, horror tales—narratives about plagues, sadistic torture, serial murder, and occultism—extend from their historical basis in mythological and medieval lore to manifest in contemporary renderings of bioterrorism, uncontrolled contagion, genetic engineering run amok, serial murder, and cannibalizing evils (41). Each part of this book contains essays that examine different incarnations of horrors made possible through the reconfiguration of monstrosity through cultural memory, the remnants of past embodied terrors grafted onto material bodies. The results are portraits of monsters signifying danger, social fear, and/or social questions specific to a particular cultural milieu. Beyond the emotional thrill of shock and horror, the monsters examined here—shape-shifting sexual beings, female murderesses, parasitic diseases, fungus-people, occult powers, traveling vampires, necrophiliacs, hauntings, snuff films, untamable beasts—enable an outlet by which writers and audiences share social anxieties.

The horrors of monsters are often imagined in how and what they threaten, from an attack on the individual to possible attacks on larger common denominators, such as family (home), city (community), nation (social order), and world (humankind). The essays in each of our book's three parts reflect such fears as well as our aim to expose the symbolic commodification of these creatures (or their engagement with the mechanisms of commodification). Many of the forgotten monsters in part one reflect transformations that individual bodies undergo sexually, spiritually, or biologically before threatening social mores. While these neo-Gothic monsters of the late-

Victorian era manifest traces of the first wave of Gothic monsters emerging in the late eighteenth and early nineteenth century, they likewise consume traditions as diverse as the ghost story and mythology. They are, in short, simultaneously simulacra and "originals" due to their socio-cultural and scientific resonances with fin de siècle concerns about embodiment, identity, and subjectivity. The essays in the final two parts implicitly justify why the Gothic monster enjoyed a resurgence of interest in the years following the global upheaval of World War II, years marked by civil, social, and racial unrest—the Vietnam War, de-colonization, the Women's Movements(s)—and the proliferation of consumerism. They interrogate gendered, spatial, and epistemological concerns through depictions of subhuman and disembodied monsters. In the second part, the essays focus on communities under siege by monsters threatening to destabilize normalcy, and they amplify the Gothic's self-referentiality and cannibalistic tendencies. As liminal figures comprised of the traces of past and present, these monsters not only consume the subjects of their fictional worlds but transgress genre boundaries with greater self-awareness than those in late–Victorian fiction. The essays focusing on millennial monsters in the third part share a different commonality—the labyrinthine designs that make fear possible are their own monstrosity, the very designs inherent in novel/genre production, war, film direction, nation-states, and economic structures. These works simultaneously offer a meditation on the Gothic monster's postmodern turn towards hyperreality and disembodiment, while simultaneously attesting to the Gothic's unbounded permeation across all forms of media (Edwards and Monnet 1–18).

The book begins with Emilie Taylor-Brown's essay on parasitism in *Dracula*, *The Beetle*, and *The Parasite*. While she tackles a familiar trio of late–Victorian texts, Taylor-Brown asks us to read them anew by placing them within the context of the "literary parasite" and demonstrating how they deviate from this trope through their overlapping Victorian scientific and imperialist concerns. Next, Sharla Hutchison continues investigating British imperialist legacies but within a very different work, Marie Corelli's reincarnation revenge narrative *Ziska: The Problem of a Wicked Soul* (1897). Hutchison's analysis resonates with and expands Taylor-Brown's discussions of the paranormal and female victimization by examining Egyptian femme fatale Ziska and her monstrous feminist legacies. Mark De Cicco, like Hutchison, also tackles a forgotten monster, albeit one whose wrath manifests itself differently than Ziska's. De Cicco examines Pan's transformation in British literature and culture from a more ambivalent pastoral deity to a queered monstrous one who anticipates the creatures in Weird Fiction and twentieth-century horror films. Our first part concludes with Anthony Camara's analysis of the Japanese horror film *Matango* (1963). As he demonstrates, the movie is an adaptation of Weird Fiction writer William Hope Hodgson's story "The Voice in the Night" (1907). The liminal embodiment De Cicco and Hutchison discuss and the anxieties concerning national identity that Taylor-Brown explores find especial significance in Camara's piece.

In part two, we largely focus on familiar texts to bring to light several tropes and anxieties associated with the fifties through the nineties in mostly American works. Jameela F. Dallis explores the Tarot as monstrous in Angela Carter's domestic vampire story "The Lady in the House of Love." As Dallis remarks, "Carter's narrative elucidates that despite the repression and exclusion of what dominant forces consider non-rational or threatening to the order of the regimes they establish, the peoples and ideas they seek to silence and contain—abject, monstrous things—remain at the root of what they strive to keep pure and unadulterated." This claim both resonates profoundly with the examinations of imperialism in part one and frames the domestic unease underlying the essays in the remainder of part two. To this end, Rebecca A. Brown links the subversive behaviors of Cold War women and teens to the figure of the vampire in Richard Laymon's freaky domestic romp *The Traveling Vampire Show*, a book that also capitalizes on the commodification of the "freak" in the sideshows of America's past. Christopher Coughlin then explores American visions of monstrosity by investigating fictional serial killers; his essay demonstrates how the commodification of female corpses in Cormac McCarthy's *A Child of God* and Bret Easton Ellis' *American Psycho* enables two nefarious male characters from different socio-economic backgrounds to construct (in)stable subject positions. Susan Poznar concludes this section by tackling Shirley Jackson's seminal novel *The Haunting of Hill House*. By investigating the house's (and by extension, the novel's) architectural disequilibrium and myriad absences, she posits that Jackson "injects distortion, instability, and uncertainty into the dynamics, not only of Hill House, but of the reading experience itself," thereby anticipating the postmodern concerns that frame the third part of our book.

Part three features a series of texts that have been subject to little academic scrutiny and that reflect the late twentieth and early twenty-first century turns towards Gothic multi-media and globalization. We begin with Bianca Tredennick's analysis of the postmodern Gothic work *White Is for Witching*, a novel that channels nineteenth- and twentieth-century vampire imagery, and casts the novel itself as a monstrous, consuming haunted house. Next, Rebecca Janicker discusses Lovecraftian graphic novel adaptations; she considers the significance of the visual in these works by investigating landscape as well as other imagery to demonstrate how the graphic novel becomes monstrous. L. Andrew Cooper shifts part three's focus from print to celluloid by interrogating *A Serbian Film* as a monster that doubles with the film's monstrous snuff director. Part three concludes with Julie Wilhelm and Steven J. Zani's Janus-faced meditation on the Gothic Bear to illustrate how this particular monster not only channels the first wave of Gothicism through the animal's embodiment of terror and horror, but also how the Bear's appropriation by artists as diverse as Pixar and Werner Herzog can render it a monster that threatens or "comforts." As Wilhelm and Zani imply, the Gothic Bear, a confluence of nature, culture, and folklore, may also harbor a capacity for hope and restoration that eludes other monsters and monstrosities.

Monsters, when understood as transgressive beings, produce an ambivalence that often introduces both subversive fantasies about chaos and conservative desires to restore social order. Many of the monsters our contributors examine leave chaos in their wake and reveal that while those restorative desires may remain, there are no simple methods for achieving social cohesion within British, American, Serbian, Japanese, or global culture more generally. Nonetheless, these texts and the monsters within them act as powerfully revelatory reflections about who we fear, who we fear we are, or who we fear we will become.

Notes

1. See also monster studies that span larger periods of time, such as the recent Interdisciplinary Press publications *Beyond the Monstrous: Reading from the Cultural Imaginary* (2013) and *Monstrous Deviations in Literature and Art* (2011) as well as Alexa Wright's fascinating study *The Human Monster in Visual Culture* (2013).

2. While we generally define the term monster within this introduction and connect the monster to an entity with a material body or a textual body with agency, we also use the term monstrous in a related, but slightly different way in this introduction and in various essays in the book. Here, the monstrous can be understood from a cultural studies/anthropological approach as an "overdetermined" image full of cultural meanings, an amalgamation of multiple social fears projected on/in/through a material body. If the monstrous is understood as abject in Kristeva's terms, then what makes the monstrous (the culturally unthinkable) thinkable are remnants of old and/or new cultural images signifying fear and monstrosity that emerge from and diverge from the past and/or present images. Certain images recognized as monsters can be understood as comfortably normative or shockingly non-normative, but the monstrous as circulated between producer and consumer, is part of a consumeristically-culturally cannibalistic process.

Works Cited

Brantlinger, Patrick. *The Reading Lesson: The Threat of Mass Literacy in Nineteenth-Century Fiction*. Bloomington: Indiana University Press, 1998. Print.

Burnett, Mark Thornton. *Constructing "Monsters" in Shakespearean Drama and Early Modern Culture*. Basingstoke: Palgrave Macmillan, 2002. Print.

Carroll, Noël. *The Philosophy of Horror or Paradoxes of the Heart*. New York: Routledge, 1990. Print.

Cohen, Jeffrey Jerome. "Monster Culture (Seven Theses)." *Monster Theory: Reading Culture*. Ed. Jeffrey Jerome Cohen. Minneapolis: University of Minnesota Press, 1996. 3–25. Print.

Edwards, Justin, and Agnieszka Soltysik Monnet, eds. *The Gothic in Contemporary Literature and Popular Culture: Pop Goth*. New York: Routledge, 2012. Print.

Halberstam, Judith. *Skin Shows: Gothic Horror and the Technology of Monsters*. Durham: Duke University Press, 1995. Print.

Hurley, Kelly. "British Gothic Fiction, 1885–1930." *The Cambridge Companion to Gothic Fiction*. Ed. Jerrold E. Hogle. Cambridge: Cambridge University Press, 2002. 189–207. Print.

_____.*The Gothic Body: Sexuality, Materialism, and Degeneration at the Fin De Siècle*. Cambridge: Cambridge University Press, 1996. Print.

Kristeva, Julia. *Powers of Horror: An Essay on Abjection*. New York: Columbia University Press, 1982. Print.

Morgan, Jack. *The Biology of Horror: Gothic Literature and Film*. Carbondale: Southern Illinois University Press, 2002. Print.

Spooner, Catherine. *Contemporary Gothic*. London: Reaktion Books, 2006. Print.

Part I

Forgotten Monsters and Social Unrest

"She has a parasite soul!"
The Pathologization of the Gothic Monster as Parasitic Hybrid in Bram Stoker's *Dracula*, Richard Marsh's *The Beetle* and Arthur Conan Doyle's *The Parasite*

Emilie Taylor-Brown

The late nineteenth century saw the publication of three texts with striking representations of social and somatic domination. In these works, the Victorian paranoia concerning social degeneration, compounded by a nexus of evolutionary, psychoanalytic and imperial discourses, was expressed as a Gothic reimagining of monstrous social hierarchies. Glennis Byron notes that "as concerns about national, social and psychic decay began to multiply in late Victorian Britain, so Gothic monstrosity re-emerged with a force that had not been matched since the publication of the original Gothic, at the previous *fin-de-siècle*" (187). Bram Stoker, Richard Marsh and Arthur Conan Doyle offer power-play narratives that combine psychological, social, and somatic threats to create just this forceful Gothic reawakening. In the late century, emergent disciplines like developmental psychology and parasitology evoked somatic anxieties, which, as I argue, might be read in these writers' use of an overtly parasitic antagonist. The parasite as a liminal and historically complex figure encapsulates anxiety about the robustness of identity at the level of the personal, the social, and the national. The reimagining of the Gothic monster as a hybrid of the social and organic parasite vocalizes the fraught relationship between what is biologically determined and what is culturally constructed. The texts' monsters have social aspirations that represent their attempts to belong to the British social world, despite their overt biological degeneration that taxonomically exempts them from it. In this way, these texts negotiate the overlapping identities of the social and biological subject.

This negotiation takes place in dialogue with a cultural context of imperialism. Increasing reports of "tropical" diseases and their translocation from the colonies back to Britain highlighted the blurred distinctions between the metropole and her colonies. Reports of, for example, African sleeping sickness[1] carried on ships from the Congo to Liverpool, enacted a pathological retort to Britain's civilizing mission. The colonization of British bodies by tropical parasites mirrored in reverse the colonization of African lands by British settlers, arguably partaking in a parallel imperial relationship. Such fears of foreign organisms—be they of the pathological agent or the human carrier—are reflected and amplified in the three late-century Gothic works.

The novels and novella differ in the attribution of home countries to their respective monsters—Stoker's vampire originates from Transylvania, "one of the wildest and least known portions of Europe" (Stoker 1), Marsh's beetle is an Egyptian goddess, and Conan Doyle's parasite derives from the West Indies; however, all enter into significant discussions concerning the infiltration of Britain by "foreign" powers. Stephen Arata has suggested, in relation to *Dracula*, that the novel enacts a narrative of "reverse colonization," citing the fear that the "civilized" world might be colonized by "primitive" forces, as symptomatic of a widespread anxiety concerning the moral, social and imperial decline of Britain as a global power (621–645). This notion of the primitive encroaching on the civilized, of infiltration, and of "imperial practices mirrored back in monstrous forms" (Arata 623), fits elegantly with the metaphor of Britain as an Imperial Parasite, parasitized. I argue in this essay for this more nuanced view borne out of the conflation of "body" and "country"[2] and intertwined with moral and social anxieties pertinent to emergent discourses on degeneration and psycho-identity. The relationship between parasite and host, as I will demonstrate, is an ancient one involving a culturally significant transfer of meaning from one sphere of language to another. The exploiter-exploited motif, of which the parasite-host dynamic becomes synonymic, is itself "colonized" by language belonging to another allied phenomenon: that of organic dependence. This in turn takes on another level of significance when employed by literary authors to explore the impact of relationships of unequal power on individual autonomy and identity.

Defining the Parasite in Literature and Culture

The parasite as archetype in the nineteenth century was a complex and hybridized figure. From the greek *para + sitos,* meaning literally "beside the grain," "parasite" was originally the name given to temple assistants who separated the grain for religious ceremonies and received, in exchange, a free meal (Phillips 482, Arnott 167). Often guests of the priest, they were not abhorred as in modern parlance, but given a title more akin to "mess-mate" (Yonge 234). Glossed variously as "a person who eats at the table of another," "a person who lives at another's expense and repays him or her with flattery," "a person who dines with a superior officer," and "a priest who is permitted meals at the public expense" (*OED*), the parasite gained fame as an exploiter with gastronomic concerns. The term was borrowed by Middle Comedy poets and fused with the *kolax* (a hungry opportunist who got what he wanted by flattery) to form a new comic character—which I shall call, for ease of reference, the social or comic parasite.[3]

Elisabeth Tylawsky charts the evolution of this character, tracing its precursors as far back as *The Odyssey*, and she points out the reliance of these hungry dependents on the social obligations that structured Homeric society to give them access to the table. Characterized as the most marginal members of society, the parasite's precursors relied on their tongues for acceptance. Tylawsky explores the tensions between these precursors and their need for a kindly host: "All subsequent descendants who were practitioners of the *techne parasitike* stood on [the] threshold between exclusion from the table and from society, and inclusion and a place in the household" (2). The comic parasite offers an exchange, often making use of his linguistic finesse; he might offer wit, praise, or jocular entertainment, even offering himself as the butt of ridicule. Robert Wilkins suggests that "[the comic parasite] translate[s] bodily needs for material fuel into social and sympotic discourse" (84).

Ultimately the social parasite gained a reputation for his ability to exploit his hosts for material gain with an unrelenting self-interest. Cynthia Damon argues that the stock character taken from Greek Middle Comedy was used by Latin authors to critique the unhealthy elements of patronage relationships and symbolized "a complicated nexus of social irritants, including flattery, favouritism and dependency" (7). In fact the comic parasite was used to reinforce correct social behavior and the proper state of social relationships as reciprocal: "the deviant [parasite] confirms the correct behavior of the other diners, who are not driven by their bellies to ignore the proper time and other proprieties, such as an invitation or the obligation to reciprocate" (Wilkins 71). Damon notes that any exchanges that are offered by the parasite cost him nothing, thus the inherently unbalanced nature of the parasitic relationship becomes its defining characteristic.

In the seventeenth century, this social archetype, represented not as a literal dinner-chaser, but a generalized "type" or set of behavioral characteristics, was transferred to a scientific sphere when proto-botanists likened certain plants to the parasite. The first such reference was probably Sir Thomas Browne's *Pseudodoxia Epidemica* of 1646, in which he characterizes plants that grow on trees, such as mistletoe on an oak as parasite-like: "such as living upon the stock of others, are termed parasiticall [sic] plants" (148). However, it was the nineteenth century that saw the full appropriation of the term in its own right to denote "an organism that lives in, on or with an organism of another species, obtaining food, shelter or other benefit, at the expense of the host organism" (*OED*). I argue that this translocation, from a social to a scientific sphere, instigated a two-way transfer of attributes, endowing the social parasite (still widely used to refer to sycophantic individuals)[4] with biological overtones and the organic parasite with a distinctly anthropocentric outlook. This phenomenon is best seen in fiction, which presents a hybridized version of the two, in what I shall call the literary parasite.

Anne-Julia Zweirlein writes convincingly on the parasite as a universally marginalized figure in the late-nineteenth century; she analyzes its representations in a variety of scientific and literary texts and makes the connection between organic parasites and the social hierarchy. However, while arguing for the biological parasite's increasing psychologization at the close of the century, she does not give due credit to its etymological heritage. Rather than simply an allegory for societal decline, I argue that the parasite is a more complex and historically significant archetype.[5] In the mid-century we begin to see narratives that deal with social parasites in this manner, arguably evoking undertones of their new-found duplicity. Honoré de Balzac's 1847 novel *Le Cousin Pons* reflects the French understanding of the parasite as "someone who makes it his profession to dine at another's table" (*OED*). It was originally titled *Le Parasite* but was changed at the request of a lover and confidante, Mme. Hanska, who considered the title "only suitable for an eighteenth century comedy," thereby acknowledging the character's comic heritage (qtd. in Sanders 279). Indeed, Cousin Pons fills the role of parasitic dinner guest, never being happier than when enjoying fine food at someone else's expense. He upholds the social relationships described in the Homeric tradition:

> The hanger-on, the prototypical parasite, represented for the audience of the *Odyssey* the most marginal member of society. He was that figure who, like Odysseus, stood at the threshold and strove to gain admittance to the household and share in the feast. In exchange he offers his wit, his praise, his news from afar, even his willingness to provide entertainment by offering himself as the butt of ridicule [Tylawsky 2].

Pons certainly suffers much embarrassment and abuse for his food: "many a time Pons ran on errands instead of the porter or the servant ... he gained no credit with those for whom he trudged about, and so often sacrificed self-respect" (Balzac 178). The ancestor of the social parasite, the uninvited dinner guest with the gift of the gab, is consciously acknowledged in the text: "To such depths had Pons fallen by adapting himself to the company of his entertainers! In their houses he echoed their ideas, and said the obvious thing, after the manner of a chorus in a Greek play" (Balzac 534). However, we might also see the beginnings of this transfer of associations and a more biological relationship to his "hosts." Pons' desire for access to the table, for example, seems to go beyond simple social aspiration or hungry necessity; he is referred to as a "digestive apparatus," and when denied access, he physically suffers—not from lack of food but from lack of host contact. It is his honor that has been wounded, his societal position taken away, an action that has a physiological effect: "that sudden flash of joy had thrown a light on the extent of the disease that was consuming Pons" (Balzac 896). He does not cause physical harm to his hosts and only exploits them materially, not somatically. In line with his social ancestor, he does offer a service, in the form of his knowledge of antiques; however, we do begin to see a blurring between the social and the biological in this mid-century representation of the parasite.

By the 1890s the transference of attributes is more overt. Arthur Conan Doyle's novella *The Parasite* (1894) does not shy away from branding Miss Penclosa as an animal parasite by likening her to a hermit crab: "she creeps into my frame as a hermit crab does into a whelk's shell" (330). Her inhumanity is emphasized as the narrative progresses by the narrator's reference to her as "the creature." *Dracula* and *The Beetle* pose similar taxonomic enigmas, producing monsters that are distinctly supernatural, while retaining (for the most part) the aesthetics of an ordinary human being. This of course is not a new phenomenon in Gothic fiction as the Uncanny relies on this ambiguous familiarity: "the uncanny derives its terror, not from something external, alien or unknown—but on the contrary—from something strangely familiar which defeats our efforts to separate ourselves from it" (Morris 307). The somatic usurpation of the organic parasite, and the societal concerns of the social, are combined to produce a terrifying hybrid. Central to this terror is an inversion of power in favor of the parasite. Its comic ancestor was presented in a variety of forms, from poor beggar standing on the threshold to obsequious sycophant whispering in the ears of the influential. W. Geoffrey Arnott suggests that the evolution of the comic archetype is indebted to Alexis' play *Parasitos* in which Alexis' nicknaming of his protagonist became associated with the archetype as a whole, while J. O. Loftberg notes the conflation of the sycophant with the parasite, producing a formidable "legal trickster" (61). This might account for the perceived danger of the social parasite in later discourse as possessing hidden power, in contrast to more pathetic representations like Balzac's Pons. However, the naming of the organic parasite adds a further dimension to the relationship between host and hanger-on, renegotiating political alliances as physical obligations.

The danger of the literary parasite is inherent in his modification of the traditional patronage relationship; what if the parasite were able to turn the tables and progress from sycophantic dogsbody to dynamic infiltrator? While the social parasite was considered to be "less gifted than his fellows" (Zweirlein 160), evolutionary discourse had highlighted the organic parasite as curiously well adapted. Charles Darwin notes that "we see beautiful co-adaptations everywhere" (132) and lists the parasite-host relationship as one such example. Indeed, Darwin lists the parasite alongside the predatory tiger—"the parasite, which clings to the hair on the tiger's body" (139)—demonstrating the impact that the organic parasite had on organisms further up the natural hierarchy. Such notions find parallel with the rising threat of social mobility—an analogy made by satirical periodical magazine *Punch* in 1867.[6] The literary parasite combines its namesakes to gain material wealth and social dominion using the efficacy of biological parasitism, thus voicing concerns over an increasingly politicized mode of behavior.

Dracula presents us with the most overt form of organic parasitism, draining the blood from his victims and infecting them with vampirism in order the gain social domination: "you and others shall yet be mine, my creatures to do my bidding" (Stoker 271). The vampire, however, is an ancient archetype with its origins in folklore, and although in this instance it has a socially-driven agenda, the vampire might be aligned more overtly with its biological equivalent. Folklorist Paul Barber notes the use of vampire stories by preindustrial societies to interpret phenomena associated with death and the decay of corpses. He writes that although incorrect, these theories are "usually coherent, cover all the data, and provide a rationale for some common practices that seem, at first, to be inexplicable" (5). The characteristics of the vampire fit it as a supernatural explanation for disease.

The late-nineteenth century interest in tropical medicine offers a framework from which to interpret *Dracula*. A number of Dracula's attributes furnish him with potency as a metaphor for the spread of parasitic disease. His fangs resemble the proboscis of the mosquito, long thought to transmit tropical diseases. Its connection to malaria (caused by the parasitic protozoan

Plasmodium spp.) and the method of transmission—biting—would be proven by Ronald Ross in August of the same year as the novel's publication.[7] The Count's ability to transform into and control other animals resembles the parasitic lifecycle, which often involves intermediate hosts. His connections in the novel to sea travel, the cultivation of soil, and miasmatic mist further fit him for the malaria metaphor: "we do not know for certain how malarial fever is contracted, whether from air, water, or the bite of mosquitoes" (Ross "Malaria"). Vampirism as a blood disease, which causes anaemia, fatigue, and fever, offers further parallels to malarial infection. The prevalence of Dracula's influence at night with the windows open, as well as the efficacy of garlic as prophylaxis, could just as easily describe the impact of the mosquito vector (which is most active at night and repelled by garlic). Thus, Dracula makes a fitting metaphor for the threat of parasitic disease, which was increasingly being registered in the bodies of British sailors and returned travellers at the Liverpool and London hospitals. Nevertheless, his social aspirations frame him as a much more complex threat to British nationhood.

Both as a personification of disease and as a social exploiter, Dracula wields the combined power of the literary parasite.[8] Although not so overtly representative of disease transmission, the antagonists of *The Beetle* and *The Parasite* also have a tangibly physical impact on their hosts. Robert Holt is described as having "little life left in him," "weak, and white and worn to a shadow" (Marsh 164) and Professor Gilroy as "feverish," his head "aching," his hands "shivering," like he is suffering from an infection (Conan Doyle 381). This physical deterioration of the victims helps further the antagonists' social aspirations. Thus the translocation of attributes between the social and the organic parasite really is bidirectional; the biological advantages of the organic parasite furnish the social exploiter with unmatched power, while the organic parasite, bolstered with the complexities of the social climber, makes a uniquely powerful vehicle for British cultural anxiety. The literary parasites presented in the three texts are products of competing fin de siècle discourses related to degeneration, psychological research, and parasitology. Their hybridity—which speaks to these competing discourses—demarcates them as "abhuman," to use Kelly Hurley's term. Dracula's ability to become mist and the Oriental's invertebrate shape-shifting perform abhuman otherings "as the human body collapses and is reshapen across an astonishing range of morphic possibilities" (Hurley 4). This morphological reshaping undermines taxonomic boundaries, echoing the multiple hosts that form the life cycle of many parasitic species, in addition to querying the social and somatic relationships that structure their positions in relation to other characters in the novels.

Degeneration and Parasitism in Dracula, The Beetle and The Parasite

In *Fors Clavigera* (1894) John Ruskin writes of "[an] extraordinary instinct for the horrible, developing itself at present in the English mind ... so that sensation must be got out of death, or darkness, or frightfulness" (372). He aligns this growing interest with the "lower forms of undeveloped creatures" and with "instinctive processes of digestion and generation" (410), connecting parasites with a decline in mental faculty. The comment refers specifically to the growing interest in the natural world, which was becoming increasingly available to the general reader, such as in Edward E. Prince's article on "Parasitic Fashions" (1892) in *The National Observer*, which talks at length about parasites and their hosts. Prince states that "parasites are verily the most despicable and degenerate of all animals" (427), attributing their degenerate nature, including the loss of "eyes, sense-organs, limbs, even mouth" to their parasitic lifestyle. "[The parasite] sinks to the lowest level of degradation," writes Prince (427). Elsewhere this biological degradation was being recognized as analogous to social degeneration. Alfred Russel Wallace, writing on biological degeneration, connects the phenomenon with its social parallel, suggesting a complex relationship between social responsibility and physiological development:

> Degeneration causes an organism to become more simple in structure, in adaptation to less varied and less complex conditions of life. Any new set of conditions occurring to an animal which render its food and safety very easily attained, seem to lead as a rule to degeneration; just as an active healthy man degenerates when he becomes suddenly possessed of a fortune; or as Rome degenerated when possessed of the riches of the ancient world [63].

He connects individual or biological degeneration with collective or historical decline, and by implication, suggests that if man is placed in too comfortable an environment, he too might physically (or at least mentally) degenerate until he is unable to survive in harder times. This phenomenon is heavily associated with the organic parasite, which is used metaphorically to critique corrupt societal relationships,[9] just as the comic parasite was used to critique unhealthy patronage relationships. Selfish or parasitic behavior then is characterized as both indicative of and responsible for degeneration.

We can see these complex ideas being negotiated in these three fictional texts. The antagonists of *Dracula*, *The Parasite*, and *The Beetle* are placed within both the social and organic hierarchies, encouraging the interpretation of analogues. Dracula is a Count, a nobleman and also a foreigner, looking to purchase a London estate. Thus he is characterized as an upper-class man attempting to enter into the British social sphere by purchasing property. However, his social foreignness is couched in biological terms. Not only is Dracula—like the "Oriental" and Miss Penclosa—described as inhuman, he is physically degenerate. During their first meeting, Jonathan Harker attempts an anatomical analysis—"I found him ... of a very marked physiognomy"— which verges from the phrenological, "lofty domed forehead," to the taxonomic, "peculiarly sharp white teeth ... his ears ... the tops extremely pointed ... there were hairs in the centre of the palm" (Stoker 15). This analysis queries the Count's position as human, while endowing him with overtones of degradation. Similarly, Robert Holt's first encounter with his host leads to an impression that suggests physiological deficiency: "the cranium and indeed the whole skull was so small as to be disagreeably suggestive of something animal" (Marsh 18).

The literary parasite modifies the template supplied by the comic parasite to express modern concerns regarding the decline of Victorian society. The domestic structure within which the comic parasite was originally conceived is upheld; however, the conventional social hierarchy is inverted, enabling the would-be parasite a position at the head of the household. Two of the literary parasites—Dracula and the "Oriental"—begin their stories as hosts. Indeed, the abnormality of the Count's social relations unnerve Harker almost as much as his physical appearance. When he first comes to Castle Dracula, he notes the coachman's similarity to the Count and the long time he has to wait to be received by his host, and wonders, "what sort of place had I come to, and among what kind of people?" (Stoker 13). The parasite's attempt to masquerade as a host is unconvincing. Later, upon failing to find a bell to alert the servants that he is done with his breakfast, he comments, "there are certainly odd deficiencies in the house" (17). The Count's deficient household here symbolically parallels his biological abnormality.[10] The antagonist of *The Beetle* inhabits a similarly abnormal household, being the only occupant in an otherwise deserted and only partially-furnished house. The sense of deformity attributed to the antagonists is in part inherited from the comic parasite: "the knisokolax ... was lame and crippled" (Tylawsky 19), but it here takes on a distinctly developmental overtone, tapping into the contemporaneous link between parasitic behavior and morphological degeneration.

Ilse Grubrich-Simitis argues that Lamarkian thought was rediscovered in the late century, following the ascendency of Darwinism (101). This kind of thinking advocated the inheritance of characteristics acquired during an individual's lifetime, and thus refocused attention onto the morphological powers of behavioral adaptation. Might our behavior affect our longstanding genetic heredity? Ray Lankester voices something akin to this when, in his book *Degeneration: A Chapter on Darwinism*, he identifies the Victorian intellectual milieu as symptomatic of degeneration, rather than of progress: "It is possible for us—just as the Ascidian throws away its tail and its eyes and sinks into a quiescent state of inferiority—to reject the good gift of reason with which every child is born, and to degenerate into a contented life of material enjoyment accompanied by ignorance and superstition" (63).

The equating of "tail" and "eyes" with "reason" ties the somatic to the mental and rallies against the vices of material indulgence and irrationality. If we are not careful, we too might meet the fate of the Ascidian, previously identified as a degenerate vertebrate ancestor. One's mental disposition and resultant behavior is conceived as a marker of one's physiological fitness and "superiority" to organisms lower down in the natural hierarchy. This sentiment is literalized in fiction to suggest that rejection of "reason" and the moral code results directly in psychological and somatic degeneration. The behavior of the parasite becomes a threat, not just to his host, but also to himself. Thus, Dracula's child-brain, Miss Penclosa's crippled leg, and the "Oriental's" androgyny might be connected directly to their immoral behavior, their physical parasitism, or their rejection of "reason"—all of which, perhaps, is synonymous with their indulgence in the Occult.

Parasitism, Mesmerism and Morality

An interest in psychic phenomena unites the three novels. Dracula's psychic abilities, despite being highlighted in the text by Jonathan Harker and Van Helsing's discussion of Charcot, are largely ignored by contemporaneous reviewers. *The Parasite*, however, is recognized as "a sensational application of the possibilities of hypnotism" ("Reviews" 2); one review even hails it as supplying the "feminine counterpart" to George du Maurier's Svengali ("My Terrible Twin" 8). In what is perhaps an amplification of the comic parasite's persuasive rhetoric, the literary parasites employ the use of mind control: a combined arsenal of hypnotism, mesmerism, and telepathy to give them the upper hand and symbolically force entry into the household. The usual sufferance of the comic parasite is reversed, and his literary reimagining asserts his psychosomatic authority with unparalleled effect. This power reversal would have been pertinent to a Victorian audience because of the controversy surrounding the widespread use of hypnosis in treating nervous disorders. In the 1880s, Jean-Martin Charcot of the Salpêtrière school proposed that only hysterics could undergo hypnosis, recognizing a confluence between the brain processes of those undergoing hypnosis and hysterical patients (Bell, Oakley et al. 332). However, Hippolyte Bernheim of the Nancy School insisted that the ability to be hypnotized, so-called "suggestibility," was a capacity shared by all human beings, not just hysterics and neuropaths (Sulloway 46). This tension between who can and cannot be hypnotized might be read in the presentation of hypnosis in the texts. It is most evident perhaps in *The Parasite* when Prof. Gilroy laments the difference between himself and Charles Sadler, who was unaffected by Miss Penclosa's hypnotic attempts: "He has to thank his phlegmatic Saxon temperament for it. I am black and Celtic, and this hag's clutch is deep in my veins" (Conan Doyle 342). The notion of individual susceptibility is evident here, but the predication of this on different reservoirs of British ancestry suggests his susceptibility is associated with his "inferior" heredity, rather than psychological abnormality—or rather that his psychological make-up is a product of his genetic inheritance. Similarly, in Marsh's novel Sydney Atherton is supposedly protected from the Oriental's power, owing to the lack of "the sensitive something which is found in the hypnotic subject" (Marsh 66). This suggests that Atherton's innate psychological makeup precludes his ability to be hypnotized.

Such an ability to be hypnotized, which includes a loss of autonomy for the subject, had an allied controversy in the field of parasitology. Was the vulnerability to parasites—like the vulnerability to hypnotism—an innate predisposition? Why did some people become infested with parasites and others not? Was it linked to a notion of morality? Was there such a thing as a "willing" host? These and other questions were being asked at a time when infestation with parasites was still being seen as a symbolic judgment. Helminthologist T. Spencer Cobbold notes in 1879, "some [people] still cling to the creed that the presence of parasites, of internal ones at least, betoken evidence of Divine disfavour" (2). This mode of thought linked immoral behavior with organic parasitism, a relationship reflected in the literary archetype. Questions of selfhood implicit in discussions concerning the origin of parasites, either generated *de nuovo* in the body or transmitted externally, might be fruitfully translocated to depictions of the literary host-parasite relationship. Although these literary parasites are undeniably external ones, they do force the hosts to question their sense of selfhood and identity. The question of where the host ends and the parasite begins might be upheld when considering the literary parasite's psychological impact, which often robs the host of bodily autonomy. Martin Willis and Catherine Wynne argue that mesmerism, which features heavily in the texts, is not a marginal or heterodox science in nineteenth-century literature, but a form of knowledge used to construct notions of the self and of society (7). In this context, the weaponization of mesmerism by the literary parasite reinforces its position as an exploiter of innate weakness or vulnerability.

The identity of the British subject is bound up with notions of the autonomous, law-abiding citizen. The influence of mesmerism in the texts directly challenges this identity by forcing its subjects to perform criminal or immoral acts. Wielded by idiosyncratically foreign "others," the mesmeric power held over the victims (all British citizens) operates as a form of psychic counter-imperialism. In this way, the literary parasite functions as a mirror through which the British subject is reflected back in monstrous form. An invading power brandishing somatic and psychic domination is a chillingly familiar conception of Britain's own international practice, which implemented ideological hegemony following geographical invasion. Furthermore, the parasites' initial refuge in the domestic space and ability to infiltrate multiple households, undermines British nationhood by threatening the sanctity of the home. The parasites' foreignness and usurpation of British property—through purchase (*Dracula*), through renting (*The Beetle*), or as a guest (*The Parasite*)—emphasizes the vulnerability of British integrity to external dangers.

The host, the household, and indeed England as a whole, are all infiltrated by the parasite—in the first instance psychologically, in the second symbolically, and in the third physically. Yet the key to the parasite's success lies within its ability to control the British subject, and this, as we've seen, relies on the victim's innate susceptibility and/or transgressive behavior.[11] For Robert Holt, it is his trespassing on an apparently empty property that enables the Oriental to take hold: "But it is well that you came through the window—well, that you are a thief—well for me! For me! It is you that I am wanting," remarks the Oriental (Marsh 25). Likewise in *Dracula*, Lucy Westenra's lamentation, "Why can't they let a girl marry three men?" (Stoker 50), exposes her unethical approach to married life and although not an explicit transgressive behavior, does gesture toward immorality (already established to thematically relate to susceptibility to parasitism). Her desire is later symbolically fulfilled when she receives blood transfusions from Arthur Holmwood, Dr. Seward, Van Helsing, and Quincey Morris in a kind of somatic matrimonial union, as underscored by Van Helsing's jocular comment, "this so sweet maid is a polyandrist" (154). However, in Lucy's case the narrative suggests that she is innately susceptible at the beginning of the novel when her psychological state is called into question; she admits, of asylum physician John Seward, "he says that I afford him a curious psychological study" (Stoker 47). A predisposition of sorts is also suggested by Mina's observation that Lucy "feels influences more acutely than other people do" (76).

Healthy and unhealthy relationships are juxtaposed in the texts in order to highlight the dangers of parasitism. Mina, who resists Dracula's power, emerges from the novel as a mother, largely unscathed and with the respect of the men; Lucy, on the other hand, is killed by the parasite, and then her body desecrated by the Crew of Light. Women's bodies are categorized as either capable of healthy reproduction—as with Mina—or condemned as a locus of pathological generation.[12] Lucy falls into the latter category, preying on children after her transformation into a vampire. In *The Beetle*, the politician Paul Lessingham's reputation, health, and relationship are jeopardized as a result of his foreign transgressions, while his fiancée Marjorie, who repeatedly defies her father's wishes, is so psychologically damaged she must spend time in an asylum, and Robert Holt, the tramp, dies. The impact of the parasite here appears to relate to the host's actions. Robert Holt, as noted previously, trespassed his way into the parasite's clutches and so suffers the greatest punishment. However, Holt's death might too be attributable to his susceptibility, which in turn is allied to the strength of his moral code or psychological robustness. In *The Parasite* Gilroy (who is demarcated as susceptible) narrowly escapes complete destruction: his reputation is in tatters, his lectureship rescinded, and his relationship almost ruined (indeed he is on the brink of marring his fiancée's face with acid). By contrast, Charles Sadler, who failed to fully succumb to Miss Penclosa, is merely "left [with] a most unpleasant impression" (Conan Doyle 246). In this way, the powers of the parasite are undermined, and blame is refracted onto the victims.

Concluding Thoughts

The inclusion of characters who have varying susceptibilities to the parasite's influence refocuses attention onto the hosts. By virtue of their poor personal choices, which are amplified by the strong moral and legal overtones in *Dracula* and *The Beetle*, or through some form of inbuilt dispositional corruptability, the parasite's victims are presented, to some extent, as self-selecting. This plays on fin de siècle preoccupations with societal and moral decline and on anxieties about the future of the British as a race and as an empire.[13] The literary parasite exploits the weakest members of British society and through them threatens the integrity of the whole: "your girls that you all love are mine already. And through them you and others shall yet be mine" boasts Dracula (Stoker 271). In addition to draining his victims of life (as is the wont of the organic parasite) and of material wealth (as is the wont of the social parasite), the literary parasite embarks on a mission to destroy the very identity of his hosts. For Lucy, this is the destruction of her identity as a monogamous fiancée and a virtuous woman by transforming her into a woman who walks the night and harms children. For Gilroy, it is the destruction of his identity as a respectable lecturer and loving fiancé by forcing him to commit crimes, sabotage his own lectures, assault colleagues, and proffer affections to another woman. Gilroy is able to retain his identity (and life) owing only to the sudden death of the parasite. Robert Holt begins with nothing. Having lost his job and his home, he has little left for the parasite to take away. Weary on his feet, almost fainting with hunger, and seeing an open window in an apparently abandoned building, he makes the decision to act. To save his own life, he enters the building. This ability to act is what the parasite takes away from Holt: "I did not obey the frantic longing which I had to flee from it ... I could not," he laments, paralyzed by the Beetle's mesmeric abilities (Marsh 13).

The parasite is depicted in opposition to scientific reason—Sydney Atherton, Professor Gilroy, and the "Crew of Light" represent versions of empirical authority. This perhaps gestures to the struggles of scientific researchers to elucidate parasitic disease and the narrativization of such struggles as a personal battle.[14] However, the failure of the protagonists to demystify their foes (the parasites' supernatural abilities are never scientifically explained) refutes the claims of Western science to intellectual authority.

Dracula, *The Beetle*, and *The Parasite* reveal a new kind of Gothic monster borne out of a complex cultural milieu concerned with psychic, somatic, and social identity. The resulting parasitic hybrid is, in part, a product of changing characterizations of inter-organismal relationships. The relationship between the comic parasite and his religious patronizer, between the shrewd gormandizer and his host, between the social climber and society, and then the newly christened relationship between the organic parasite and its animal or plant host, all form the parentage of the literary parasite. The hydridization of these varying conceptions of the parasite-host relationship are represented in the literary parasite as a physical draining of the host's energy, life, or blood, in order to secure material gain and social domination. The literary parasite retains the powerful rhetoric of the comic parasite, amplified by the infiltrative physicality of the organic. This is recognizable in his potent mesmeric or hypnotic ability. The physical deficiencies of the comic parasite, often used as a disguise in order to gain access to the household, are here transformed into a physiological or developmental atavism. The complex societal structuring is retained in the domestic settings and preoccupations of these stories, as represented by the purchase of property, the infiltration of households, and the presence of marriage proposals.

Sean Corner discusses the comic parasite as both an "other" of the aristocrat, "his inferiority constituted in relation to and affirming the superiority of an elite," and as an "other" of the citizen, arguing, "the social boundaries, relations, and values that define the parasite are those of the middling civic society of the polis" (45). The literary parasite upsets these demarcations by subverting the very boundaries that purport to define the social world in which it operates. By embodying the degenerate aristocracy (the crippled mystic and the primitive goddess) and preying on the innocent young woman (the respectable professor and the lowest member of British society, the unemployed homeless tramp), the literary parasites function as the quintessential face of counter-imperialism. The ideological epitome of the foreign, uncivilized cultures that the British empire had attempted to "sanitize" under imperial rule came to invade England in fiction and attack society at all social levels—a reverse-colonization anxiety personified and underscored by imperial guilt. Thus, newly imbued with cross-disciplinary cultural significance, the literary parasite more than ever embodies, as Corner argues of the comic, "a figure belonging to the social imaginary, to an image of the world by which a society represents itself to itself" (43).

Notes

1. African sleeping sickness, or trypanosomiasis, is a parasitic disease caused by the protozoan parasite *Trypanosoma* spp. and spread by the bite of the Tsetse fly.

2. Prof. Gilroy notes the conflation of body and landscape in the opening of *The Parasite*: "Green shoots are peeping out everywhere ... the moist, heavy English air is laden with a faintly resinous perfume ... I can see it without, and I can feel it within. We also have our spring, when the little arterioles dilate, the lymph flows in a brisker stream ... nature readjusts the whole machine" (loc. 14). Ioana Boghian reviews the body as a house metaphor prevalent in nineteenth century fiction—a concept that will take on increasing significance as this essay progresses. See Ioana Boghian, "The Metaphor of the Body as a House in 19th Century English Novels," *Styles of Communication* 1 (2009): 1–13. Web. 11 November 2014.

3. NB. By "comic parasite" I refer specifically to the archetype in Greco-Roman comedy, whereas by "social parasite" I mean the real-life counterpart, which the comic parasite satirizes.

4. See Samuel Robertson, *A Dictionary of the English Language in which words are deduced from their originals and illustrated in their different significations by examples from the best writers, to which are prefixed a history of the language, and English grammar* (London: J.F. and C. Rivington, 1810). Print.

5. While Zweirlein notes that "an ancient literary topos gives a name to a newly emerging subfield of biological inquiries [and] the literary stock figure of the sponger-parasite ... attains very concrete biological overtones" (158), she does not fully bring to light the complex social and political relationship between the comic parasite and the household on its literary and biological descendants.

6. *Punch* published two articles in 1867 that made the connection between social and organic parasites. Both of these articles presented organic parasites as circumventing

the social hierarchy and gaining access to high society balls. See "A Sweet Thing in Chignons," *Punch, or the London Charvari* 52 (1867): 89 and "A Parody Upon a Parasite," *Punch, or the London Charivai* 52 (1867): 196.

7. Although experimentally proven after the publication of *Dracula*, the connection between malaria and mosquitoes had been speculated on for a long time, their connection to fever diseases dating back to around 800 BCE. In 1877 Patrick Manson identified the mosquito as the vector for the filarial nematode responsible for the parasitic disease Elephantiasis. The mosquito-malaria connection was resurrected by Albert King in 1883 (published in the American magazine *Popular Science Monthly*), by Charles Laveran in 1884 and by Manson in 1894, before being proven by Ross in August 1897.

8. Dracula's position as a transmitter of disease is recognized by a review in *The Era* (7 August 1897): "Count Dracula is a vampire of the most malignant and dangerous kind. The worst of it is he carries contagion with him."

9. See "Parasites," *The Leicester Chronicle and Mercury,* Saturday, 17 November 1883; "Monarchs—their Parasites and their Victims," *Reynolds's Newspaper*, Sunday, 7 October 1885.

10. Dracula's peculiar behavior does not go unnoticed by the general reader, as one reviewer in *The London Standard* (11 August 1897) notes: "This Vampire Count ... conducts his domestic arrangements with an ease and swiftness that would strike despair into the heart of an English housewife."

11. One might argue that the two are intimately linked.

12. Carol Senf's "'Dracula': Stoker's Response to the New Woman," *Victorian Studies* 26.1 (1982): 33–49; Christopher Craft's "'Kiss Me with Those Red Lips': Gender and Inversion in Bram Stoker's *Dracula*," *Representations* 8 (1984): 107–133; and Stephanie Demetrakopoulos' "Feminism, Sex Role Exchanges, and Other Subliminal Fantasies in Bram Stoker's *Dracula*," *Frontiers: A Journal of Women Studies* 2.3 (1977): 104–113, laid the foundations for conversations about gender in relation to Stoker's text. Such conversations, which recognize a categorization of "good" and "bad" women, as well as questioning the innate moral virtues of "femininity," might be further critically elaborated on by looking at them through the lens of the literary parasite and its victims.

13. Arguably, however, the parasites themselves ultimately retain the blame for their actions and pay for it with their deaths (however intangible or contested). Those victims considered most transgressive are not always punished most severely, and those killed by their interactions with the parasites are noted for their naivety (Lucy Westernra) or dire circumstances (Robert Holt). This reinforces the parasite as an exploiter.

14. See Emilie Taylor-Brown, "(Re)Constructing the Knights of Science: Parasitologists and Their Literary Imaginations," *Journal of Literature and Science* 7.2 (2014): 62–79.

Works Cited

Arata, Stephen. "The Occidental Tourist: 'Dracula' and the Anxiety of Reverse Colonization." *Victorian Studies* 33.4 (1990): 621–645. Print.
Arnott, W. Geoffrey. "Studies in Comedy, I: Alexis and the Parasite's Name." *Greek, Roman and Byzantine Studies* 9.2 (1968): 161–168. Print.
Balzac, Honoré de. *Cousin Pons*. Trans. Helen Marriage. Kindle file.
Barber, Paul. "Vampire Stories and Beyond." *Why Sex Matters: A Darwinian Look at Human Behaviours*. Ed. Bobbi. S. Low. Princeton: Princeton University Press, 2000. Print.
Bell, Vaughan, David A. Oakley, Peter W. Halligan, and Quinton Deeley. "Disassociation

in Hysteria and Hypnosis: Evidence from Cognitive Neuroscience." *Journal of Neurology, Neurosurgery and Psychiatry* 82 (2011): 332–339. Print.
Browne, Thomas. *Pseudodoxia Epidemica*. 1646. Ed. Robin Robbins. Vol. 2. New York: Oxford University Press, 1981. Print.
Byron, Glennis. "Gothic in the 1890s." *A New Companion to the Gothic*. Ed. David Punter. Chichester: Wiley-Blackwell, 2012. 186–196. Print.
Cobbold, T. Spencer. *Parasites; a treatise on the entozoa of man and animals including some account of the ectozoa*. Internet Archive. 2001. Web. 20 June 2013.
Conan Doyle, Arthur. *The Parasite*. Westminster: Archibald Constable & Company, 1894. *Project Gutenberg*. 2008. E-book.
Corner, Sean. "The Politics of the Parasite (Part One)." *Phoenix* 67.1 (2013): 43–80. Print.
Damon, Cynthia. *The Mask of the Parasite: A Pathology of Roman Patronage*. Ann Arbor: University of Michigan Press, 1997. Print.
Darwin, Charles. *On the Origin of Species by Means of Natural Selection, or the Preservation of Favoured Races in the Struggle for Life* in *Evolutionary Writings*. Ed. James A. Secord. 1859. Oxford: Oxford University Press, 2008. Print.
Grubrich-Simitis, Isle. "Metapsychology and Metabiology." *A Phylogenetic Fantasy: Overview of the Transference Neuroses*. Cambridge: Belknap Press, 1987. 75–107. Print.
Hurley, Kelly. *The Gothic Body: Sexuality, Materialism and Degeneration at the Fin de Siècle*. Cambridge: Cambridge University Press, 1996. Print.
Lofberg, J. O. "The Sycophant-Parasite." *Classical Philology* 15.1 (1920): 61–72. Print.
Marsh, Richard. *The Beetle*. London: Skeffington & Son, 1897. Kindle file.
Morris, David B. "Gothic Sublimity." *New Literary History* 16.2 (1985): 299–319. Print.
"My Terrible Twin." *Glasgow Herald*, 3 July 1896. Print.
"Parasite, n." *OED. Oxford English Dictionary*. Web. 25 Feb. 2014.
Phillips, Edward. *The new world of words; or, universal English dictionary*. Vol. 1, 7th ed. Ed. J. K. Philobibl. London: J. Phillips, 1720. Eighteenth Century Collections Online. Web. 25 Feb. 2014.
"Reviews." *Morning Post*, 25 Jan. 1895. Print.
Ruskin, John. *For Clavigera: Letters to the Workmen and Labourers of Great Britain*, Vol. II. New York: Bryan, Taylor, 1894. Print.
Sandars, Mary F. *Honoré de Balzac, His Life and Writings*. New York: Dodd, Mead, 1905. Internet Archive. Web. 25 Feb. 2014.
Stoker, Bram. *Dracula*. Westminster: Archibald Constable & Company, 1897. Kindle file.
Tylor-Brown, Emilie. "(Re)Constructing the Knights of Silence: Parasitologists and Their Literary Imaginations." *Journal of Literature and Science* 7.2 (2014): 62–79.
Tylawsky, Elisabeth Ivory. *Saturio's Inheritance: The Greek Ancestry of the Roman Comic Parasite*. New York: Peter Lang, 2002. Print.
Wallace, Alfred Russel. "Degeneration." *Science* 1.6 (1880): 63. Web. 14 Apr. 2014.
Wilkins, John. *The Boastful Chef: The Discourses of Food in Ancient Greek Comedy*. Oxford: Oxford University Press, 2000. Print.
Willis, Martin, and Catherine Wynne. Introduction. *Victorian Literary Mesmerism*. Eds. Martin Willis and Catherine Wynne. New York: Rodopi, 2006. 1–17. Print.
Yonge, C.D., trans. *The Deipnosophists or the Banquet of the Learned of Athenaeus* Book Six. London: H. G. Bohn, 1854. Attalus.org. Web. 20 Feb. 2014.

Marie Corelli's *Ziska*
A Gothic Egyptian Ghost Story

SHARLA HUTCHISON

Bertha Vyers's memoirs concerning Marie Corelli offer entertaining anecdotes about a personal life shared with the best-selling, late–Victorian fiction writer. Because of Corelli's interest in ancient Egypt, it is not surprising that Vyers recounts a supernatural, celebrity-rich anecdote about Corelli's visitation by a four-thousand-year-old Egyptian ghost in 1903. Apparently, Corelli was given an ancient Egyptian necklace (c. 4000 BC) that was unearthed during construction efforts along the Nile. At some point after she assumed ownership of the artifact, Beerbohm Tree, the English actor and theater manager, invited Vyers and Corelli to his staging of *Antony and Cleopatra*, and the actress playing Cleopatra, Constance Collier, asked to borrow the necklace to wear on stage. However, the night before the play, the original and "rightful" owner of the necklace, a four-thousand-year-old Egyptian spirit, visited the popular writer in her dreams, instructing her that bad luck would befall her should she allow the actress to wear it. As a result, she rescinded her offer to Collier. During the play that next evening, Collier, acting as Cleopatra, ripped her costume necklace from her throat resulting in it breaking into tiny pieces. In Vyers's own words, Corelli then turned to her and exclaimed, "'How lucky it was not my necklace!'" (187).[1]

The story of a four-thousand-year-old Egyptian ghost issuing a warning about a necklace seems rather preposterous, and especially so in this case where it is difficult not to be suspicious of a story that would conveniently keep a favorite piece of jewelry out of harm's way. However, the sorts of tales where English citizens were visited by the spirits of ancient Egyptian kings, queens, princesses, and priests became fashionable and circulated regularly during England's occupation of Egypt (1882–1914) as well as during periods of archaeological excavation such as the one performed on King Tutankhamen's tomb (1922). The era stands out as a time when ordinary English citizens felt qualified to become armchair Egyptologists and images of Egypt became appropriated and projected into English popular culture. It was also a time when late-Victorian interest in psychic research took root in popular fiction, reframing the ghost story with the theories and jargon of psychic researchers.

Six years prior to Corelli's visit by the Egyptian ghost, she published *Ziska* (1897), a best-selling Gothic Egyptian ghost tale that fabricates the story of love and life in ancient Egypt during the days of Amenhotep, where an unresolved love plot between two principle characters, Ziska and Araxes, causes the two lovers to be spiritually reincarnated and transported to an English tourist community in Cairo at the fin de siècle. Corelli borrows from two popular Gothic trends at the end of the nineteenth century—mummy narratives and ghost stories—to create an ambivalent portrait of the New Woman in the Egyptian ghost and glamorous femme fatale, Ziska, who operates as both an agent of the scales of spiritual justice and as a horrifying supernatural predator. Using a reincarnation plot, Corelli conceives of a supernatural, spiritual method to punish the men who abuse women, and in this case, that man is Araxes.

Corelli's novel stages the story of a scorned ancient Egyptian concubine, Ziska-Charmazel, whose spirit returns to Cairo in the late nineteenth century to seek a just form of retribution against her former lover, the great warrior Araxes, who resides reincarnated in the body of Armand Gervase, a French atheist. The transgressions of Corelli's supernatural heroine—particularly her brazenness—approximate characteristics similar to the sexually liberated protagonists of New Woman fiction as well as the dangerous femme fatale that inhabited popular fiction at the fin de siècle. Ziska, a femme fatale archetype, merges feminine beauty with adventure, danger, and sexual allure. Simply put, Corelli's novel is not just the "melodramatic," "exotic and erotic" orientalist romance critics understand it to be (Felski 138–39). Rather, it also functions as a vehicle to imagine and validate female desire while also attacking gender inequities. Corelli draws on the appetites wetted by Egyptomania, fusing a variety of cultural trends—orientalism, occultism, and spiritualism—to the mass appeal of Gothic plots, and consequently, she creates a reading pleasure for her audience in a variety of popular fantasies: a fantasy about unsuppressed power manifest in a glamorous female body, an orientalist fantasy about discovery and adventure in Egypt, and a romantic fantasy about love setting the human soul free. In doing so, she creates a style of feminism that reaches as broad an audience as the masculine adventure fictions published by the likes of Henry Rider Haggard or Rudyard Kipling.[2] However, unlike the femme fatales of Haggard's imperial fictions, Ziska does not act as a colonizing threat that potentially destabilizes English masculine authority as Ayesha does in *She* (1887). Additionally, Ziska's status as a powerful female figure does not lead to the downfall of civilization as it does in Haggard's *Cleopatra* (1889). Instead, Ziska's vengeance, acted out in her violent murder of Armand, becomes an act of karmic retribution sanctioned and orchestrated by greater spiritual powers, imbuing her character with a frightening but intoxicating new power.

Corelli's Ziska *and New Woman Fiction*

As many scholars note, Corelli often articulates a contradictory feminist position. Publicly, Corelli's feminist stance was problematic, for she voiced support for women pursuing intellectual endeavors but criticized the suffragist movement. Janet Galligani Casey argues that Corelli's writings embody the ambivalent attitudes toward female equality expressed by an English culture in transition, a social world on the brink of change (164). Nicola Diane Thompson suggests that while Corelli embraced the notion of equality, she objected to New Woman feminism because of its lack of femininity: "It is not so much the New Woman's politics that Corelli objects to—she believes in women's equality and when she sees sexism she names it—but she views the New Woman's apparent betrayal of feminine culture and a female aesthetic as a misguided allegiance with men rather than a commitment to women" (245). However, Corelli was deeply committed to the equality of the sexes, and this position manifested in fictional heroines who were independent, self-assured, unmarried, adventurous, virtuous, sometimes superior to men, and even, at times, scientifically-minded. Corelli vocalizes her feminist concerns in fiction, especially in romance plots where she more comfortably expresses "anger at male privilege and [where] her desires for sexual fulfilment can be given free play" (Thompson 243). Corelli perhaps felt the future of gender equality could be better achieved through the "emotional power of literature" (Frederico 242). So although Corelli seems like an unlikely candidate to construct a character modeled after the "New Woman," *Ziska* poses new possibilities for viewing Corelli's position on this controversial figure, especially as she melds a critique of male privilege with the actions of a beautiful femme fatale.

Between 1880 and 1918, the debate over the social and political rights of women played out in mass culture in a variety of forums, including fiction, film, and print media. New Woman fiction incorporated female characters who rejected the traditional marriage plot and created public debate about women's domestic rights and private concerns, often challenging, as Ann Ardis stresses, the labels differentiating "pure" from "fallen" women (61). A variety of feminist positions describing the New Woman proliferated in public discourse, but two predominant New Woman archetypes defined the poles of feminist debate in New Woman fiction: the "sexual liberationist" feminist and the "social purist" feminist (Ledger 160). George Egerton (Mary Chavelita Dunne) presents the most renowned sexual liberationist views in *Keynotes and Discords* (1893), a series of short stories featuring unvarnished depictions of female sexual fantasy, lesbian awakenings, the ennui of domestic life, and realistic depictions of domestic abuse. Sarah Grande (Frances Elizabeth McFall) is best recognized for social purity feminism in *The Heavenly Twins* (1893), a best-selling novel that addresses the rights of wives to protest a husband's infidelity on moral grounds.

The female characters of New Woman fiction were independent, intelligent, and honest about their desires, even when those desires were taboo. Corelli's character Ziska is not terribly different. Similar to a sexual liberationist feminist, Corelli voices female sexual desire in the development of a character who takes pleasure in making her body an object for voyeurism, a desire expressed in Egerton's "A Cross Line" (1893), a short story that boldly magnifies a fantasy about female sexual prowess. To date, no scholar has examined *Ziska* within the framework of New Woman fictional archetypes, but the novel's "Dance of Thebes" scene is tinged with allusions to Egerton's story. Like a social purist feminist, Corelli decries the sexual licentiousness of men in her novel, imagining, through Ziska, a powerful female who actively seeks reprisals for male abuses.

In her characterization of Ziska, Corelli goes to great lengths to avoid the unflattering social caricatures of the New Woman that populated nineteenth century public discourse, stereotypes such as the anti-marriage "wild woman," the bookish bore, or the "mannish" female (Ledger 153). As an ultra-feminine and charming woman, Ziska becomes a safe mechanism to explore female power, a figure Corelli can use as a centerpiece in a novel that packages consumer fantasies in exotic settings, enticing treasures, and occult dangers—all of which make the novel's place within New Woman fiction less obvious. Perhaps, then, Ziska can also be understood as a manifestation of the femme fatale, a beautiful, taboo-breaking woman, who, as Elizabeth Carolyn Miller notes, became an archetype celebrated and mediated in popular fiction, often representing the financial freedoms women exercised in an expanding consumer market.[3] Ironically, though, Corelli's protagonist also functions to induce anxiety since, like any Gothic monster, she is clearly capable of unspeakable violence.

Popular Plots and Popular Culture: Mummies and Feminism in Ziska

Corelli's tale of an Egyptian love gone awry begins with the novel's short prologue introducing her narrative as the recovery of an untold tale. Just as an archaeologist discovers and decodes ancient hieroglyphs, the narrator of *Ziska* begins with a small fragment of the past to unlock the narrative that follows. In the prologue, Corelli establishes a portrait of ancient Egypt as a mysterious, alien, and powerful supernatural world. The reader, transported thousands of years in the past, becomes quickly captivated by a panoramic view of the pyramids against the darkness of the desert night. Suddenly, a woman's voice cries out in agony, "Araxes! Araxes!" Next, a wind simulating the painful wailing of a woman blows sands across the desert, and a vaporous form emerges from an underground tomb, her eyes "flash[ing] with an unholy fire" (5). In a vengeful shriek, the shadowy figure vows to pursue Araxes to the end of time.

The reading audience quickly pieces together that the shadowy figure is the vengeful spirit of a female lover who has been murdered by Araxes. In the following chapter, the readers flash forward to Cairo during the English occupation, where the undead Ziska-Charmazel poses as a flesh and blood Russian princess while scheming to avenge herself with an elaborate plot to torture the reincarnated soul of Araxes now manifest in the body of Armand Gervase, a self-proclaimed atheist and an egotistical womanizer. Meanwhile, Dr. Maxwell Dean, an armchair Egyptologist and spiritualist, perceptively observes that Ziska is a protoplasmic spirit, a ghost who must right the scales of justice and attain inner-peace before she can transcend into the universal spirit of life. Conveniently, Dean sits on the sidelines rather than giving away the secret of her identity, and Ziska achieves her goal by using her womanliness and supernatural power to bewitch and mesmerize the overconfident Armand/Araxes, driving him to despair. By the novel's end, Ziska kidnaps Armand/Araxes and forces him to beg for forgiveness before plunging a knife into his heart. However dastardly this act might seem, it becomes clear that her actions release Araxes's soul from Armand's body, enabling him to gain wisdom and humility so that he, too, can transcend with her into the spiritual realm.

Playing to many a woman's fantasy to come back and haunt the man who scorns her, Corelli incorporates feminism and trendy, turn-of-the-century spiritualism as she manages to reinvent and recombine some of the conventions distinct to mummy fiction. Corelli's Gothic framework enables her to carefully glamorize female sexuality and imbue the protagonist, Ziska, with the frightening attributes of a mummy avenger.

Mummy revenge narratives existed as part of the larger Egyptomania and mummymania trends surfacing during the English occupation of Egypt. As Edward Said has famously argued, the rise of Orientalism in the West occurred as a set of political, educational, cultural, and aesthetic discourses that generated, organized, and disseminated details about ancient Egypt and promised to explain the mysteries and secrets of Pharaonic dynasties in ways that subordinated the actual occupation of Egypt by foreign governments to the educational projects touted to preserve history. Consequently, Orientalism consumed the Orient and "domesticated this knowledge to the West, filtering it through regulatory codes, classifications, specimen cases, periodical reviews, dictionaries, grammars, commentaries, editions, translations, all of which together formed a simulacrum of the Orient and reproduced it materially in the West for the West" (166). Said does not elaborate on the role that English popular culture played in the construction of a simulacrum of the Orient, but images of Egypt resurface time and again in mass culture at the fin de siècle, and mummy narratives became one such avenue for projecting a simulation of Egypt as a source of material splendor and exoticism, one that offered consumers the fantasy that they participated in the discovery of archaeological secrets and far-away adventures experienced by wealthy aristocrats.

In popular fiction, writers cultivated tales about archaeologists discovering a Pharaoh's tomb or deciphering ancient hieroglyphs, acts that promised readers they, too, could uncover the true stories of politics and love that defined the lives of ancient Egyptians. Dozens of newly published novels and short stories showcased mummies and/or ancient Egyptian spirits coming to life, often raising ethical concerns about archaeological practices as well as ethical questions about the nature of England's relationship to Egypt, revealing that Egyptomania and mummymania consumer practices did not occur without a certain amount of social anxiety. The two defining plots employed in this body of fiction are the mummy revenge plot (otherwise known as the mummy's curse) and the mummy romance plot. The mummy revenge plot is more relevant to Corelli's novel precisely because Ziska's role, like that of the mummy spirit avenging wrongdoings, is to punish the brutish behaviors of Araxes.

In the mummy revenge plot, an English Egyptologist disturbs an Egyptian tomb, resulting in either the resurrected mummy or its reincarnated spirit coming to life with the sole purpose of exacting punishment on the Englishman. The plot of "Lot 249" (1892) by Arthur Conan Doyle rests upon the horrors of a mummy escaping the sarcophagus and terrorizing Oxford students. In Richard Marsh's *The Beetle* (1897), an Egyptian entity invades London and colonizes the minds and bodies of citizens in a plot to exact revenge on Paul Lessingham, a prominent English politician who escapes the sacrificial rituals of an Isis cult in Cairo. Bram Stoker's *Jewel of the Seven Stars* (1903) features the disembodied Queen Tera who murders tomb-robbers and, in the first ending Stoker concocted, destroys the English Egyptologist who unwraps her mummified corpse and dares to look upon her naked body. In "The Nemesis of Fire" (1908) by Algernon Blackwood, an Englishman transports a mummy to his country home, only to unleash its dangerous spirit which seeks revenge by killing family members and burning parts of the estate. Sax Rohmer's "In the Valley of the Sorceress" (1916) illustrates the basic mummy revenge plot when an English Egyptologist is threatened by the spirit of Queen Hatsu while excavating her tomb. In the revenge plot, the mummy or its spiritual counterpart, awakened by the misdeeds of the Egyptologist, colonizer, or irreverent traveller, exacts punishments in the form of invasion, death, bodily harm, or destruction of property.

This body of fiction is often seen to signify cultural paranoia over what Stephen Arata calls "reverse colonization" or what Patrick Brantlinger identifies as the "invasion of civilization by the forces of barbarism," a defining characteristic of the "Imperial Gothic," a subgenre of Gothic fiction in which imperial ideology and the occult merge to express a variety of anxieties over British imperialism, specifically in themes where the "Orient takes its revenge" (Brantlinger 227–230).[4] More generally, though, the mummy revenge narrative can be understood to express anxiety over the archaeological practice of disinterring sacred graves. The practice was at odds with Victorian moral values, and there were English citizens who abhorred the sacrilege of ransacking graves and exploiting the dead. The questionable ethics of archaeological practices, according to Jasmine Day, played out as the Victorian "conflict between moral and material values" in mummy revenge narratives where the activities of obsessive Egyptologists are countered by the very bodies they rob (47).

Oddly enough, scholars investigating Egyptian themed literature have largely ignored *Ziska*. To date, Roger Luckhurst's *The Mummy's Curse: The True History of a Dark Fantasy* is one of the most extensive and thorough studies regarding mummy revenge narratives and the historical and cultural events influencing them, but even this important study only gives a brief mention to Corelli.[5] However, Corelli clearly modifies the mummy revenge plot in *Ziska* to suit her purposes, namely developing a narrative framework in which a female spirit returns to exact punishment on her male oppressor. It is significant that Corelli favors the mummy revenge plot over the mummy romance plot to launch an imaginative warning about the consequences of spousal abuse, for in mummy romance plots, the female mummy becomes both an "erotic love object" and an imperial conquest (Macfarlane 6).[6] Female mummies, in these stories, represent male desire for an "unknowable" female body, a body that the Egyptologist claims, possesses, studies, unwraps, and fondles (Macfarlane 7). In other words, female mummies are most often represented as passive objects rather than acting subjects. In contrast, Corelli's character, Ziska, treks new fictional ground in such Gothic tales. With a little help from the spiritual world, she plays both the object of desire and the agent of action, directing her own journey and that of Araxes/Armand.

Mummy narratives, whether filled with horror, romance, or both, usually direct readers to identify with the English Egyptologist who acts as a "tamer," a "slayer," or a tragically lost soul when confronted with the unwieldy magic of the Orient (Day 93). Such identification, as Karen E. Macfarlane notes, often depends upon mummy fiction casting women in one of two stereotypical roles: the emasculating monster who threatens to undo the authority of the male Egyptologist or the beautiful object men desire to possess (7). In *Ziska*, however, the Egyptologist takes a backseat and the female Egyptian spirit takes the lead.

Ziska's Orientalist Accoutrements, Sexual Desire and the "dance of Thebes"

Drawing on Egyptomania and mummymania trends at the end of the nineteenth century, Corelli manipulates popular images derived from mummy excavations, museum exhibitions, and popular entertainment, orientalist images that cast Egypt as an exotic, supernatural, and adventurous world, but two key scenes in the novel frame Ziska as a spectacle of Egyptian-inspired high-fashion, an exotic yet wealthy Cleopatra-type seductress. The first scene occurs at the Gezireh Palace Hotel and the second at an ancient Egyptian palace. Ziska conveys glamor and adventure for readers—first, as a woman who oozes the glitz and opulence of Egyptian wealth and second, as a woman who takes control of male admirers. Corelli positions Ziska as a beautiful woman who dominates Armand/Araxes with her intelligence and sexual allure. It is in these scenes that Corelli engages the orientalist and consumer fantasies rendering Egypt as a wellspring for the lifestyles of the rich and famous, and consequently, the sexual overtones referenced in Egerton's "A Cross Line" appear elegant when mixed with fashionable Egyptian images signifying aspirational wealth. In other words, *Ziska* redefines sexually assertive female behavior by linking it to beauty and consumer luxury.

The costume ball at the Gezireh Palace Hotel in Cairo resembles the opulence manifest in one of Lawrence Alma-Tadema's orientalist paintings, and Ziska makes a grand entrance in which she appears more like Cleopatra than a former harem girl. Ziska glides into the room, and her voice, "rarer than song," "soft and silvery," "a magic flute," grabs the attention of Armand immediately (25). She appears "clad in gleaming gold tissues" (25) with a "jewel-winged scarabei on her breast" and an "emerald-studded serpent in her hair" (27) while servants with vaguely mummy-like features fan her with "peacock's plumes" (25).

Capturing the fantasy and adventure of mummy fiction, Corelli carefully attends to detail as she presents Ziska to the audience for the first time, depicting her character in spectacular fashion. Ziska is seen as "the very beau-ideal of an Egyptian Princess"(26), "dazzling yet enigmatical," "wild and voluptuous," and "loaded with quaint Egyptian gems" (27):

> the figure of a woman clad in gleaming golden tissues and veiled in the old Egyptian fashion up to the eyes, with jewels flashing about her waist, bosom and hair,—a woman who moved glidingly as if she floated rather than walked, and whose beauty, half hidden as it was by the exigencies of the costume she had chosen, was so unusual and brilliant that it seemed to create an atmosphere of bewilderment and rapture about her as she came. She was preceded by a small Nubian boy in a costume of vivid scarlet, who, walking backwards humbly, fanned her slowly with a tall fan of peacock's plumes made after the quaint designs of ancient Egypt [25].

Here Ziska embodies one of the popular images of Egypt at the turn of the century: a mythic and dangerous Cleopatra temptress symbolizing ancient splendor in the form of material wealth. She is sensual, exotic, and sultry, an enchanting woman who gives Armand a "dizzying shock" (27) to his senses, eventually rendering him "stupefied ... and mute" (64). Bejeweled and beautiful, she enters the scene as one would imagine Cleopatra would—with her entourage, servants fanning the queen. Here, however, Corelli also celebrates Ziska's sexual dominance over Armand, depicting her erotic dress as a self-directed spectacle designed to attract the wicked soul of Araxes.

Just like a scene from Guiseppe Verdi's *Aida* (1871), Ziska's elaborate costume as Araxes's concubine coupled with Armand's appearance as a Bedouin chief remarkable for his "half-savage type of beauty" and "fierce black eyes," transports the crowd back to ancient Egypt (21). First staged in Cairo, *Aida* debuted in London in 1876, astounding audiences with spectacular sets and costume designs that were modeled on ancient Egyptian architecture and archaeological discoveries, making viewers feel as though the age of Egyptian pharaohs had been revived on stage. The dramatic sets and lavish costumes impressed upon audiences the imperial power of the Pharaonic dynasties, while the love story featured in the opera cemented the association of the Orient with romance and unbridled passion.

In *Aida*, considerable care was given to the artistic craft of costume designs that made use of headdresses, headgear, sandals, tunics, plumed fans, ankle bracelets, arm bracelets, cymbals, breastplates, necklaces, and harp-like instruments—many of which were finely detailed and ornamented with scarabs, snakes, hieroglyphic designs, and symbols of Egyptian gods (Humbert, Pantazzi, and Ziegler 427). After *Aida*, costume designs for Egyptian-inspired theater figures like Cleopatra followed suit, spotlighting the glamor of imperial Egypt. Corelli stages a similar mise-en-scène for her audience, drawing out the details of her heroine's costume design, ornamental jewelry, and servants.

Onlookers watch "open-mouthed" and enraptured as Ziska takes the floor with Armand, awestruck by her authentic costume featuring tiny bells that tinkle when she moves, sandals embellished with ribbons and jewels, and gold ankle bracelets (46). Drawing on the "oriental stereotypes of the mesmeric foreigner," Corelli invites the reader, like Armand and the onlookers at the ball, to view the spectacle as a rare offering of what was previously inaccessible to their imaginations (Luckhurst, *The Mummy's Curse* 173). Charmed and thrilled, Armand remains enthralled by Ziska's company, while the "authentic" dress of an ancient Egyptian woman captures a live re-enactment of a museum exhibition for the English tourists.

The second scene that stages Ziska as an aficionado of Egyptian fashion occurs at a social event Ziska organizes at her ancient Egyptian palace. There, Ziska throws a party, one that provokes the former memories of Araxes whose soul now resides in Armand. During these festivities, the novel's femme fatale is, perhaps, even more recognizable as a figure combining a myriad of social changes specific to Corelli's time: the spectacle of high fashion and commodity fetishism, the fear and celebration of criminal disguise, and the sexual female subject. At an old Egyptian palace, Ziska makes another grand appearance, entering her party wearing Egyptian-inspired Western fashion:

> A sudden blaze of light flamed on the scene, and twenty tall Egyptian servants in white, with red turbans, carrying lighted torches and marching two by two, crossed the court.... The Princess Ziska, attired wonderfully in a dim, pale rose colour, with flecks of jewels flashing from her draperies here and there, waited to receive her guests. Like a queen she stood,—behind her towered a giant palm, and at her feet were strewn roses and lotus-lilies. On either side of her, seated on the ground, were young girls gorgeously clad and veiled to the eyes in the Egyptian fashion [95].

The initial portrait of Ziska here, just as at the costume ball, is that of an Egyptian queen receiving guests with a full entourage at her disposal, only now she models Egyptian-themed Western fancy dress adorned with expensive accessories and stands coolly in front of a palm tree and lotus flowers.

Corelli also allows readers to partake in the fantasy that they are participants in archaeological discovery. At the party, Ziska reveals to guests an ancient bas-relief from the time of King Amenhotep that introduces the story of Araxes and Ziska-Charmazel (99). More sure than ever that the spiritual universe designed the reunion of Ziska and Armand, Dr. Dean remarks on the uncanny resemblance between the image of Araxes in the bas-relief and Armand.

Returning to the party wearing gold and white veils and "gleaming with jeweled bangles," Ziska performs the erotic "dance of Thebes" for the crowd (103), which ends with a gender role-reversal as Armand swoons like a hysteric. The dance, highly erotic, showcases music played from antique lutes and harps. A group of servants, many of whom resemble mummies brought back to life, unfold a special carpet for the dance. Ziska dances like a "bright, wild, wanton thing" (104), a "wild bacchante" (106). Using cymbals, she dances faster and wilder, brazenly stripping off her veil and part of her dress (104). Some of the guests, offended by her overtly sexual dance, begin to disperse, but Armand remains, his mind and heart completely surrendered to Ziska.

The fantasies undergirding the party activities—Egyptology adventures and consumer luxury—do not overshadow the shocking sexuality displayed in Ziska's dance of Thebes, a dance that recalls the fantasies of Egerton's unnamed female protagonist in "A Cross Line." In her short story, Egerton reveals the ruminations of a woman who, bored with her life, flirts with thoughts about a passionate affair. She expresses her erotic desires in daydreams where she plays the role of Cleopatra, swept into the arms of Antony. Such musings metamorphosize into sexual fantasies in which she, like Ziska, gains sexual pleasure by dancing erotically before men:

> Then she fancies she is on the stage of an ancient theatre out in the open air, with hundreds of faces upturned toward her. She is gauze-clad in a cobweb garment of wondrous tissue; her arms clasped by jewelled snakes, and one with quivering diamond fangs coils round her hips; her hair floats loosely, and her feet are sandal-clad, and the delicate breath of vines and the salt freshness of an incoming sea seems to fill her nostrils. She bounds forward and dances, bends her lissome waist, and curves her slender arms, and gives to the soul of each man what he craves, be it good or evil [8–9].

The racy, bodice-ripping fantasy laid bare to Egerton's readers illustrates a female sexual passion complete with "parted lips and panting, rounded breasts"

(28). Ardis refers to this scene in Egerton's short story as the "infamous dream sequence," one that shocked readers (115). Luckhurst claims Egerton's scandalous representations of sexual liberation became the "centre of the New Woman storm" at the turn of the century (*The Invention of Telepathy* 220). Curiously, though, scholarship focused on Corelli's novel is scant, and this is, perhaps, the reason readers fail to pick up on the parallels that can be found between Egerton's short story and Corelli's dance of Thebes, particularly the orientalist venues imagined, the gauzy Egyptian dress, the exotic jewelry, and the overtly pleasurable depiction of voyeurism and striptease.

Notably, the sexualized notion of striptease became a common feature in mummy narratives where a male Egyptologist unwraps a female mummy and uses his powers to control her, a feature that Corelli clearly alters to empower the Egyptian woman in her tale. Corelli deviates from mummy narratives further as she seemingly borrows from Egerton's forthright presentation of female desire as inspiration to project a psychologically unfettered female sexuality in Ziska. It is fair to say that Corelli evades some of the social controversy of Egerton's frank portrayal of English marital boredom by engaging plots dependent on Gothic fantasy. An interesting point of contrast between Corelli and Egerton, however, exists in that Egerton's protagonist merely fantasizes, while Corelli's protagonist, albeit as ancient spirit, actually performs the dance for a crowd in order to captivate Armand. In response to Ziska's dance, a mesmerized Armand faints, declaring, "I feel that she holds my life in her hands!" (110). His defenses diminished by her sexual prowess, Armand is easily lured away by one of Ziska's servants, at which time he is kidnapped and brought to the catacombs leading to the burial place of none other than Araxes.

As part of her scheme, Ziska uses her servants to orchestrate the capture of Armand, who is then blind-folded and brought to the underground tomb of Araxes. There, Ziska confronts Armand about his true identity as Araxes and reveals her own as the ancient Egyptian Ziska. She summons eternal spirits that work with her to bring justice from beyond the material world. Shocked, Armand remembers his past life and repents, begging for Ziska's love and forgiveness. Mysteriously, the light in the tomb suddenly goes out, and when the light of his soul illuminates the tomb, it becomes clear he has been stabbed with the same dagger used by Araxes to murder Ziska thousands of years ago. His change of heart awakens him to what Dr. Dean previously explains to readers as the Divine Spirit, a force that intervenes to lift the curse on the two lovers, so that both spirits may transcend into the spiritual universe together, a climactic ending that ambiguously affirms the practices of scandalous dancing and murder.

Equity and the Afterlife: Dr. Dean on Psychic Research, Theosophy and Ziska

It is among the social coterie of English tourists in Cairo that Ziska meets Dr. Dean, a learned English physician, Egyptologist, and psychic researcher. As previously mentioned, it is Dr. Dean who first recognizes Ziska as a "scientific ghost," a spiritual entity existing as part telepathic astral projection, as part "protoplasmic machine" (a phrase used by psychic researcher turned spiritualist Richard Hodgson), and as part good old-fashioned ghost (Luckhurst, *The Invention of Telepathy* 231). Acting as a psychic detective, Dr. Dean describes Ziska as a "scientific ghost," a spiritual entity who appears as flesh and blood human (protoplasmic) but exists as part of the psychic matter that makes up the universe (49). According to Dr. Dean, Ziska is controlled by a pan-religious force referred to as the "Intelligent Principle," "Spiritual force," or "Invisible Mind" (51). The scientific ghost, as Dr. Dean theorizes, acts as an agent of the Spiritual Force, exacting punishment for the sins that went unpunished in the material world. Ziska, he suggests, is on a mission acting on behalf of the "Spiritual law of vengeance," an element of the "psychic law of equity"—a concept perhaps best understood as the scales of karmic justice presiding in the psychic universe (52). Ziska confirms as much when, in a conversation with Dr. Dean, she admits that she is, indeed, an "avenger[s]" of "wicked deeds" (139). In Corelli's novel, Dr. Dean's role is to serve as a learned, reliable intellectual authority who can inform audiences about the mystical forces that demand justice, if not in a present human life, then in the next life experience. The weird mix of psychic research and theosophy vocalized by Dr. Dean enables Corelli to illustrate the significance of equitable and fair treatment between men and women, for crimes that go unpunished in one life will surely be punished in the next. His philosophical dialogues act as a mouthpiece for a range of popular beliefs about psychic research and spiritualism, ideas that blend the scientific dignity of the psychic detective with the mysticism of Madame Blavatsky's theosophy.

By the late nineteenth century, popular culture acted as a crossroads in which occult, imperial, and scientific discourses merged. The Society for Psychic Research, an organized conglomerate of intellectuals who documented, classified, and compiled hundreds of paranormal accounts, eventually published some of their findings in Edmund Gurney's *Phantasms of the Living* (1886). Borrowing from emerging discussions in biology, chemistry, and psychology, the SPR adapted and transformed the ideas and language of scientific research to investigate and explain the paranormal, developing, in a short period of time, a series of theories explaining ghost sightings. The proceedings of the SPR detailed a variety of psychic phenomena—trances, clairvoyance, dream-states, and thought-reading (telepathy)—all of which were theorized as the untapped spectrum of consciousness available to human brains (Luckhurst, *The Invention of Telepathy* 109). Gurney, along with SPR members Frederick Myers and William Barrett, proposed that apparitions were actually messages sent from one living person to another, messages activated by the hidden powers of the human brain. Such theories effectively reduced the ghosts of spiritualism to mere neurologic-telepathic experiences. However, the SPR's findings and scientific jargon ultimately entered mass culture through the journalism of William Stead, a psychic enthusiast who popularized the ideas of the SPR in *Real Ghost Stories* (1891–1892). Reaching more than a half-million readers, Stead's plain-spoken dissemination of psychic research ultimately became coupled with occult spiritualism in popular fiction, particularly in the figure of the psychic-detective, a Sherlock Holmes-like figure inhabiting ghost plots between 1880 and the 1920s.[7] For example, Algernon Blackwood's *John Silence, Physician Extraordinary* (1908) stars a philanthropic doctor turned psychic detective who takes medical cases only solved by the expertise Dr. Silence possesses, namely the ability to diagnose and differentiate patients with legitimate psychic maladies from patients suffering psychological disease. William Hope Hodgson's *The Casebook of Carnacki: The Ghost-Finder* (1913) features a psychic detective who solves a vast array of ghost mysteries by combining modern technological tools, such as a camera and phonographic recording device, with long-standing methods for supernatural discovery, specifically a protective pentacle and obscure historical knowledge. Alice and Claude Askew's *Aylmer Vance: Ghost Seer* (1914) presents a series of titillating ghost mysteries solved by Vance, a detective who uses the depth and breadth of his knowledge to uncover paranormal explanations for events that might be otherwise explained as criminal events. Approximately a decade prior to the development of psychic detectives as a new subgenre, Corelli's Dr. Dean, acting as psychic detective, solves what otherwise might be unsolvable: Ziska's mission to avenge wicked deeds and lift a centuries old curse.

Dr. Dean's educated musings about the occult activities transpiring before the very eyes of the English tourists also resemble the writings of the infamous Madame Blavatsky (Helena Petrovna Blavatsky), especially in the descriptions of a universal spirit and reincarnation. Known for relentless self-promotion and, at times, accused of being an imposter, Blavatsky traveled to London in 1887 to market theosophy, an occult philosophy described by Heather Ingram as "a heady mix of Neo-Platonism, Buddhism, and Kabbalistic mysticism" (187). In *The Secret Doctrine* (1888), Blavatsky describes a "divine spirit" or "divine intellect" that orders the universe—spiritual and terrestrial (73–74). She goes on to outline a progressive "karmic evolution" (248) for the universe in which the spirit passes through various forms on its way to perfection (261). Blavatsky borrows from Eastern religious philosophy, and in *Isis Unveiled* (1877), she explains the role of reincarnation as part of progressive spiritual development, one where an individual who violates "the laws of harmony" by committing a grave sin must relive an "earth-life" to "restore its disturbed equilibrium" (231). In *The Key to Theosophy* (1889), she proposes that the ego can exist as a being forced into reincarnation (78), and she claims it has the capability of retaining a "memory of the soul" (76).

In *Ziska*, Dr. Dean's "Intelligent Principle" and "Spiritual Force" operate as a stand-in for Blavatsky's "divine intellect" that orders the spiritual universe and the progress of karmic evolution, including reincarnation. Araxes becomes reincarnated and is forced to relive his life in the terrestrial form of Armand to restore the balance of harmony in the universe, and Ziska, acting as an agent of the spiritual universe, forces him to remember his grave and violent sins of the past. However, Corelli diverges from the Eastern underpinnings of theosophy a bit in that her scientific ghost acts slightly more like a warrior archangel who does God's bidding to restore the scales of justice, but Ziska's actions as a scientific ghost are beneficial since they force Araxes/Armand to remember his past sins and repent, releasing his spirit for transcendence. In the spiritual world of the novel, all of Ziska's behaviors which might be deemed inappropriate or "un-lady-like" are actually part of a grand spiritual design in which the roguish, disloyal, and abusive behaviors of men are criticized and resolved for the betterment of all.

In her criticism of the mistreatment of women, Corelli uses the less-than-sympathetic characterization of the reincarnated Araxes who, fused with the French atheist Armand, comes across as nothing less than a scoundrel. Through a series of conversations, the reader learns that Araxes murdered Ziska simply because he had grown tired of her; she was no longer beautiful to him. The great warrior Araxes was cruel, disloyal, and violent, and Armand is no different. In an initial conversation, Ziska brings Araxes's "infidelities" (29) to light, and Armand admits later that he, too, is "cruel and unprincipled" regarding women (44). Taking no responsibility for his behavior, Armand excuses himself as fulfilling a transhistorical male prerogative to use "women as toys or slaves" (45). Ziska then bitterly complains about the brutality of men as she declares, "Man's idea of love is to take all he can get from a woman, and give her nothing in return but misery sometimes, and sometimes death" (65). In response, Armand confesses that, like Araxes, he also values women only for their beauty and argues that he would repeat the actions of the ruthless Araxes, sentencing women to death when their "beauty began to wane" (67). Araxes/Armand is consistently depicted as "cruel," "remorseless," and "selfish," so when Ziska mercilessly kills him by the novel's end, readers, as uneasy as they may be about a woman wielding such power, feel little regret (134). It is in this regard that his dastardliness tempers Ziska's characterization as a dangerous predator eyeing her prey, and consequently, readers may desire to witness his comeuppance.

Gothic Monsters and Monster Romances

If, as Judith Halberstam asserts, the Gothic monster represents multiple forms of criminality and desire, including the perverse, unsanctioned expressions of human sexuality, then Ziska does signify monstrosity, but it is a monstrosity best understood as an amalgamation of social differences unique to Corelli's historical moment, and that moment was rife with discussions about female transgression and fears about ethnic difference as evidenced in New Woman fiction and Imperial Gothic fiction (6). Inspiring fear in others is an integral part of the femme fatale archetype in Gothic fiction, and Ziska does not disappoint. Compared to wild animals and demons, she induces fear and admiration in all who encounter her. Various characters note her resemblance to other dangerous women like Medusa (69) and Cleopatra (134), but Corelli also conjures images of predators to define the awesomeness of her power, such as the "splendid tigress" (65), "ravenous bird of prey" (150), and "the spider who wove the web" (34). To emphasize Ziska's single-minded vision in stalking and hunting Araxes, Corelli incorporates the recurring image of Ziska's gleaming, glittering, fire-filled eyes, which are compared to the "eyes of a vampire bat" (35), "eyes of a hawk gleaming on its prey" (63), and "eyes of an angry snake" (68). Her power is supernatural, lending comparisons to a witch (131) and demon (150).

Corelli's portrait of Ziska does seem to fit Halberstam's monster as the "negative of human description," but Corelli also glorifies the female supernatural and humanizes the negative with Ziska's cursed love story, and in so doing, fabricates a romance fiction with moral undertones (22). If Gothic fictions become "technologies" and the monsters permeating them are the "meaning machines" that combine numerous cultural fears in a singular body (Halberstam 22), then Corelli's characterization of Ziska as mummy avenger, ghost, atavistic primitive beast, and wanton concubine certainly mixes the fearful visions of devolving civilization specific to the Imperial Gothic, while also sensationalizing, with titillating delight, the sexual taboos broken by the main character, a femme fatale who also represents the new freedoms available to women.[8] However, it is the pathos manifest in a fable of cursed love and the righteousness of a spiritual mission that softens Ziska's brash behaviors.

Using her reincarnation plot, Corelli conceives of a spiritual method to punish men who abuse women. The transgressions of her supernatural monster/heroine, seen by the novel's end as serving the greater good, provide a glimpse of Corelli's own unique feminism, one defined by an appeal for equality based on the importance of spiritual harmony in the afterlife. In the course of the novel, Ziska alters the conventions of mummy revenge narratives in which female Egyptian mummies malevolently seek to harm and harass Englishmen, having instead, shifted the roles to focus on Egyptian feminist vengeance acted upon a contemporary French misogynist/ancient Egyptian master. If, as Ardis contends, New Woman fiction contains female protagonists reimagined outside the doldrums of domestic life, then *Ziska* can be classified as New Woman fiction. As is the case with many New Woman fiction writers, Corelli also challenges the idea of the "fallen" woman by redefining Araxes as having the original "wicked" soul. The origin of the sin that sets the couple's curse in motion is Araxes's murder of Ziska, the culmination of his egotism, infidelities, and abuse. With a few fictional manipulations, Corelli reverses the biblical mythos of original sin and projects it onto her personally engineered legend about Egypt. Yet in spite of Corelli's transformation of mummy fiction into feminist fiction, various popular romance conventions deployed in the novel limit its subversiveness.

As Janice Radway argues in *Reading the Romance*, women use romance reading as a way to reject their prescribed roles as wives and mothers by living vicariously through the adventures of romance heroines. Radway notes, however, that the romance text always contains dominant or hegemonic cultural threads that maintain "the ideological status quo" (217). So even as Corelli creates an exciting presentation of female sexuality and power, she also draws on ideas more recognizable as traditional, romantic clichés. For instance, the heroine of the romance plot frees her romantic hero to be his true, sensitive self, but only after much suffering on her part (Radway 216), and in the case of Ziska, that suffering transpires over more than a millennium. Similar to romance novels, *Ziska* also includes the basic message that the heroine's role is to transform a bad man into a good one—even if it takes thousands of years. So although Araxes has the wicked soul capable of the sin that spawns an extraordinary curse, it is Ziska who unfairly suffers the consequences and must wait thousands of years to free them both.

One of the earlier origins for the word "monster" derives from the Latin word "monere" or "to warn." Ziska's conduct unambiguously warns audiences not to underestimate women, but Corelli's feminist message mixes with a more ambivalent tone in the novel as the unrepressed admiration for and monstrous presentation of the heroine's libidinal energies and execution-style strength suggests. Significantly, the writer diverges from the Gothic genre as she warns readers about refraining from exploiting women rather than regurgitating the nearly universal victimization of women in Gothic texts. It is important to note, too, that Corelli's representation of freely expressed libidinal desires in *Ziska* is quite unlike Bram Stoker's obviously sexist portrayal of Lucy Westenra, a weak, undisciplined woman who, because she lacks physical and moral strength, becomes doomed to vampiric existence. This is worth noting because it suggests that, even though Corelli inexcusably partakes in the orientalist trappings that saturated mummy narratives at this time, she was adapting the Gothic genre to engage broader social discussions about female sexuality and the mistreatment of women, conversations that were, perhaps, more easily imagined and more easily made palatable in popular fiction at the fin de siècle than other outlets available to the English populous.

Notes

1. See Bertha Vyers, *Memoirs of Marie Corelli*. Biographers have yet to conclusively determine whether the relationship between Vyers and Corelli can be best described, to paraphrase Annette Federico, as sexually intimate, "romantic" friends, loyal companions, or family (176).

2. According to Annette R. Frederico, Corelli's book sales averaged 100,000 per year. One of her novels, *The Sorrows of Satan*, sold 25,000 copies in a mere week's time (7).

3. In *Framed: The New Woman Criminal in British Culture at the Fin De Siècle*, Elizabeth Carolyn Miller argues that a "New Woman Criminal" emerged in various genres of popular fiction during the 1880s and 1890s, a fantasy figure that functioned to naturalize the changes of modern life: feminism, consumer culture, and new imperialism. Miller characterizes this figure as a femme fatale.

4. For an explanation of reverse colonization, see Stephen Arata's "The Occidental Tourist: *Dracula* and the Anxiety of Reverse Colonization."

5. As the famous story goes, in 1922 the archaeologist Howard Carter and his financial backer, Lord Carnarvon, excavated King Tutankhamun's tomb, and during his trip to Egypt, Carnarvon developed septicemia from a mosquito bite. His death became a sensation, retold in the press as the consequence of a "pharaoh's curse." Corelli did not hesitate to share her own concerns quite openly, even publishing her thoughts on Carnarvon's demise, claiming that she warned him about the deadly risks of exhuming a Pharaoh's tomb. This anecdote about Corelli is mentioned by several critics, but her novel, *Ziska*, rarely is.

6. As many critics attest, the mummy romance narrative normalizes the exploitation of Egyptian tombs by portraying the archaeologist's transgressions as his love for the object of study. Such narratives abound. H.D. Everett's *Iras: A Mystery* (1896) spotlights

a supernatural romance between an English Egyptologist and an ancient Egyptian woman he resurrects. Henry Rider Haggard's "Smith and the Pharaohs" (1912) tells the story of an Egyptologist who falls in love with an Egyptian queen after observing her likeness in a museum. He then travels to Egypt where excavates her tomb, meets her spirit in the Cairo museum, and discovers he is none other than the reincarnated spirit of an Egyptian artist.
  7. For information about William Stead's work at *The Review of Reviews*, see p. 126 of Roger Luckhurst's *The Invention of Telepathy*.
  8. See p. 21 of Judith Halberstam's *Skin Shows*.

Works Cited

Arata, Stephen. "The Occidental Tourist: *Dracula* and the Anxiety of Reverse Colonization." *Victorian Studies* 33.4 (1990): 621–45. Print.
Ardis, Ann. *New Women, New Novels: Feminism and Early Modernism*. New Brunswick: Rutgers University Press, 1990. Print.
Askew, Alice, and Claude Askew. *Aylmer Vance: Ghost Seer*. 1914. London: Wordsworth Editions, 2006. Print.
Baudrillard, Jean. *Simulacra and Simulation*. Trans. Sheila Faria Glaser. Ann Arbor: Michigan University Press, 2004. Print.
Blackwell, Algernon. "The Nemesis of Fire." *Out of the Sand: Mummies, Pyramids, and Egyptology in Classic Science Fiction and Fantasy*. Ed. Chad Arment. Landisville: Coachwhip, 2008. 174–238. Print.
Blavatsky, H.P. *Isis Unveiled*. 1877. Radford: Wilder Publications, 2007. Print.
_____. *The Key to Theosophy*. 1889. New York: Theosophical Publishing Company, 1889. Print.
_____. *The Secret Doctrine: The Synthesis of Science, Religion, and Philosophy*. 1888. London: Newnham, Cowell & Gripper, 1893. Print.
Brantlinger, Patrick. *Rule of Darkness: British Literature and Imperialism, 1830–1914*. Ithaca: Cornell University Press, 1988. Print.
Brier, Bob. *Egyptomania*. Middlesex: Brockville, 1992. Print.
Casey, Janet Galligani. "Marie Corelli and Fin de Siècle Feminism." *English Literature in Transition, 1880–1920* 35.2 (1992): 163–78. Print.
Conan Doyle, Arthur. "Lot No. 249." *Late Victorian Gothic Tales*. Ed. Roger Luckhurst. Oxford: Oxford University Press, 2009. 109–140. Print.
Corelli, Marie. *Ziska: The Problem of a Wicked Soul*. 1897. Ed. Curt Herr. Kansas City: Valancourt, 2009. Print.
Daly, Nicholas. *Modernism, Romance, and the Fin de Siècle: Popular Fiction and British Culture, 1880–1914*. New York: Cambridge University Press, 1999. Print.
Davison, Carol Margaret. "Marie Corelli: A Critical Reappraisal." *Women's Writing: The Elizabethan to Victorian Period* 13.2 (2006): 181–87. Print.
Day, Jasmine. *The Mummy's Curse: Mummymania in the English-Speaking World*. New York: Routledge, 2006. Print.
Deane, Bradley. "Mummy Fiction and the Occupation of Egypt: Imperial Striptease." *English Literature in Transition, 1880–1920* 51.4 (2008): 381–410. Print.
Egerton, George. *Keynotes and Discords*. Ed. Sally Ledger. London: Continuum, 2006. Print.
Felski, Rita. *The Gender of Modernity*. Cambridge: Harvard University Press, 1995. Print.
Frederico, Annette R. *Idol of Suburbia: Marie Corelli and Late Victorian Literary Culture*. Charlottesville: University of Virginia Press, 2000. Print.
Grand, Sarah. *The Heavenly Twins*. 1893. London: Forgotten Books, 2012. Print.

Gurney, Edmund. *Phantasms of the Living*. 1886. London: Forgotten Books, 2012. Print.
Halberstam, Judith. *Skin Shows: Gothic Horror and the Technology of Monsters*. Durham: Duke University Press, 1995. Print.
Hodgson, W.H. *The Casebook of Carnaki: The Ghost Finder*. 1913. London: Wordsworth Editions, 1987. Print.
Humbert, Jean-Marcel, Michael Pantazzi, and Christiane Ziegler. *Egyptomania: Egypt in Western Art 1730-1930*. Ottowa: Éditions de la Réunion de Musées Nationaux Paris/National Gallery of Canada, 1994. Print.
Ingram, Heather. "Religion and the Occult in Women's Modernism." *The Cambridge Companion to Modernist Women Writers*. Ed. Maren Tora Linett. Cambridge: Cambridge University Press, 2010. 1–16. Print.
Ledger, Sally. "The New Woman and feminist fictions" *The Cambridge Companion to the Fin De Siècle*. Ed. Gail Marshall. Cambridge: Cambridge University Press, 2007. 153–168. Print.
Luckhurst, Roger. *The Invention of Telepathy: 1870-1901*. Oxford: Oxford University Press, 2002. Print.
_____. *The Mummy's Curse: The True History of a Dark Fantasy*. Oxford: Oxford University Press, 2012. Print.
Marsh, Richard. *The Beetle*. 1897. Ed. Julian Wolfreys. Ontario: Broadview, 2004. Print.
Mcfarlane, Karen E. "Mummy Knows Best: Knowledge and the Unknowable in Turn of the Century Mummy Fiction." *Horror Studies* 1.1 (2010): 5–24. Print.
Miller, Elizabeth Carolyn. *Framed: The New Woman Criminal in British Culture at the Fin de Siécle: Popular Fiction and British Culture, 1880—1914*. Ann Arbor: University of Michigan Press, 2008. Print.
Radway, Janice. *Reading the Romance*. London: Verso, 1987. Print.
Richards, Thomas. *The Commodity Culture of Victorian England: Advertising and Spectacle 1851-1914*. Stanford: Stanford University Press, 1990. Print.
Rohmer, Sax. "In the Valley of the Sorceress." *Out of the Sand: Mummies, Pyramids, and Egyptology in Classic Science Fiction and Fantasy*. Ed. Chad Arment. Landisville: Coachwhip, 2008. 355–368. Print.
Said, Edward. *Orientalism*. New York: Vintage, 1994. Print.
Stead, William T. *Real Ghost Stories*. 1891. London: Forgotten Books, 2012. Print.
Stoker, Bram. *Dracula*. 1897. New York: W.W. Norton, 1997. Print.
_____. *Jewel of the Seven Stars*. 1903. New York: Penguin, 2008. Print.
Thompson, Nicola Diane. *Victorian Woman Writers and the Woman Question*. Cambridge: Cambridge University Press, 2012. Print.
Vyers, Bertha. *Memoirs of Marie Corelli*. London: Alston Rivers, 1930. Print.

The Queer God Pan
Terror and Apocalypse, Reimagined

Mark De Cicco

Pan—last and youngest of the Olympian gods, guardian of shepherds and flocks, of wild natural spaces, and of rustic music—had become something of a phenomenon in much of Europe and North America by the turn of the twentieth century. Imagery of the goat-footed god could be found across literature and popular culture: from children's stories to Gothic horror; in painting, music, and dance; in advertisements on posters and in periodicals; and even on books of matches. This fascination has rightly been deemed a "Pan craze" (Owens 120). By the fin de siècle, the ancient god Pan, the source of panic terrors ("panic" means literally to fall under the influence of Pan [*OED*]), had become one of the era's defining monsters. This nineteenth-century Pan is a dark, vengeful, disruptive being: a monstrous prophet of apocalypse and queer embodiment of the death drive, and of the unknowable, incomprehensible abyss of deep time.

In this essay, I argue that this darkly reimagined Pan queers both the ancient mythological figure and the conventions of the Gothic monster while feeding off of the anxieties and desires of a disenchanted and secularizing Western world. Through a critical analysis of the depictions of the god in a selection of literary texts, including two poems by Elizabeth Barrett Browning, Algernon Swinburne's late work "A Nympholept," and Arthur Machen's fin-de-siècle novella "The Great God Pan," I will highlight the range of queer activities and possibilities represented by this darkly transformed ancient myth and attempt to trace the development of Pan as a queer, and queering, figure in popular English literature of the nineteenth century. As an attempt to catalog fully every instance of the dread-inducing Pan across the long nineteenth century would perhaps prove tedious, I will instead examine these representative works in order to provide what Judith/Jack Halberstam terms "a symptomatic history" (26) of Pan's development as an image of terror, disruption, and violence in English literature, culminating in the Gothic demonization of the figure by the fin de siècle. I will also consider Pan's cultural significance as a reflection of an increasingly apocalyptic view of the course of modern civilization that takes root by the turn of the twentieth century. As humanity hurtles toward a dark, unknown future, the ancient god Pan emerges from the shadows, becoming simultaneously a harbinger of horrifying death and rebirth into new, queer possibilities. In these works, Pan burns through the masks of the everyday, revealing a creeping horror that has threatened humankind through the ages. By broadening the impact of the monstrous Other, Pan effectually queers the Gothic monster of the nineteenth century and paves the way for the more chaotic monsters of the twentieth and twenty-first centuries. Reborn in the nineteenth century, Pan gestures simultaneously to the past, present, and future of the Gothic, Fantastic, and Weird genres.

The Queer Gothic Pan

Halberstam defines the Gothic "as the rhetorical style and narrative structure designed to produce fear and desire within the reader" (2). This fear "emanates from a vertiginous excess of meaning" and results in an "experience of horror" intimately linked to the "realization that meaning itself runs riot" (2). The figure that I term the "queer Gothic Pan" embodies an excess of meaning so potent that he is perceived as a serious threat to normative order and categorization. Those who encounter the queer Gothic Pan are caught in a maelstrom of conflicting emotions, hovering between horror and desire, panic fear and exultation. I believe this amorphous gray area between clearly definable emotional states can best be described as queer. As Hughes and Smith note in their seminal anthology *Queering the Gothic*, queerness refers to "a sense of difference" or "deviance from perceived norms" that both encompasses and transcends sexual behavior (3). While Pan is certainly a sexually queer figure, his queerness transcends the bodily. His appearance in English literature is almost universally disruptive and disturbing psychologically, temporally, spiritually, and sexually. Seen in this light, the queer Gothic Pan is a remarkable manifestation of societal anxiety over the place and function of the non-normative. Pan projects onto the "civilized" Victorian age an image of ancient chaotic forces that continue to shadow modern industrialized society, threatening disorientation should that chaos break through into the rational, physical world.

In *Queer Phenomenology*, Sara Ahmed argues that the encounter with the queer or unexpected is a disorienting experience that upsets our accepted worldview. This is followed by what Ahmed terms a "queer orientation"—a reorientation toward a "'slantwise'" view of the world which "put[s] within reach bodies that have been made unreachable" and objects previously unattainable or invisible under conventional circumstances (107). In the literature and art of Pan, the god functions as a disquieting figure that shatters accepted notions of civilized order and reorients those he encounters towards new, queer possibilities or orientations. Eating through the decaying walls of civilized modernity, Pan is a Freudian oceanic force of repressed, chaotic, queer drives that besiege civilized humanity, threatening to overwhelm the norm-enforcing superego with the limitless desires of the id. Pan's queerness is in this way a multifaceted, amorphous entity, like a raging body of water. It sexually and behaviorally queers the individual who ventures near, it swallows and disintegrates logic and order, and finally it washes away the moral, religious, sexual, and social structures that anchor Victorian society. This is the ultimate threat posed by the queer Gothic Pan: a subversion of Victorian normativity at micro and macro, individual and societal levels.

The queer Gothic Pan also queers the conventions of the Gothic monster, who is typically confined by some limitations or vulnerabilities. Pan lacks such restraints. He infects the Gothic victim with his monstrously overwhelming queerness, resetting that person's relationship to physical and spiritual experience. The queered, slantwise view of the world that Pan consequently reveals to his victims is an exhilarating and frightening experience of boundary-free limitlessness akin to hovering over a vast abyss. This overpowering revelation of the infinite compels the victim to confront the disturbing possibility that not all things can be explained or comprehended within the limited scope of science and materialism. Moreover, she or he must acknowledge that dark and terrible things have always existed, obscured but present, alongside the mundane and familiar. This deeply unsettling realization epitomizes the uncanny effect that Pan exerts over those he encounters. Pan's monstrous ability to reorient and queer the victim in this manner is a manifestation of what Paulina Palmer terms the "queer uncanny." Palmer posits that the queer uncanny is the experience of those slantwise, unsettling Gothic moments in literature, art, and film in which queerness and the Freudian uncanny overlap (6–8). While Palmer primarily uses the queer uncanny as an interpretive lens for modern Gothic works, I believe that the queer Gothic Pan is a queerly uncanny predecessor of the modern Gothicized figures that she studies. Pan's queerly uncanny effects on his victims, when combined with the figure's behaviorally and sexually queer activities, work to construct a new kind of monster that is both original and an amalgamation of older traditions.

An Ancient Nightmare: Pan and Terror Through the Ages

Pan has always been potentially terrifying. Though commonly depicted as a pastoral and benevolent (albeit mischievous) figure, the earliest recorded stories and traditions from antiquity also refer to Pan's power to frighten and cause panic. These attributes, combined with Pan's frequently horned and goat-footed appearance, and his association with unrestrained sexuality, fertility, and wild music led, during the Middle Ages, to the superimposition of the Christian Devil on to Pan (Russell, *The Devil* 126). Though Pan's association with evil and terror solidified in the Western imagination during the Christian era, the roots of this darker image of the god reach deep into antiquity. Several ancient literary and historical sources stand out for their depictions of threatening Pans: the Greek pastoral poet Theocritus' *Idylls* (third century BC), which describes a menacing entity who causes panic among shepherds, the sinister and vengeful undertones of Longus' depiction of the god in *Daphnis and Chloe* (second-third century AD), and the warrior–Pan who breeds panic terror among his enemies in Herodotus' *Histories* (fifth century BC). The threatening, ominous renditions of the god in these ancient works serve as prototypes and points of reference for the darker re-envisionings of the god that appear centuries later. As early examples of Pan's sinister behavior, they also show that more benevolent depictions of the god have always been shadowed by something darker—a queered reflection of a mythological figure that could already be considered queer. Like a monstrous mask glimpsed in a funhouse full of mirrors, Pan becomes ever more disturbing by a multiplication of the bizarre. Deflecting direct lines of sight, he avoids clear definition and thereby becomes exponentially more terrifying.

Pan's reappearance as a literary figure in early Victorian Britain will be the focal point of this study. Earlier in the nineteenth century, writers like Wordsworth, Shelley, and Keats invoke a pastoral, gentle Pan in works like Shelley's "Hymn of Pan" (1820) and Keats's "Hymn to Pan" (1818). Sublime and mysterious yet nonetheless a benign force, the Romantic Pan is a mystical embodiment of the spirit of animate nature and poetic inspiration, "occasionally heard, but almost never seen" (Merivale 76). This Pan is not a bodily presence, but rather a spiritual influence intimately connected to place and natural space. Over the course of the nineteenth century, literary depictions of Pan gradually shift away from this conceptualization of a rustic, benevolent nature god and muse. By mid-century, "the Victorians eschewed the abstract concept of Pan as a spirit of the place" (Chapman 273) for what Merivale calls a "concrete and sharply visualized Pan" (qtd. in Chapman 273). This is Pan the goat-god—a tangible and increasingly terrifying physical presence. Simultaneously, many writers and artists seize on more sinister strands of the ancient myth, like those found in Theocritus and Longus, as well as on medieval artistic conventions of depicting the Devil with Pan-like features such as the horns, shaggy legs, and cloven hooves of a goat (Russell, *The Devil* 126). The darker, classically-inflected aspects of the god also begin to merge with elements of then-contemporary Gothic literary conventions to create a modern monster that echoes ancient and medieval traditions, while embodying nineteenth-century fears and anxieties over social changes and threats like secularization, sexual liberation, degeneration, and the rapid societal changes undergone since industrialization. Pan speaks to a sense of unease over an uncertain future in which traditional beliefs and ways of living have (perhaps prematurely) been cast aside.

The queer Gothic Pan is a monster of an increasingly anxious age in which science and materialist conceptions of the universe had gradually begun to break down centuries-old religious structures and understandings of the world. He appears at a time when, as Hobsbawm puts it, "God was not merely dismissed, but actively under attack" by forces of science, modernity, and secularization (271). Nonetheless, there remained "a nostalgia for religion" (273) that could no longer be quenched by traditional religious beliefs. The "Pan craze" of the late-nineteenth and early-twentieth centuries and supernaturalist phenomena, like the rise of spiritualism, the appearance of occult organizations like the Hermetic Order of the Golden Dawn, and the Cottingley fairies incident,[1] suggest a popular desire for fantastical re-enchantment in an increasingly disenchanted world.[2] The queer Gothic Pan is a refraction of older traditions, reoriented through Gothic and fantastical, supernatural tropes—a queered, Gothicized monster haunting ancient pagan (rather than medieval Catholic, as in traditional Gothic writings) ruins, artifacts, and places of power that lie beneath the surface of a disenchanted, secularized modern life. This sense of a mystical, superstitious past that continues to echo in the present directly connects the literature of Pan to both the Gothic tradition and to contemporary issues and discourses that haunted Victorian Britain.

Elizabeth Barrett Browning and the Death and Life of Pan

The darker Pan notably resurfaces in the midcentury poetry of Elizabeth Barrett Browning. Barrett Browning's reimagined Pan is both terrifying and sexually and behaviorally queer. Her Pan, like that of Swinburne and Machen later in the century, is a harbinger and queer agent of a deconstructed modernity, demolishing boundaries between animal and human, inside and outside, male and female, homosexual and heterosexual. Pan wields his queerness as a weapon, smashing heteronormative structures in his path.

Though Barrett Browning's early piece, *The Battle of Marathon* (1819), is her first work to feature the god Pan (and to depict him as monstrous),[3] it is her mature poems "The Dead Pan" (1844) and "A Musical Instrument" (1860) that bring renewed attention to Pan's sinister features. These works are two of her most popular and frequently anthologized pieces and arguably did more to color public perception of Pan in Victorian Britain than those of any other author. In "The Dead Pan," the god is cast as a corrupting, behaviorally non-normative anti–Christ figure. His death symbolizes the passing of the ancient gods, which makes way for the ultimate triumph of Christianity. Morality has changed, and Pan's death signals an end to the behaviorally and sexually queer practices and celebrations of the pagan gods of Greece and Rome with their lusty "revels" (8) and excessive, inebriating "libations" (214). The ancient gods' wine that "crawls in the dust" (215), and their "Wormlike" glories (216) can be read with reference to the original archaic meaning of the Old English word "wyrm": according to the OED, "a serpent, snake, dragon," traditional embodiments of evil and/or the Christian Devil. Like her medieval predecessors, Barrett Browning diabolizes Pan. Furthermore, she shows how the sinister, sexually and behaviorally queer pagan gods are routed by the normative benevolence and austere love of Christ:

> Earth outgrows the mythic fancies
> Sung beside her in her youth,
> And those debonair romances
> Sound but dull beside the truth.
> ....
> Christ hath sent us down the angels;
> ....
> And Pan is dead [232–245].

Against this Christianizing backdrop Pan can no longer be seen as a harmless god of nature, but rather as a false idol that can potentially lead humanity astray from the straight and narrow. The refrain "Pan, Pan is dead" (or some variation of this) is repeated at the end of every stanza, and by repetition becomes a prayerful celebration of Christ and the imposition of a new, hegemonic Christian order that sheds the queer trappings of the pagan past.

Barrett Browning returns to the Pan myth sixteen years later in "A Musical Instrument." This poem retells the ancient myth of Pan and Syrinx popularized by Ovid in Book One of *Metamorphoses*. Pan pursues the nymph Syrinx to the bed of a river, presumably to rape her. Just before catching her, sympathetic river deities transform Syrinx into "a bunch of marsh reeds" (March 117). Unlike Ovid's gentler and more sympathetic portrayal of Pan, in Barrett Browning's version "Pan has returned as 'the great god Pan' vibrant, but violent and destructive: 'Spreading ruin' ... and tearing out a reed from the river" (Davies 565). Here Pan is a force of queerly disorienting sexualized violence who frightens away dragonflies and leaves dead flowers in his wake. He makes his pan-pipes from the reeds into which Syrinx has been transformed and forcefully blows into the shell of her body, out of which comes "piercing sweet" music (Barrett Browning, "A Musical Instrument" 32). The language Barrett Browning uses illustrates the violent rending of barriers and the breakdown of order: Pan "hacked and hewed as a great god can, / With his hard bleak steel" (15–16), cutting away leaves and any other signs of generative life from the reed. The sexual implications of this language are difficult to miss. Mermin describes this episode as a "deliberate articulation of sexual assault" (243). This contrasts sharply with Ovid's original in which Pan, more than Syrinx, is the object of pity and suffering. Barrett Browning flips reader's and speaker's sympathies, rewriting a classic from the perspective of a wronged female. In doing this she has effectually queered the Ovidian myth from a male-oriented adolescent fantasy of "the one that got away" to a frightening tale of sexual violence perpetrated by a powerful male god against a helpless female.

In "A Musical Instrument," Pan is a sexualized monster: his forceful hacking of the reed/Syrinx obliquely reflects a rending of the hymen, while his subsequent playing of the torn reed suggests a final expression of mastery over the already violated female. Syrinx's plaintive cry emitted through Pan's piping of the reed is, however, more ambiguously described as both beautiful and painful, reviving the natural life that died or fled upon Pan's arrival:

> Piercing sweet by the river!
> Blinding sweet, O great god Pan!
> The sun on the hill forgot to die,
> And the lilies revived, and the dragon-fly
> Came back to dream on the river [32–36].

Pan's sexual violence is orgasmic—a temporary "little death" that both kills and creates. From Syrinx's agony, Pan makes beautiful, rather than sorrowful, music (Chapman 283). This music is an example of what Chapman calls the "destruction and inexpressible delight" (279) that are simultaneously expressed through Pan in this work. Barrett Browning's retelling of the Pan and Syrinx myth illustrates the disturbing mixture of pain and pleasure that Pan has come to symbolize. Reborn in mid-nineteenth-century Britain, Pan has become a monstrous queering force of violent and terrible jouissance. As Mermin remarks, with "A Musical Instrument" Barrett Browning "introduces into English poetry the idea of Pan as a sexually brutal creature that became commonplace afterwards but had rarely appeared before" (243). Barrett Browning's Pan has become a pagan beast-god, a violent *wilder mann* of nightmare and prehistoric mythic memory. This Pan is exponentially more terrifying than before, for his motivations and very existence lie in the realm of the irrational and inexplicable, buried in the depths of the pre–Christian past.

The horror of Pan's irrationality seems inextricably linked to these pagan origins. I see a parallel between Pan's irrational, bacchanalic features as depicted by Barrett Browning and Nietzsche's exploration of Western society's Dionysian elements (which he argues stand opposed to the Apollonian features of Christianity). As Russell explains, "Nietzsche identified the Devil with Dionysius, who was for him the rich, ambivalent, but generally positive symbol of creativity, chaos, fertility, destruction, sexual license, and courage. Under the influence of Nietzsche and Romanticism, Dionysius and Pan became popular symbols in the art and literature of the end of the [nineteenth] century" (*Mephistopheles* 226). Pan, traditionally depicted as a friend and follower of Dionysius, and Christ, who in the early Christian era took on aspects of the ancient Apollo, stand juxtaposed in "The Dead Pan" and "A Musical Instrument." In these poems, Barrett Browning contrasts spiritually luminous Apollonian Christ-figures against dark, earthy Dionysian Pans. This counterpointing of Pan/Dionysius and Christ/Apollo is implied, for example, in "A Musical Instrument" when "the true gods sigh" (40) for lost Syrinx while Pan laughs. More dramatically, in "The Dead Pan," Pan dies at the moment of Christ's sacrifice:

> 'T was the hour when One in Sion
> Hung for love's sake on a cross—
> ....
> When his priestly blood dropped downward
> And his kingly eyes looked throneward—
> Then, Pan was dead [183–189].

While Pan dies, the heroic risen Christ replaces Phoebus (a Latin name for Apollo "in his capacity of god of the sun" [Smith 343]) in the heavens, for "Phoebus' chariot-course is run" (236). The speaker encourages poets to look toward Phoebus' former domain ("Look up, poets, to the sun!" [237]), which has been filled by Christ: "And the whole earth and the skies / Are illumed by altar-candles / Lit for blessèd mysteries" (240–242). Having taken on the mantle of Phoebus/Apollo, Christ lights up the world as the new God of light. This example of the dynamic tension between Christianity and paganism reflects Barrett Browning's personal struggle as a Christian in accepting the classical heritage of authors whom she admires. Homer and Ovid, whose works feature an understanding of morality often markedly different from Christian beliefs, haunt the margins of Barrett Browning's poems, attracting and repelling simultaneously. Indeed, several of Barrett Browning's works are accompanied by some sort of denial, refutation, or apology for the pagan subject matter. And yet again and again she returns to Pan. I believe this can be partially explained by the appeal of Pan's dual monstrous and benevolent nature, which itself parallels Barrett Browning's feelings of attraction and repulsion for the classical heritage. After Barrett Browning, the Romantic Pan of benevolent nature vanished (at least for a time), replaced by the animalistic, horned—and horny—goat-god, a being utterly lacking in empathy and driven by an untamed, hyper-sexualized id.

Swinburne and Sexual Obsession

Though Barrett Browning popularized a darker, hyper-sexualized Pan, it would be Swinburne and Machen who would bring the figure to a fever pitch of demonic intensity. Swinburne's depiction of the god in particular is more overtly, irresistibly seductive and irrationally terrifying than earlier incarnations. In contrast with the devoutly Christian Barrett Browning, whose Pans function as queered shadows of Christ, for the atheist Swinburne there is no Christ-figure to temper the pantheistic paganism represented by Pan. Rather, in Swinburne the paganistic becomes a virtue opposed to a restrictive sense of Christian morality. Swinburne was unabashedly open in his admiration for ancient myth and culture, and many of his works (and the poet himself) have been described by contemporaries and modern critics as neo-pagan. Hutton argues that it is Swinburne who re-stoked pagan fires in Victorian Britain, first raising "the standard of paganism in the field of revolt" in the 1860s with *Atalanta in Calydon*, which was styled after ancient Greek drama (25). The ancient gods of Greece and Rome frequently figure in Swinburne's works, and Pan is no exception.[4] The darker, Theocritan vision of Pan in his late poem "A Nympholept" (1891) is especially striking, as it emphasizes unmoderated emotional responses to the god that "are of the two extremes of ecstasy and terror" (Merivale 96). "A Nympholept" features both foreboding tones of doom and sublime feelings of awe at the workings of life, death, love, and divinity. This awe becomes intimately tied to the pagan gods, and particularly to Pan, who intensifies these already overwhelming sensations into a deep, terrifying, and powerful experience of divinity in and through nature. Swinburne's Pan is an overwhelming force that, while located externally, is experienced internally, affecting the subject simultaneously from inside-out and outside-in. The awe, panic fear, and terror inspired by a wild, animalistic natural world is expressed through Pan and experienced physically and psychologically through enraptured figures like the nympholept.

"A Nympholept" depicts the approach of Pan and his nymphs from the perspective of a nympholept: a person (typically a man) paralyzed in sexual thrall to a nymph or nymphs. Swinburne's Pan is "a demonic overlord"—sadistic, amoral, and horrible (Wilson 64). In this daymare, the rays of the fierce Mediterranean sun bring "awareness of [Pan's] cruelty" (64). Swinburne's language describing the sunlight is evocative of this demonic Pan: "fierce," "fearful," "unmerciful," "loveless," and "naked," while the light "pervades, invades, appals" (85–88). As in Barrett Browning's Pan poems, a monstrous Pan threatens to overwhelm any sense of order or equilibrium. This time, however, no reformative rays of Christianity appear to banish Pan's queering, chaotic influence. Instead of looking to the heavens, the nympholept calls "on the gods hard by" (43)—the physically grounded gods present in nature, like Pan, who are "at hand" (44) and can be *felt* rather than merely worshipped. This desire for a tactile deity—a god that can be physically experienced—is for the nympholept personified by a Pan that inspires powerful emotions, like terrific fear and intense sexual desire, which are manifested bodily.

As Pan approaches, the nympholept experiences primal panic terror tinged with desire. The queerness of this sexualized desire is revealed by the conflicting emotions of extreme fear and lust that course uncontrollably through the nympholept's being. He is unsure if he suffers from "panic dread" or "panic passion," to use Swinburne's language (qtd. in Fisher 795). The nympholept's uncertainty regarding his own feelings, as well the resistance he encounters in trying to linguistically define them, are signs of the inherently queer nature of Swinburne's Pan, who functions as a catalyst of queer desires—in this case, sexual obsession and masochistic thralldom. The distinctly non-normative sensations experienced when touched by Pan result in Ahmedian "queer disorientation": the nympholept's perspective has shifted, and a set of hybridized alternative pathways that were once obscured have opened before him. As Fisher remarks, "terror and delight merge repeatedly in 'A Nympholept'" (795) as the terrible, queerly disorienting jouissance of Pan is taken to new heights. Pan's queerly painful and ecstatic pleasures can also be read as a product of what Dollimore terms "sexual dissidence." Sexual dissidence is a way of queering the subject "by claiming non-normative desires as essential to one's nature" (Denisoff 432). Pan causes his subjects to feel that their own queer, uncontrollable desires—e.g., panic dread/passion—are inherent and inescapable. Pan queers the subject by exposing the sexual dissidence that lies dormant within the individual.

Pan's ability to encompass difference, or what we might term a panchotomous "all"—pleasure and pain, queer and heteronormative desires of all kinds—is an essential aspect of the god's attractions. Ridenour suggests that the appeal of Pan in "A Nympholept" is the promise of union with the divine: with the god, with the nymph, and with nature itself (7). Those who seek Pan desire a sense of wholeness and at-oneness that only he can provide. Pan, like the modern paganism that so attracted Swinburne, offers "a spiritual dissipation of the self within a natural collective" (Denisoff 435). However, this potential union is also destructive to the individual, as it threatens to erase the boundaries of individual identity. As Ridenour argues, by the end of "A Nympholept" the potentiality of union "dissolves almost instantly ... [for] in Pan the quality of terror is too great to be assimilated" by any individual (7). Yet it is already too late for the nympholept, who cannot flee. This phenomenon of inescapability—the inability to break one's thrall to the monstrous Pan—is the figure's strongest link to contemporary Gothic monsters like Dracula, Mr. Hyde, or Dorian Gray.

Many late-Victorian Gothic works feature moments in which the victim completely submits to the monstrous Other, as a willing vampiric victim of Dracula, or Dr. Jekyll's surrender to the temptations of the progressively uncontrollable Mr. Hyde, or Dorian Gray's submission to the horrific portrait that mirrors the fate of his soul. The Gothic victim loses control over his destiny, enthralled as he is to the monster that threatens to engulf him. What makes Pan effectually different from other monsters is the god's inexplicability. Dracula is physically described and observed by many people and scientifically studied by Van Helsing. Richard Marsh's "Beetle" is also described in detail and confronted with science, and we are even given some physical descriptions of Mr. Hyde. Such descriptions and characters' attempts to understand or counter the monster provide at least some sense of control over it. However, if one wishes to remain sane, one must never catch even a fleeting glimpse of Pan, which is often enough to drive one to babbling madness (as occurs repeatedly in Machen's "The Great God Pan"). Even mere contemplation of Pan, as in "The Nympholept," leads to terrified paralysis.

Unlike Dracula or other late Victorian Gothic monsters, Pan can never be comprehended or effectively combated with rational means, for science breaks down when confronted with Pan's queer monstrosity. Pan's utter incomprehensibility, and the way that his irrationality overwhelms the individual, make him unique among contemporary Gothic monsters. Pan is more than just a being with a monstrous physical body. He is a chaotic force that comes crashing through the veneer of civilized modernity. Pan tempts, invites, and enraptures the curious souls who seek him out in the hope of eternal union with the divine and infinite, only to reveal his irrational, queerly disruptive and destructive nature to the helpless subject. In doing this, Pan opens to them a slantwise view of the universe that is too much for mortals to bear. Pan then destroys the individual by overwhelming her or him with the chaotic force of life unrestrained.

Peering Over an Abyss: Machen's Apocalyptic Pan

Arthur Machen's novella "The Great God Pan" (1894) is the culmination of the queered Gothicization of Pan that begins with Barrett Browning and Swinburne. This Pan reborn into the fin de siècle is nastier, more horrifying, and more overtly sexualized than his predecessors. Machen amplifies the darker aspects present in earlier writers' depictions of Pan, such as the god's violent tendencies and his ability to inflict panic fear, while intensifying his queer sexuality. In this work, Pan and his kin become sexualized terrors that force human beings to confront unveiled horrors beyond their comprehension.

To briefly summarize the plot, Dr. Raymond seeks to lift the veil between material and spiritual worlds by way of an experimental neurosurgical procedure performed on his orphaned ward, Mary. As Raymond boasts to his friend Clarke, "'for the first time since man was made, a spirit will gaze on a spirit-world. Clarke, Mary will see the god Pan!'" (Machen 4). After the operation, Pan presumably appears to Mary, impregnating her in the process. Mary consequently enters a catatonic state, never regaining her senses. Though she dies in childbirth, Mary is survived by a daughter named Helen, who grows up among mortal folk. Once Helen reaches young adulthood, Pan apparently reveals himself to her, his presumed daughter. Thereafter Helen becomes a living terror—a manifestation of Pan in human form—and uses the potent sexuality of her queer, hybrid body to seduce modern British men, women, and children. Helen compels her victims to face the horror and chaos of the deep past and forces them to choose between infernal union with the infinite (which threatens loss of the self in the vastness of time and the ubiquity of evil) or death by their own hands. Madness, moral degeneracy, and suicide follow. Machen's Pan hovers over the text like a half-forgotten nightmare, glimpsed and referred to, but never described in great detail. His threatening presence, however, is always at hand. As Dr. Raymond explains, the physical world is no more than "dreams and shadows: the shadows that hide the real world from our eyes. There *is* a real world, but it is beyond this glamour and this vision ... beyond them all as beyond a veil.... [I]t may be strange, but it is true, and the ancients knew what lifting the veil means. They called it seeing the god Pan" (2). Pan is revealed to be a symbol of something greater and more horrifying than merely a mythological figure. He is a demonic force of pure evil that has *always* existed just beyond human perception—pan-evil, existing across pan-time, only now physically appearing in fin-de-siècle London in female form. Pan's spatial, physical, and temporal shifts underscore the transformation of the god of antiquity into the great god Pan: a queer Gothic monster and modern embodiment of evil.

The queer Gothic Pan exists within and without human perception. He is both dream and waking nightmare, male and female, and inhabits the modern world and the ancient past simultaneously. Worth argues that the horror of Pan is owing to his embodiment of the abyss of "deep time," a "kind of terrifyingly expansive past that had forced itself into the Victorian consciousness during the previous decades" (216) due to new conceptions of geological and evolutionary time. By the century's close these new areas of study had already actively "undermined or actually disproved" many of the "verifiable statements in the Judeo-Christian holy scriptures" (Hobsbawm 271). Pan, whose name has (albeit through etymological error [Boardman 26–27]) traditionally been understood to mean "all," personifies the monstrous horror integral to this sense of immeasurably deep time that threatened established understandings of temporality. As Cohen posits, "the monster is a category that is not bound by classificatory structurations, least of all one as messy and inadequate as time" (ix). Machen's Pan monstrously transcends time, crushing humankind with the vastness and inconceivability of the infinite. By continuously existing in the deep past, present, and future, Machen's Pan queers understandings of "straight" time—linear, teleological, and diachronic—and introduces a queered sense of time.

I define this queered sense of time as synchronic, immeasurable, and lacking a clear beginning or end. Thus Pan, existing in a queered sense of time, can simultaneously appear as a modern human woman (Helen) and as a creature of the deep past (Helen's atavistic transformations). This queered, synchronic temporality, shifting forward, backward, and sideways in time, is illustrated by Helen's unstable body: "I saw the form waver from sex to sex, dividing itself from itself, and then again reunited. Then I saw the body descend to the beasts whence it ascended, and that which was on the heights go down to the depths, even to the abyss of all being" (Machen 46). Pan's influence has fundamentally queered Helen's body. Helen's wavering, morphing form, moving through a reverse or parallel evolutionary process, signals the collapse of traditional modes of interpreting and regulating conceptions of time, species, gender, sexuality, the body, and human nature itself. Regulation and categorization disintegrate, leaving chaos in their wake.

Helen awakens dormant memories of this primordial chaos which "inhere in every human" (Fox 66). She rips away the veil concealing "the horror which underlies the quiet surface of life" (Punter 22) and reveals that humanity exists tenuously in a state of siege from ancient "dark forces" (Punter and Byron 146). Chaotic life itself, unmediated by constructed civilized perceptions, becomes the ultimate horror (Fox 66–67). Helen is the queer agent of chaos who provides the lit fuse to this primordial bombshell that lies underneath the fortification of civilization. Helen's inherent queerness lies in this ability to wreak disorienting chaos as she undermines normative structures of marriage, sex, power relations, and generative potential. This Pan in drag sabotages heterosexual relationships and destroys the possibility of futurity by leading heterosexual British men and women to suicide or madness. Like the ghost or revenant of the Gothic tale, Helen is "a kind of transvestite, destabilizing gender as [she] terrorizes the straight subject" (Fincher 10), particularly the aristocratic bachelor-detectives who attempt to reassert heteronormative authority over her queer, resistant body.

The havoc Helen causes among British male aristocrats, her primary targets, reflects contemporary real-life male anxiety in Europe and North America caused by the "New Woman." The New Woman was a term used in the latter half of the nineteenth century to refer to sexually and behaviorally liberated women who felt emancipated from male domination. Popular press and literature responded (often hysterically) to the perceived threat that the New Woman posed to traditional society, leading to what Showalter terms a "masculinity crisis" in the West (10). In art and literature of the fin de siècle, this crisis is often dealt with imaginatively through depictions of powerful femme fatales whose "castrating potential" produces "an exaggerated horror" in the viewer (10). Machen's Helen is an über-New Woman of nightmares: a queer being that fulfills paranoid male anxieties over the castrating female who has come to strip aristocratic men of the keys to the kingdom.

Helen's body itself is the locus of this sexual panic surrounding the queer (and especially the queer female) in this work. All who interact with her experience distress, confusion, intense fear, and disorientation, as men, women, and children are drawn to her in spite of themselves. Helen's unrestrained sexuality—queer for her time and place—causes a particularly riling panic in the heterosexual men, and a consequent reaction that is both fearful and vengeful. This pandemic of panic is the most powerful manifestation of Helen's monstrosity. Such disorienting "impact(s)," as Mittman argues, are "rooted in the vertigo of redefining one's understanding of the world" and caused by the encounter with the monstrous (7–8). Helen defies traditional Victorian gender and sexual roles, her queer body casting a monstrous shadow, invisible but subliminally perceptible to the straight men who pursue her.[5] They, in turn, experience a panic of category crisis upon encountering Helen, for they are unable to classify and thereby exert control over her body:

> Every one who saw her at the police court said she was at once the most beautiful woman and the most repulsive they had ever set eyes on. I have spoken to a man who saw her, and I assure you he positively shuddered as he tried to describe the woman, but he couldn't tell why. She seems to have been a sort of enigma; and I expect if that one dead man [one of the suicides] could have told tales, he would have told some uncommonly queer ones [Machen 20].

These "uncommonly queer" tales would likely be colored by the queerly uncanny feelings of unease that Helen triggers in others. Helen forces a new, queered orientation onto those she encounters—a slantwise view of the world which reveals ancient horrors coexisting in the same space as a mortal human woman. Pigeonhole conceptions like beauty or ugliness lose significance in her presence. The straight men that see Helen, like those at the police court, become disoriented and unsettled by her queer body's resistance to categorical interpretation. Fincher argues that Gothic writings are marked by "the multiplicity of potentially conflicting interpretations" which is mirrored in "the fear of ... queer bodies whose gender or sexuality cannot be easily read and who remain suspicious" (67). At once physically female, but imbibed with the dark powers of a male Pan, Helen's body queers any attempt to categorize or exert control over it, and this, according to Fincher's criteria, "signifies a queerness in [its] resistance" to external control and heteronormative power structures (67). This resistance to control, according to Mittman, is a hallmark of the monstrous: the monster "is outside of ... definitions; it defies the human desire to subjugate through categorization. This is the source, in many ways, of their power" (7).

Helen's subversion of Victorian conceptions of patriarchal sexual hierarchy is horrifyingly demonstrated in the novella's final scenes, when her body undergoes transformations before the group of straight men who have come to oversee her execution/suicide as punishment for her crimes. Rational comprehension and conventional means of communication, like speech and writing, break down in the face of the transmutations, as the narrative begins to shatter into fragments (indeed, Chapter VIII is entitled "The Fragments"). Dr. Matheson's manuscript describing Helen's monstrous transformation is scribbled in Latin and "was only deciphered with great difficulty, and some words have up to the present time evaded all the efforts of the expert employed" (Machen 45). Clarke's letter to Raymond and Raymond's to Clarke are likewise fragmentary. Helen's queer monstrosity defies not only reason but also the men of science who impose reason upon Victorian society. This demolition of rationality clears a path for the incomprehensible and inexplicable queerness of the shadow-world embodied by Pan.

Machen's Pan is made even more terrifying because of his proximity to humankind, not to mention his capability to affect them psychologically, spiritually, and physically. Through scientific procedure, he can be touched and is biologically capable of impregnating a human woman. Yet Pan remains a mystical being and a cultural entity associated with Western antiquity. The boundaries between these many personae are not clearly defined, and the end effect of an encounter with the boundary-less Pan is uncanny and extraordinarily discomfiting. Like more traditional monsters, Pan is a liminal being that exists along the gray, amorphous borders between the physical and spiritual worlds, in a "sphere unknown" (Machen 3) to a humanity limited to the tangible. The terror of Pan is thus of the chaotic, incomprehensible infinite which threatens to expand out of the liminal borders and swallow the finite being in its horrible vastness—an impression experienced by Machen's Clarke, who "'has peered over an abyss, and has drawn back in terror'" (qtd. in Worth 217).

Pan reveals that the world at the turn of the twentieth century is fundamentally queer, albeit in a way that is horrifying rather than liberating. Murder, suicide, madness, rampant sexuality—Pan breaks down the walls that separate rational, modern humanity from these socially unacceptable behaviors. He is a reminder of what Punter and Byron refer to as "past, half-hidden memories that remain lodged in the individual psyche" which are "inseparable from humankind's bloody history" (146). Pan revives these ancient memories, heretofore buried in deep time. His ability to reach into the mind of the individual, overriding their will and accompanying mechanisms of psychological repression, exposes humanity's inability to resist Pan's grasp.

Destabilizing nature, history, power structures, and sexual and gender norms, Machen's Pan inflicts chaotic mayhem on a world hurtling towards an apocalyptic twentieth century. He is the culmination of the terrifying

Gothicization of Pan that began with Elizabeth Barrett Browning and would later be explored by writers as diverse as Algernon Blackwood, Saki, E. F. Benson, E. M. Forster, and D. H. Lawrence. Through Machen, Pan truly becomes a queer being, exploding any attempts to classify or understand him in normative terms. Machen's demonic, terrifying, and queerly disruptive, Gothicized Pan foreshadows the coming of a new age, when humanity's sins against the natural world and against the instinctual, innate desires and needs of the individual will be reckoned.

Conclusion: Queerly Weird

In the essay "Weird Fiction," China Miéville argues that Machen's "The Great God Pan" is marked by a horror of the failures of "democracy and the perceived vulgarities of modernity's 'disenchantment'" (513). I argue that Pan is the figurehead of this disenchantment and a harbinger of coming crisis in the Western world. His reappearance in Britain in the nineteenth and early-twentieth centuries speaks to a sense of cultural and societal dis-ease that would soon culminate in world war. As Miéville argues, "the growing proximity of this total crisis—kata-culmination of modernity, ultimate rebuke to nostrums of bourgeois progress" is expressed in the monsters of nascent Weird fiction ("M. R. James and the Quantum Vampire" 111). Though Pan is a traditional mythological figure, he shares many similarities with the creatures of Weird fiction as defined by Miéville. I see the queer Gothic Pan as a precursor to the monsters of the Weird. Like Lovecraft's hybrid monstrosities, Pan is god, demon, and mortal, humanoid and animal with origins that extend into prehistory. Like Cthulhu, Pan inspires inexplicable panic terror in those he encounters. Pan literature, like Weird fiction, is marked by the shattering of natural law and the divide between inside and outside ("Weird Fiction" 510–511). Both share an "obsession with numinosity under the everyday" and at the same time "focus ... on awe and its undermining of the quotidian" (510). Finally, Pan literature, like the Weird, expresses a literary moment marked by "upheaval and crisis" (513). And while Miéville argues that the creatures of the Weird harken back to the horrors of World War I, I suggest that Pan literature prophetically looks ahead to the coming cataclysm. Like a dark, pagan reflection of John the Evangelist, Pan foretells a reckoning of sinners (and sins): the inexplicable, a-rational terror that Pan inspires thus prefigures the agonies experienced on and off the battlefields of World War I.

However, unlike John's *Book of Revelation*, Pan's message is not one of ultimate salvation but rather of apocalypse. This Pan is a harbinger of the gathering storm of world war and the end of a Western hegemony and way of life that has become unsustainable. The queer Gothic Pan reflects a dark vision of the future and of a chaotic past that has returned to wreak havoc upon the material world. Queer, Gothic, and proto–Weird, Pan embodies the fears and desires of transformational times. He is a transitional figure that speaks to the past and the future and as a cultural phenomenon paved the way for the next breed of Weird and transformational fictional monsters that still stalk our bookshelves and video screens today.

Notes

1. For more on these phenomena, see Alex Owen's *Place of Enchantment: British Occultism and the Culture of the Modern* and article "'Borderland Forms': Arthur Conan Doyle, Albion's Daughters, and the Politics of the Cottingley Fairies," Antonio Melechi's *Servants of the Supernatural: The Night Side of the Victorian Mind*, and Peter Washington's *Madame Blavatsky's Baboon: A History of the Mystics, Mediums, and Misfits Who Brought Spiritualism to America.*
2. For a more detailed discussion of the concepts of disenchantmant and re-enchantment during the long nineteenth century, see *The Magical Imagination: Magic and Modernity in Urban England 1780–1914* by Karl Bell.
3. *The Battle of Marathon* is based on an incident reported by Herodotus in his account of the Persian Wars of the fifth century BC. Barrett Browning embellishes Herodotus' relatively sparse text with dramatic detail. This is evident in her description of Pan, which strongly emphasizes the god's brute physicality and monstrosity: he is described as "the monster Pan" (2.668), "dreadful" (2.669), "awful" (2.678), and "grim" of visage (2.673). This terrifying, corporeal figure is echoed in Barrett Browning's later Pan poems.
4. Between 1887 and 1893 Swinburne wrote several Pan poems, including "Pan and Thalassius," "The Palace of Pan," and "A Nympholept" (Merivale 96).
5. Helen's monstrous shadow can be read as a dark double, a trope common to late Victorian Gothic works like Robert Louis Stevenson's *The Strange Case of Dr. Jekyll and Mr. Hyde* (1886) and Oscar Wilde's *The Picture of Dorian Gray* (1891). For more on the double as a literary trope, see Karl Miller's classic *Doubles: Studies in Literary History.* For more in-depth intertextual readings of *The Great God Pan* alongside other late Victorian Gothic works, see *The Literature of Terror, Vol. 2: The Modern Gothic* by David Punter, *The Gothic Body: Sexuality, Materialism, and Degeneration at the Fin de Siècle* by Kelly Hurley, and my article "'More than Human': The Queer Occult Explorer of the Fin-de-Siècle."

Works Cited

Ahmed, Sara. *Queer Phenomenology: Orientations, Objects, Others.* Durham: Duke University Press, 2006. Print.
Bell, Karl. *The Magical Imagination: Magic and Modernity in Urban England 1780–1914.* Cambridge: Cambridge University Press, 2012. Print.
Boardman, John. *The Great God Pan: The Survival of an Image.* London: Thames and Hudson, 1997. Print.
Browning, Elizabeth Barrett. "The Battle of Marathon." *The Poetical Works of Elizabeth*

Barrett Browning: Cambridge Edition. Ed. Ruth M. Adams. Boston: Houghton Mifflin, 1974. 485–489. Print.

_____. "The Dead Pan." Browning, *Poetical Works* 188–191. Print.

_____. "A Musical Instrument." Browning, *Poetical Works* 437–438. Print.

Chapman, Alison. "'In our own blood drenched the pen': Italy and Sensibility in Elizabeth Barrett Browning's Last Poems (1862)." *Women's Writing* 10.2 (2003): 269–286. Print.

Cohen, Jeffrey Jerome. "Preface: In a Time of Monsters." Preface. *Monster Theory: Reading Culture.* Ed. Jeffrey Jerome Cohen. Minneapolis: University of Minnesota Press, 1996. vii–xiii. Print.

Davies, Corinne. "Two of Elizabeth Barrett Browning's Pan Poems and Their After-Life in Robert Browning's 'Pan and Luna.'" *Victorian Poetry* 44.4 (2006): 561–569. *ProQuest.* Web. 20 Nov. 2012.

De Cicco, Mark. "'More than Human': The Queer Occult Explorer of the *Fin-de-Siècle.*" *The Journal of the Fantastic in Arts* 23.1 (2012): 4–24. Print.

Denisoff, Dennis. "The Dissipating Nature of Decadent Paganism from Pater to Yeats." *Modernism/Modernity* 15.3 (2008): 431–446. *ProQuest.* Web. 17 Jan. 2013.

Fincher, Max. *Queering the Gothic in the Romantic Age: The Penetrating Eye.* New York: Palgrave Macmillan, 2007. Print.

Fisher, Benjamin F. "Swinburne's 'A Nympholept' in the Making." *Victorian Poetry* 47.4 (2009): 787–800. *Project Muse.* Web. 20 Nov. 2012.

Fox, Paul. "Eureka in Yellow: The Art of Detection in Arthur Machen's Keynote Mysteries." *Clues* 25.1 (2006): 58–69. *ProQuest.* Web. 14 Dec. 2012.

Halberstam, Judith. *Skin Shows: Gothic Horror and the Technology of Monsters.* Durham: Duke University Press, 1995. Print.

Herodotus. *The Histories.* Trans. Aubrey De Selincourt and John Marincola. London: Penguin, 1996. Print.

Hobsbawm, Eric. *The Age of Capital: 1848–1875.* New York: Vintage, 1975. Print.

Hughes, William, and Andrew Smith. Introduction. *Queering the Gothic.* Ed. William Hughes and Andrew Smith. Manchester: Manchester University Press, 2009. 1–10. Print.

Hurley, Kelly. *The Gothic Body: Sexuality, Materialism, and Degeneration at the Fin de Siècle.* Cambridge: Cambridge University Press, 1996. Print.

Hutton, Ronald. *The Triumph of the Moon: A History of Modern Pagan Witchcraft.* Oxford: Oxford University Press, 1999. Print.

Machen, Arthur. "The Great God Pan." *The Three Imposters and Other Stories: The Best Weird Tales of Arthur Machen, Volume 1.* Ed. S. T. Joshi. Hayward: Chaosium, 2007. 1–50. Print.

March, Jenny. *The Penguin Book of Classical Myths.* London: Penguin, 2008. Print.

Melechi, Antonio. *Servants of the Supernatural: The Night Side of the Victorian Mind.* London: Arrow, 2009. Print.

Merivale, Patricia. *Pan the Goat-God: His Myth in Modern Times.* Cambridge: Harvard University Press, 1969. Print.

Mermin, Dorothy. *Elizabeth Barrett Browning: The Origins of a New Poetry.* Chicago: University of Chicago Press, 1989. Print.

Miéville, China. "M.R. James and the Quantum Vampire: Weird; Hauntological: Versus and/or and and/or or?" *Collapse: Philosophical Research and Development* 4 (2008): n. pag. *Weird Fiction Review.* Web. 17 Jan. 2013.

_____. "Weird Fiction." *Routledge Companion to Science Fiction.* Ed. Mark Bould and Sherryl Vint. London: Routledge, 2008. 510–515. Print.

Miller, Karl. *Doubles: Studies in Literary History.* Oxford: Oxford University Press, 1985. Print.

Mittman, Asa Simon. "Introduction: The Impact of Monsters and Monster Studies." *The Ashgate Research Companion to Monsters and the Monstrous.* Ed. Asa Simon Mittman and Peter J. Dendle. Farnham: Ashgate, 2012. 1–14. Print.

Owen, Alex. *The Place of Enchantment: British Occultism and the Culture of the Modern.* Chicago: University of Chicago Press, 2004. Print.

_____. "'Borderland Forms': Arthur Conan Doyle, Albion's Daughters, and the Politics of the Cottingley Fairies." *History Workshop* 38 (1994): 48–85. *JSTOR.* Web. 15 July 2014.

Owens, Jill Tedford. "Arthur Machen's Supernaturalism: The Decadent Variety." *The University of Mississippi Studies in English* 8 (1990): 117–126. Print.

Palmer, Paulina. *The Queer Uncanny: New Perspectives on the Gothic.* Cardiff: University of Wales Press, 2012. Print.

"Panic, adj. and n.2." *Oxford English Dictionary Online.* Oxford University Press, 2013. Web. 29 Jan. 2014.

Punter, David. *The Literature of Terror: A History of Gothic Fictions from 1765 to the Present Day, Vol. 2: The Modern Gothic.* 2d ed. London: Longman, 1996. Print.

Punter, David, and Glennis Byron. *The Gothic.* Oxford: Blackwell, 2004. Print.

Ridenour, George M. "Swinburne in Hellas: 'A Nympholept.'" *The Victorian Newsletter* 64 (1983): 4–8. Print.

Russell, Jeffrey Burton. *The Devil: Perceptions of Evil from Antiquity to Primitive Christianity.* Ithaca: Cornell University Press, 1977. Print.

_____. *Mephistopheles: The Devil in the Modern World.* Ithaca: Cornell University Press, 1986. Print.

Showalter, Elaine. *Sexual Anarchy: Gender and Culture at the Fin de Siècle.* New York: Viking, 1990. Print.

Smith, William. Ed. *Dictionary of Greek and Roman Biography and Mythology, Vol. 3.* Boston: Little, Brown, 1870. Print.

Swinburne, Algernon Charles. "A Nympholept." *Selected Poems.* Ed. L. M. Findlay. Manchester: Fyfield, 1982. 232–240. Print.

Washington, Peter. *Madame Blavatsky's Baboon: A History of the Mystics, Mediums, and Misfits Who Brought Spiritualism to America.* New York: Schocken, 1993. Print.

Wilson, F. A. C. "Indian and Mithraic Influences on Swinburne's Pantheism: 'Hertha' and 'A Nympholept.'" *Papers on Language and Literature* 8 (1972): 57–66. Print.

"Worm, n." *Oxford English Dictionary Online.* Oxford University Press, 2013. Web. 30 June 2013.

Worth, Aaron. "Arthur Machen and the Horrors of Deep History." *Victorian Literature and Culture* 40 (2012): 215–227. *Cambridge Journals.* Web. 14 Dec. 2012.

Attack of the Mushroom People
Ishirô Honda's *Matango* and William Hope Hodgson's "The Voice in the Night"

Anthony Camara

Virtually unknown except to aficionados of Asian cult cinema, fans of Weird literature, and sleepless consumers of late-night television programming, Ishirô Honda's 1963 *tokusatsu* (special-effects) film *Matango*, produced by the Toho company, deserves wider recognition as one of the most visually provocative and thematically unsettling horror movies made in Showa-era Japan.[1] Sean Kotz compares the film to genre classics like Kaneto Shindo's *Onibaba* (1964), Nobuo Nakagawa's *Jigoku* (*The Sinners of Hell*, [1960]), and Hajime Sato's *Kyuketsuki Gokimidoro* (*Goke, Body Snatcher from Hell*, [1968]).[2] Kotz even proposes that the film is "probably the most significant, disturbing and influential of Japan's 60s horror/sci-fi psychodramas." Indeed, many American viewers who were introduced to *Matango* in 1965, when it was released directly to television under the title *Attack of the Mushroom People*, vividly remember its grotesque, human-fungus hybrid monstrosities, as well as its baleful atmosphere of physical and spiritual degeneration. Despite the film's merits, which include a sharply-written screenplay by Takeshi Kimura and impressive visual effects by long-time Honda collaborator Eiji Tsuburaya (who worked with the director on his popular *Gojira* [Godzilla] films), *Matango* has attracted relatively little scholarly attention, save that from Peter H. Brothers, who devotes a chapter to the movie in his detailed study *Mushroom Clouds and Mushroom Men: The Fantastic Cinema of Ishiro Honda* (2009; revised 2013). Stuart Galbraith IV also includes an entry on *Matango* in his critical filmography of Japanese horror, fantasy, and science-fiction films (84–7). By and large, however, reviewers and fans have been quickest to respond to the incitements of *Matango*.

While various aspects of the film invite investigation, it is particularly significant that *Matango* was loosely based on William Hope Hodgson's maritime short story, "The Voice in the Night," which first appeared in the November 1907 *Blue Book Magazine*. Hodgson, a British pioneer of the Weird horror literature that is today widely associated with H.P. Lovecraft, wrote prolifically and for a living.[3] Before his life was cut short in World War I, Hodgson published a multitude of short stories in popular periodicals and four novels, among them the cosmic horror masterpieces *The House on the Borderland* (1908) and *The Night Land* (1912). In "The Voice in the Night," a seaman onboard a vessel in the Pacific is awakened by a voice "curiously throaty and inhuman" (15),[4] issuing from the darkness surrounding the boat. From deck, the sailor listens to the visitor's chilling narration. The voice (which gives its Christian name as John) and his fiancée were *en route* to their wedding in the *Albatross*, which was demolished in a tropical storm. The lovers drifted to an island blanketed in a vile fungus quivering with life. Exposed to the organism's spores, they soon found birthmark-like growths dotting their skin. As the transmutation took hold of their bodies, the couple watched themselves becoming less human with each passing day. John speculated that this calamity was a punishment from God—a conclusion evidently supported by the discovery of his companion eating the fungus, like Eve in the Garden of Eden. True to biblical type, John also partook of the forbidden fruit. The voice relates that he and his fiancée swore never to go among healthy humans again. He then thanks the sailor for sharing his provisions, bids farewell, and rows off toward the island. As dawn breaks, the seaman glimpses "John," or whatever remains of him, in the distance. Hodgson writes that he resembles a "great, grey nodding sponge" (24) with a bulbous head bereft of any human features.

The central question of this chapter inheres in the relationship between Hodgson's short story and Honda's film. How and why, I ask, is Hodgson's pre–World War I tale adapted for post–World War II Japanese cinema? I respond to this question by arguing that the metamorphic human-fungus bodies of "The Voice in the Night" provide Honda with a powerful imagery for the rapidly transforming Japanese social body, which had not only undergone drastic cultural, political, and economic changes in the years immediately following World War II, but continued to do so in the mid–Showa period around the film's release, during the so-called "era of high-speed growth" that lasted from 1955 to 1974. These two decades saw Japan rebound from the devastation of World War II with a surging economy that stimulated profound alterations in the structure of society, not the least of which included a massive population influx into urban centers. Gary D. Allinson writes that "[f]ew nations had ever undergone such an extensive economic transformation in such a short period of time. England took almost a century to reduce its agricultural sector from 40 percent of the labor force to 15. Japan compressed this change into twenty short years" (122).[5] Allinson notes that the Japanese economy seemed to come "out of nowhere to surpass Canada, France, Great Britain, and West Germany. By the mid-1970s Japan's GNP was second only to that of the United States" (122). With economic prosperity came a demand for more secondary and postsecondary educational institutions capable of offering the training required to secure a newly-minted, high-salary career in one of the big cities. In the 1960s, Japanese consumers also began purchasing household appliances such as vacuum cleaners, washing machines, refrigerators, and sewing machines (Allinson 118).

Japan's speedy transition from the ruins of the postwar years to the prosperity of the 60s suggests the complex symbolism of the volatile, monstrous bodies on display in *Matango*. Due to the crucial physiochemical role that it plays in ecosystems as a decomposer, fungus has long been associated with death and decay in mythology, folklore, and literature.[6] I argue that the fungal body in Honda's film registers a fear of the dissolution of traditional Japanese culture and values in the midst of the sweeping changes following World War II, in particular those that took place in the "era of high-speed growth." And yet, as Hodgson's short story attests to, with its sprawling fungal jungle and tenaciously-spreading specimen, the fungus is also marked by its potential for explosive and unlimited growth. Consequently, I show that the mycological body also signifies a hastily emerging, modernized Japanese society with different social and labor relations, material conditions, lifestyles, and values, especially those of the youth that pertain to recreational drug use, dating, and sexuality. As in Hodgson's tale, the frighteningly dynamic morphology of the creatures in *Matango* couples the decomposition of the human form with the simultaneous (re)production of the monstrous body, thereby suggesting the breakdown of the old society and the concomitant (re)formation of a new and hideous, yet patently regressive one. Thus *Matango* powerfully critiques Japan's so-called "Golden Years." Honda is not, of course, attacking wealth and improved material conditions *per se*; rather, his target is the degraded human monsters that create, and are created by, excessive wealth and its trappings. To that end, for a work evidently focused on bodies, *Matango* is strongly concerned with psychology. The film explores how changes in material conditions, graphically registered as symptoms on the monstrous body, influence perception, thought, and identity (this theme is also developed through the film's extensive, and inevitable, engagement with psychoactive substances). Therefore, *Matango* is not a simple body horror film,[7] nor could it be said that its creatures solely reflect Cold War anxieties about thermonuclear apocalypse and proliferating radioactive waste, as is the case for many *kaiju* (giant monster) films.

Matango *and Life in Showa Japan*

The film begins with a nighttime shot of the Tokyo skyline (actually a miniature created by Tsuburaya) streaked with neon lights and smog. The clamor of traffic and machines suggests that "the very heart of the city is cold, mechanical and hollow," writes Brothers (217).[8] As the camera tracks backward, the cityscape becomes framed in the window of a dark room, and an off-screen voice intones, "[t]his is the psychiatric ward. Yes, I know that. And you think that I'm insane, don't you?" The camera continues to track backward into the room, bringing a figure into view with his back toward the audience. "All of my friends died," he says, "every one of them. No—I'm the one who died. It's true, they're alive. Then you want to know why they didn't return, don't you? I don't want to tell you the story because it would only convince you that I really am insane." This figure—who sounds like an unreliable narrator from one of the fictions of H.P. Lovecraft or Edogawa Ranpo—is the film's protagonist, Dr. Kenji Murai (played by Akiro Kubo), who was once a professor of psychology at Jonan University. Like John, who tells of his transformation to the sailors in "The Voice in the Night," Honda sets up Murai in this opening scene as a frame narrator who relates the events that follow. (At the end of the film, we discover that Murai's auditors are the psychiatrists engaged in studying him.) Murai's cryptic use of life and death in this monologue complicates his status as the sole survivor of the film's events. Although he is the only one who made it back to Tokyo, he insists that he is dead and his friends are alive. Kotz writes that Murai "is physically alive, so life and death in this context mean something else." Recalling the fate of Murai's fictional counterpart, John, indicates what life and death mean in the context that Murai uses them here. Murai has "died" in the sense that he has lost his identity, if not sanity, in the process of becoming-fungus (a twist revealed at the conclusion of the film), with the implication that he has not only transformed physically but also psychologically. In any case, whatever it is that lives and breathes inside the hospital cell no longer considers itself to be Dr. Kenji Murai, even though it possesses his memories. Thus, the first scene of *Matango* introduces the film's major thematic concern: the relationships between one's physical or material condition, mental state, and identity.

Honda follows this scene with a shot of a yacht cruising over the sea on a sunny day, signaling that Murai is now narrating the events of the film in flashback. As the opening credits roll over paintings of garishly colored sails, the buoyant saxophones and trumpets of the title track strike hollow notes in the wake of the film's gloomy opening and the foreknowledge that this excursion is about to take a horrifying turn. The discordance between the grave beginning and exuberant sequence that follows implies the falsity of appearances, especially social ones, and thereby primes the viewer for the film's critique, which exposes the rottenness behind the seductive wealth of Showa Japan. Rich industrialist and nightclub owner Fumio Kasai (Yoshio Tsuchiya) has invited some friends out on his new yacht, the *Ahodori* (Japanese for "Albatross," which is the name of the ship destroyed by the hurricane in "The Voice in the Night," leaving John and his fiancée stranded on the cursed island[9]). Along for the voyage are Murai; Akiko Soma (Miki Yashiro), a university student and Murai's fiancée; Kasai's current love interest, Mami Sekiguchi (Kumi Mizuno), a popular singer, television personality, and performer at Kasai's nightclubs; Etsuro Yoshida (Hiroshi Tachikawa), an up-and-coming writer of mystery novels; Naoyuki Sakuta (Hiroshi Koizumi), a relative and employee of Kasai's who is an experienced seaman; and Senzo Koyama (Kenji Sahara), a sailor who is hired help on the vessel.

Kotz writes that the passengers aboard the *Ahodori* form "an interesting cross section of early 1960s Japanese society." He notes that "Kasai, the successful businessman, reflects Japan's rapid rebirth as an economic power and the central role of businessmen in post–Imperial Japan ... every other character is dependent upon him to some degree just as Japanese society was dependent upon its newfound wealth." Although details in the film indicate that Kasai possesses exceptional wealth that may have originated from an inheritance, as a prosperous businessman, he also more generally suggests the emergence of the enviable white-collar professional known as the *sararii-man* (salary man). Allinson writes that the salaried worker "became the symbol of a new social category to which many now aspired.... The historical rarity of achieving such a position made it an object of desire for young company workers in the 1960s" (111).[10] The two artists, Mami and Yoshida, seemingly occupy a social station opposite that of Kasai's. Mami, however, has relied upon Kasai's patronage to launch her career, and Yoshida may have profited by knowing the industrialist. Whatever the case, the narcissism and hedonism of Mami and Yoshida exemplify the "escapism and indulgence of the post-war generation," Kotz claims. Ironically, the same could be said of Kasai; unlike the prototypically hard-working salary man, Kasai delegates all his work to employees while he enjoys the returns on their labor and his investments.

The scholars, Dr. Murai and Akiko, also indicate a major change in the social body of 1960s Japan. As more families moved into urban zones, obtaining secondary and post-secondary education for children became a top priority, as such training conferred social prestige and a competitive edge in the marketplace. Gains in the public and private sectors fueled an expanding network of high schools and colleges. The captain of the *Ahodori*, Sakuta, is also a product of this new educational system. Kasai funded his studies and granted him employment, with the result that Sakuta is a liminal figure marked by socioeconomic ambiguity: while he makes his living as the skipper of Kasai's yacht, he seems to draw a salary uncharacteristic of a sailor, and he no longer fits in socially with his seafaring counterpart, Koyama. An outcast on the ship, Koyama is onboard to handle the unsavory and dangerous tasks of sailing befalling members of his class. The blue-collar work that Koyama does represents the kind of physical labor that was by and large left behind by the modernized Japanese economy.

In addition to establishing the characters as a representative cross-section of society, the scenes on the yacht reveal fissures among the group that will cause it to fracture under the pressures of starvation, greed, desire, and threats from the island's mutants. Cinematographer Hajime Koizumi's first shot onboard the *Ahodori* captures the passengers in a top-down view from the ship's mainmast. Brothers compares this vantage point to "the perspective of an indifferent god" (216), yet this omniscient view overlaps with the audience's gaze, suggesting that it is the viewer who stands in moral judgment of the characters. By presenting the clique from above, the shot visualizes internal divisions among the group that contradict its supposed solidarity. Koyama, the second-class citizen, is at the rear of the ship, while Mami and Yoshida are set apart from the rest of the group. The distance separating them from the other travelers foreshadows their exile from the group and willingness to become mushroom people.

As Mami flirts with both Yoshida and Kasai, Akiko watches her with a look of scandal (and envy) on her face, before storming off below deck with Murai. Meanwhile, Mami charms her admirers by breaking into song. Smitten, Koyama asks Sakuta whether he knows if the entertainer is single or married. "Not exactly," replies Sakuta, his vague answer intended to convey Mami's ambivalent relationship status, as she is Kasai's personal guest, but she is also evidently attracted to Yoshida. Koyama's response is deaf to Sakuta's nuance and overly literal: "Oh, so she's somebody's mistress?" Sakuta responds by lifting his hat and running his fingers through his hair—a gesture that relates his frustration with Koyama's denseness and exasperation at the sailor for entertaining the notion that someone of his social class stands even a chance at romance with a celebrity "top girl" like Mami. This somewhat humorous exchange hints at the class distinctions that exclude Koyama from the group, not to mention how Sakuta's education and blood relatedness to Kasai have distanced him from his fellow seaman. The characters' differences in fashion bring these socioeconomic disparities into relief. Koyama wears a weather-beaten tank top, trousers, and baseball cap, while Sakuta, befitting his class ambiguity, sports a black turtleneck, matching military hat, and wayfarer sunglasses—an ensemble simultaneously maritime and "mod." Additionally, all the revelers onboard the *Ahodori*, with the exception of Koyama, wear gold chains with nautical steering wheel pendants, signifying membership in Kasai's exclusive yacht club. This gaudy jewelry suggests their distasteful elitism. The various socioeconomic and sexual conflicts foregrounded in these scenes do not just represent the fault lines along which the group will crumble. Considering that the passengers form a microcosm of 1960s Japanese society, Honda suggests that these tensions threaten the group's collective identity as *Nihonjin*—a coherent, unified Japanese people.

After a hurricane ravages the vessel, lack of food and water and extreme heat cause Yoshida to hallucinate a giant ship bearing down on the *Ahodori*—a scene that foregrounds the film's interest in abnormal psychology and foreshadows the writer's taste for psychotropic mushrooms. Kasai, Sakuta, and Mami argue over who is responsible for their situation, while Koyama is afflicted by being at sea in close quarters with women—an indication of sexual frustration that becomes physically hostile on the island. Before the group implodes, Koyama glimpses a fog-choked island mottled with jungle. The characters gather on deck, with Mami asking, "Is that Japan?" In the context of the group's plight, Mami's line expresses hope that the vessel has drifted back home; to the viewer, however, her question suggests that the remote island and its grotesque denizens somehow represent Japan, querying the viewer to recognize similarities and form associations between the two locales and their respective inhabitants. As this scene unfolds, the viewer simultaneously realizes the startling extent of the ship's ruination. The beautiful yacht that graced the opening scenes is now hardly recognizable as such, its masts shattered, sides streaked with rust, and exterior strewn with tattered sails and ropes that resemble masses of vines. The overall appearance of the boat generates an impression of almost organic decomposition, consistent with the decayed, fungus-clotted settings of the island. If the film's critique uses putrefying bodies and environments to graphically register the degeneracy of 1960s Japanese society, then the blighted *Ahodori* serves as a subtle but nevertheless telling visual cue that the characters, whom we have seen form a miniature of society, are the true source of the film's prolific rot, which they in essence bring to the island along with themselves.

Ashore, the characters find that the island bears water but little food. They soon come to a derelict run aground on a strip of beach. As they enter it, Koizumi shoots the characters from an angle that occludes the vessel's sides, giving the impression that the group is heading into the ruins of a forgotten metropolis[11]—a hint that the target of Honda's criticism is the unsavory side of modern urban existence and the base life-forms that it cultivates. The interior of the boat is coated with dust, refuse, cobwebs, rust, and various lividly-colored patches of fungi. The excruciating naturalistic detail that art designer Shigekazu Ikuno's sets achieve might be described, flatly, as nauseating. Brothers refers to the derelict ship as "the central character [of *Matango*].... The vessel seems not a dead but a living thing" (220). Consistent with the growth rate and morphological changes of fungi, during the film, the interior of the ship progressively blooms with diverse mycological life: ropy mycelia, carbuncle-like mushroom caps, and gill ridges that sprout from the walls. Perhaps even more than the film's creatures, *Matango* derives its effectiveness as a horror movie from this setting, which presents the viewer with the appalling vision of human beings living and dying in abject filth.[12] This spectacle would have been even more psychologically charged for viewers who witnessed the nuclear devastation at Hiroshima and Nagasaki and who were accustomed to the cleanliness of traditional Japanese aesthetics and the premium *Shinto* religious beliefs place on physical purity.

The ship presents a Weird permutation of horror's traditional Gothic settings. Instead of a rotting ancestral manor haunted by undead specters, *Matango* largely transpires inside a ship overrun with an immanently present and vitalized biological horror. The fungus in the ship's mess hall, which queasily overflows from pots and pans, is neon green, suggesting unnatural radiological fecundity and potential for growth. As they investigate the surroundings, Murai, Sakuta, and Kasai discover a laboratory complete with chemical apparatuses, a Geiger counter, and a cabinet of scientific curiosities. Murai opens the latter and finds a taxidermic marine turtle without eyes— "a good example of mutation caused by radiation," he observes—as well as specimens of monstrous fish in jars. More distressing than these strange births, however, is the gruesomely oversized mushroom that they find in a crate labeled "Matango." The characters surmise that the ship was an internationally-funded research vessel studying the mutagenic effects of nuclear radiation. While these scenes register Cold War fears of nuclear conflict and teratogenic radiation contamination—as do the fully-transformed creatures, which resemble atomic mushroom clouds—the film cannot be reduced to an allegory for these anxieties. As Brothers points out, radiation is but "a minor subtext" in the film (215), predominately limited to this short scene. If anything, the presence of radioactivity marks the "there" of the remote island as the "here" of the island of Japan, thereby encouraging 1960s Japanese audiences to connect the film's bizarre forms and modes of life with those prevailing around them. The scene suggests a powerful analogy: just as a nuclear explosion catalyzed the emergence and growth of the giant mushroom called "Matango," the nuclear blasts at Hiroshima and Nagasaki provided the historical preconditions for the explosively-growing economy and society of 1960s Japan, the real focus of the film's critique.

Social Rot

After foraging for edibles, Murai returns to the ship with some roots, which he proudly displays to the women in the kitchen. Just then, Koyama, beaming, enters with turtle eggs (a portion of which he has secretly consumed and stashed) and a sack of roots. Koyama's larger, phallic roots cause Murai to blush while the women look on. Beneath the humor of this scene, Honda suggests that the island operates according to a Darwinian economy of survival that is the inverted image of the modernized economic system that emerged during Japan's "era of high-speed growth." Within this primitive economy, the hardened Koyama out-competes the intellectual and professional men who out-earn him back home. According to the island's Darwinian laws, Koyama's ability to thrive under harsh conditions makes him fitter and a better provider, thereby increasing his access to females—hence the phallic roots and Koyama's lascivious grin when the women react with pleasure to his cache of food. Contrary to Sakuta's earlier disparagements, Koyama's desire for Mami now seems anything but hopeless. Although nothing could appear more at odds with the modern market, the regressive island economy reflects contemporary forms of economic participation in Japan. Koyama sells his surplus turtle eggs to Kasai at outrageous prices, extorting millions from the industrialist. Although Koyama seems to achieve socioeconomic mobility by fleecing the robber-baron and nearly securing Mami's affections, Koyama's actions nevertheless replicate the abusive capitalism that Kasai preaches. As the sailor increasingly resembles Kasai, the lowest socioeconomic stratum displaces the highest, revealing the primitive economy to be nothing but the modern one turned upside-down. Moreover, just as Kasai's economic dominance permitted him to exploit Mami, Koyama's monopoly on island resources indicates that he will do likewise. The economy of the island and mainland Japan, therefore, are fundamentally identical, operating according to the same logics of relentless competition, individualism, mindless accumulation (sounding like Kasai, who makes more money than he can spend, Koyama muses that he probably will not live to spend his fortune) and extortion of the highest price. To highlight that such economic exploitation is a literal dead end, when Yoshida murders Koyama, Koizumi's camera focuses on the worthless yen notes that come to rest around the sailor's corpse.

The last visitor to the kitchen is an empty-handed, drugged Yoshida, who has consumed mushrooms. At night, Koyama catches Yoshida and Mami engaged in foreplay and proceeds to attack the writer. Koyama does so not simply out of jealousy or anger that Yoshida broke a pact by the men to restrain their sexual urges; he presumably feels entitled to Mami's body because, as the best provider, he thinks that he has earned it. The men separate Koyama and Yoshida, but the writer reappears with the rifle and declares that he will kill the men and have the women, especially the virginal Akiko, to himself. Epitomizing individualism taken to inhuman extremes, Yoshida has decided that all males must be eliminated, which he later does to Koyama, the fittest man on the island. When Murai calls him a madman, Yoshida responds, "Yeah, I ate mushrooms ... I read in a book a long time ago that the Mexicans used to eat them in order to enhance their perception and get a sense of well-being ... Japanese legends mention laughing mushrooms, so I'm in good company. The people who went out to gather the mushrooms danced in high spirits in the mountains and were in touch with the infinite." The legend to which Yoshida refers forms part of the *Tales of Long Ago* (*Konjaku Monogatari*), an eleventh-century collection of folklore. In the tale, some woodcutters wander into a forest and encounter a group of singing and dancing nuns, who they assume "are certainly not human beings, but must be goblins or demons."[13] The nuns explain that they went into the forest to gather flowers to honor Buddha, but became hungry and ate mushrooms, which caused them to sing and dance uncontrollably. The starving woodcutters consume the fungus and experience the same effects. When the intoxication wears off they leave the forest, but not before naming the mushrooms *maitake* (*mai*, "dance" + *take*, "mushroom") (Sanford 174). Sanford refers to multiple sources that propose the *maitake* in the narrative are actually *waraitake* (*warai*, "laughter"), a different type of psychotropic fungi commonly known as "laughing mushrooms" (176). Indeed, the shots of growing mushrooms and hybrid monsters featured near the end of the film are accompanied by peals of mad laughter.

By referencing this folktale in the story, Honda stresses that the fungus is a psilocybin mushroom and should be interpreted as a representation of hallucinogenic drugs rather than just a supernatural plot device that induces fantastic corporeal transformations. *Matango* also reinterprets this lighthearted folktale in the vein of the Weird body horror that characterizes Hodgson's "The Voice in the Night." While the nuns and woodcutters indulge their appetites for food and revelry and then leave the enchanted space of the forest with their humanity intact once the psychoactive effects of the mushrooms abate, in *Matango*, consumption of the fungus irreversibly dehumanizes the characters, turning them into something not at all unlike the "goblins or demons" that the woodcutters mistake the nuns for. As such, the mushroom men are creatures that can never leave the island and rejoin humanity (to his detriment, Murai is able to do the former but not the latter). Accordingly, Yoshida culminates his paean to the entheogenic fungus by emphasizing its power to consummate inhuman becomings, exempting him from the constraints of all-too-human moral considerations: "Matango according to your understanding means a person who is no longer human. That's just fine by me because when I kill you, I won't be committing any crime." While this homicidal intent amplifies the violent and sacrificial dimensions to ritual that persist as traces in the involuntary and furious dancing recounted in the folktale, Yoshida's murderous impulses belie the humor and joyfulness of the experience that creates social cohesion among the nuns and the woodcutters in the *Tales of Long Ago*.

Yoshida's reference to the folktale is even more ironic when one considers that he relates its narrative, which depicts the formation of a social whole, at the very moment that he is threatening to sunder the group of friends, and to do so by means of murder and rape, the acts most inimical to society. This discrepancy between the folktale and the events of the film underscores *Matango*'s interest in processes of societal degradation, and more specifically, its concern with the deleterious effects of psychoactive substances. Refusing to reduce the film to simplistic anti-drug propaganda, Kotz writes that *Matango* can nevertheless be read as a cautionary parable, "especially since there was much international debate about the mind-altering effects of psilocybin mushrooms in the late 1950s and early 1960s. At that time, hallucinogens and Zen began to be tied loosely together and trippers were showing up high in Japanese temples by the early sixties." Hence Yoshida's speech alludes to the freewheeling, experimental spirituality of the counterculture, which mixed Eastern religious traditions with hallucinogens: "enhance their perception," "a sense of well-being," "high spirits," "in touch with the infinite," etc. (Kotz). Brothers notes that Akira Kubo, the actor who played Murai, recalled that Honda made the film during a phase of disillusionment with Japanese culture. Reflecting on *Matango* decades after its release, Honda wrote that "the film commented on the then 'Rebel Era' in which people were becoming addicted to drugs. Once you get addicted, it's a hopeless situation.

And, as among all human beings, no matter how good friends people are, even if they're the very *best* of friends, under certain conditions things can get very ugly" (Brothers 228).[14]

Just as Honda foregrounds the discordance between the folktale and Yoshida's own murderous intentions, thereby emphasizing his critique of the drug counterculture, the director also exploits contradictions between Yoshida's body and his discourse to much the same end. The folktale of the mushrooms is not simply about social formation; rather, it is about social formation *through transcendence*. Here, transcendence functions in multiple registers: having a bona-fide spiritual experience; transgressing human mental and corporeal limits; escaping into a higher metaphysical reality; achieving a state of blissful cosmic oneness; and overcoming the differences constitutive of personal and societal forms of identity, such as feudal station and gender. As we have seen, Yoshida's dialogue leans heavily on the language of transcendence, yet such speech is sorely at odds with his debased existence. Many of his lines are delivered in close-ups, which reveal beads of fever sweat, dark circles around his mad eyes, and a facial lesion crusted over with fungus and ringed by necrotic flesh. Considered on its own, Yoshida's language might lead one to believe that his transformation is spiritual and exalting, yet his decaying body indicates he is in the process of undergoing a metamorphosis that is thoroughly material and degrading in nature. Yoshida's words suggest that he believes himself to have become an enlightened spiritual creature, but the spectacle of his putrefying body signifies that the creature he is becoming is in fact nothing more than mindless, filthy base matter. After all, if Yoshida had stumbled into nirvana rather than just tripped on some *very* bad mushrooms, then why would he be caught more than ever in the undertow of the lowest carnal desires for drugs, sex, and homicide? Yoshida's rotting form, alongside Murai's warning that the fungus damages the central nervous system, implies that any pretensions the novelist has to ecstatic spiritual experience are, at bottom, demented illusions and perverse sensations caused by the breakdown of his own brain tissue. Descending into base matter rather than ascending into spiritual refinement, Yoshida has not transcended the human condition as much as sunk beneath it. His becoming, Honda suggests, is not just inhuman but subhuman.

Yoshida exemplifies how the monstrous bodies in *Matango*, which decompose under the corrosive powers of the fungus, register anxieties about spiritual, moral, and physical ruination, especially so when these pathologies are effected by drug abuse. Nevertheless, the fungal body also indexes fears of widespread societal ruination, which should hardly be surprising given that individual bodies collectively constitute the larger Japanese social body, and contamination of one reciprocally taints the other. From this perspective, Yoshida can be read as a morbid case study that graphically embodies the corruptive influences of 1960s trends in psychedelic drug use. And yet, the fungal body also symbolizes other species of societal rot even more pervasive than substance abuse, hence Kotz's insistence that the film cannot be dismissed as mere anti-drug propaganda. For instance, the infected Yoshida's appetite for sex (with both Mami and Akiko) and killing suggests lust, greed, and viciousness. By exploiting somewhat stereotypical associations of these vices with particular socioeconomic figures—the promiscuous nightclub singer, the avaricious capitalist, and the bloodthirsty writer of murder-mystery novels—and then dramatizing how they cut across such class distinctions, the film acknowledges these vices as epidemic ills that afflict the whole of the social field.

The film betrays its overriding concern with degeneration even when it turns its attention away from vice and towards virtue. For instance, shortly after the men lock up Yoshida, Honda includes a distant shot of Murai and Akiko attempting to gather food on a dreary beach. During this scene, the former, in a voice-over, proclaims that the "weak restraints of society disintegrate in the face of the will to survive in harsh circumstances. Man's power must be turned to creative action, his reason must grow stronger, if we are to continue to progress." The subtitled version is simple and plaintive: "[u]nder trying conditions, man tends to become selfish and cruel. That's when we must act in a rational manner. We must help each other." The scene extols the goodness of the protagonists while accentuating the wickedness of their counterparts. The lovers' work ethics, perseverance, love, and reasonableness contrasts the slothfulness, despair, hedonism, and irrationality of the others. This distant shot turns Murai and Akiko into tiny figures inhabiting a forlorn, desert island landscape. Honda thus implies that, as the only two ethical subjects on the island, the lovers are otherwise and for all intensive purposes alone—a bitter reflection on the scarcity of virtue in Showa Japan.

This scene and its voice-over would not be out of place in a World War II drama exploring how the values of Japanese civilians enabled them to survive the aftermaths of the Allied fire-bombings and nuclear tragedies at Hiroshima and Nagasaki. Honda[15] proposes that the ideals and virtues of the post-war generation—which not only sustained the Japanese through the traumas of World War II and the hardships of the MacArthur years, but also enabled them to build the infrastructure that paved the way for prosperity in the "era of high-speed growth"—have been lost on the spoiled, individualistic generation coming of age amidst the surplus wealth and goods of the 1960s. Here, Honda's film echoes right-wing critics who, as Andrew Gordon writes, "celebrated the growing power of the economy ... [but] lamented the way affluence threatened to undermine what they described as traditional Japanese values of endurance and sacrifice to a larger collective" (266).[16] Therefore, this scene on the beach articulates the film's critique of a modern, moneyed Japan on the verge of losing its foundational values—a decay that finds its most vivid expression in the progressively decomposing anatomies of the mushroom men. As per Gordon's quotation, they are avatars of a materialistic age in which society rots under the weight of its own accursed share of excess wealth. They prefigure a victory of materialism so absolute as to abolish everything that is not base matter itself, leaving both the individual and society bereft of spirit, form, and identity.

The Prolificacy of Decadence

The fungal body personifies a manifold of degenerative processes, yet in the final part of this paper, I consider how *Matango* deploys the *productivity* of the monstrous body in its allegory of Showa-era social realities. I demonstrate that (de)generative fungal bodies dramatize the emergence of a lucrative economy during the boom years of the "era of high-speed growth" and that the liminality of these bodies bespeaks a process of mass cultural homogenization that threatens personal and collective forms of Japanese identity. *Matango* foregrounds these concerns in its treatment of the wealthy industrialist Kasai, suggesting that in many ways, his character maps to Japan's national character. This congruity is nowhere more evident than in the sequence depicting Kasai's consumption of the mushrooms and resulting hallucinatory fantasy. As the drug's effects take hold, Honda cuts from a delirious Kasai to a patch of mushrooms that shimmer with multicolored lights, indicating that the audience is "experiencing" Kasai's drug trip via a first-person perspective. Honda uses a fade-in that superimposes Kasai's hallucination of the gaudy interior of a nightclub, likely the one that he owns, over the patch of shiny toadstools; the "lights fantastic" that Kasai sees in the mushroom patch effectively become the lights illuminating the nightclub—a continuity that prompts the audience to associate the fungal grotto with Kasai's den of iniquity in Tokyo. A spotlight switches on, revealing a showgirl who does inverted splits, followed by a procession of female burlesque dancers, one of whom repeatedly executes split-legged flips. All the while, Honda incorporates shots of a neon-lit Tokyo skyline, creating a montage of imposing buildings and sexualized bodies that would neither be out of place in Shibuya, Tokyo's business district, nor Kabuki-Cho, its pleasure district. Kasai's fantasy culminates with the reappearance of a dancer who has seemingly morphed into Akiko.

This hallucination indicts the capitalist's superficiality and materialism, as it reveals that what Kasai values most are the emptiest pleasures of life back home: the tawdry glitz of Tokyo nightlife, and using his nightclub, not to mention his money and power, to procure sexual trysts with women he employs. But it is important to recognize the correspondences this hallucination creates between life-forms on the island and lifestyles in Tokyo. In addition to the way special-effects lighting connects these locales, the images of buildings awash in neon use the same color palette as the creatures and their wretched environs. Concrete grays match the dingy tones of fungal growths, while the neon signs recall the blotches of lurid color on the mushroom men and toadstools. Brothers writes that the creature suits "were constructed out of latex and coated in fluorescent paint to give the impression of phosphorescence" (220). Honda thus identifies the neon glow of the city with the bio-luminescence of the fungal body, implying that the city and its residents are no different from the jungle and its denizens: a degraded superorganism, a sprawling form of lower mycological life radiating a sickly, unnatural glow of vitality.

In the hallucination, Honda further entwines the prolific fungal body with modern metropolitan life by incorporating images that stress Tokyo's emergence as an international business powerhouse. Many of the shots comprising Kasai's fantasy feature multi-story commercial buildings—likely in Shibuya—covered with advertisements, suggesting not only Japan's thriving 1960s economy but also the ways in which said economy was profoundly transforming public social space. This procession of urban scenes reflects the Showa-Era proliferation of buildings and zones dedicated to commerce, yet the proximity of these images to the fetishized showgirls and their frenzied dancing suggests that the forces driving this economic expansion have become obsessional and out of control—an instance of "bad growth" that recalls the pervasively spreading fungal body. Steering the audience towards this interpretation, shortly before Kasai's hallucination, Honda shoots toadstools growing in the rain at a freakish rate, accompanied by crazed laughter and eerie organ music that emphasizes the anomalous nature of the organism's powers of increase. Thus Honda likens an economically surging Japan to the fungus—an organism that, due to its preternatural capacity to spread and (re)produce, is profoundly successful. Yet this outrageous success is simultaneously an ecological catastrophe, as the fungus decomposes complex, conscious human and non-human organisms and then reassembles their biomolecules into a lower, less organized form of life. In effect, this prosperous, evolutionarily fit organism perversely ensures the succession of a less sophisticated, regressive species dangerously close to the base matter that life arose from in the very first place.

Consequently, in the fungus and its *modus viviendi*, Honda devises metaphors powerfully critical of capital and its *modus operandi*. *Matango* proposes that commercial success in the "era of high-speed growth" has passed into the realm of excess, creating a dehumanizing economic system that does not just sustain itself on commerce, but parasitically feeds on the cultural substrate of Japanese values, traditions, and ways of life, only to replace them with a formless, homogenized, and decadent agglomeration of materials that in no way resembles civilization. And so, Honda stresses the barbarous and regressive nature of life on the island, where the Darwinian dynamic prevails. In a time of unparalleled fiscal prosperity, *Matango* defies commonplace assumptions that growth and wealth always translate to progress, asserting that the price of excess is not only the loss of Japan's identity but also its fundamental humanity. Reiterating this point, Kasai is frightened out of his reverie by a leering Yoshida, further "advanced" in his transformation and squatting in the mushroom patch as his body becomes a toadstool. Kasai runs headlong into some mushroom men and prostrates himself in fear, suggesting that the industrialist is an even lower form of parasitic life than they are.

Another aspect of Kasai's fantasy cites social problems contingent on Japan's economic productivity. As corporations burgeoned, salary men spent increasing amounts of time away from their wives and children, socializing afterhours with co-workers and clients at bars and nightclubs. Gordon points out that white-collar workers customarily drank in the presence of female bar hostesses, which drove the growth of the "water trades"—so named because the hostesses poured the men's cocktails—into a multi-billion dollar industry between the 60s and today (255). Gordon writes that the water trades mixed aspects of 1920s café culture with *geisha* entertainment, "generally stopping short of prostitution but not ruling out occasional liaisons with customers" (255). In addition to taking place inside a club, Kasai's fantasy is filled with images of neon-lit nightclub marquees. Considering that Mami likely traded sexual favors with Kasai to jump-start her career and to obtain residence at his nightclub—not to mention the way Akiko is enmeshed in Kasai's fantasy—*Matango* underscores the illicit side of the water trades, portraying the nightclub world as sexually corrupting Mami and threatening Akiko's virginity. Indeed, on an individual level, the celebrity chanteuse embodies the same mixture of exalted success and moral depravity that the film proposes is characteristic of the 60s Japanese economy as a whole. With regards to Akiko, a flashback depicts Murai introducing his fiancée to the group in Kasai's nightclub, where Mami is singing. As the scene ends, Koizumi's camera rests on Yoshida, who glances at Kasai and raises his eyebrows as if to acknowledge Akiko's attractiveness. The ruination and peril resulting from contact with Tokyo's seedy nightclubs indicates that such places are degenerate zones of male sexual incontinence—therefore featuring prominently into Kasai's fantasy—that constitute a threat to female sexual virtue, and by extension, marriage-ability. This suggests that there is far more at stake, thematically, in Murai's efforts to protect his fiancée from the depredations of the mushroom men than just building audience suspense.

Brothers remarks that *Matango* is "Honda's most erotic film, although the sexual subtext is not stimulating or enticing as it is degrading and indecorous" (227). This statement is especially true insofar as the seamy world of Tokyo nightlife brings the film's vision of eroticism into focus. Recall that Kasai's drug fantasy begins with a female contortionist doing inverted splits and centralizes a dancer robotically executing split-legged somersaults. The speed and repetitiveness of these salacious flips bespeaks a sexuality that has become mechanical, banal, and inhuman, insinuating how prostitution associated with the water trades, and the Showa "adult entertainment" industry more generally, has degraded sex into an automated bodily routine and a for-pay service with hitherto unseen destabilizing effects on social relations. Moreover, the fantasy's juxtaposition of the erotic and the economic does not only imply that sex has become another consumer good, but also that the downward spiral into decadence, which passes through excess, is fueled by libidinous energies—a notion evinced by the simple insight that decadence *feels good*. As the dancer performs flip after flip, her erotically charged body traces out a circular path that proposes desire and pleasure as the rotary forces driving a perpetual cycle of economic growth, birthing the clubs and businesses in Kasai's fantasy.

Thus *Matango* sexualizes its fungal transformations, especially that of the virginal Akiko. As Brothers writes, when Akiko, clutching two phallic roots, recommends that she and Murai give in to their hunger and eat mushrooms, the psychologist "promptly slaps her in the face as if her proposal had been a crudely carnal one" (227). Murai reacts with uncharacteristic violence to this idea because Akiko is voicing her desire to be sullied by the fungus—a thought unbearable to Murai because it means that his fiancée is only too willing to surrender her virginity to the vilest of rivals and that the fungus will despoil her flesh before he can consummate their marriage. Amplifying Murai's fears of a filth-loving, debased sexuality, Mami and Yoshida emerge in the mushroom men's den when he finds his fiancée eating toadstools. The hedonistic pair of infected lovers constitutes a shadow doubling of the hitherto abstinent Akiko and Murai. As they look on Akiko's Eve-like fall from innocence and the couple's dissolution, their sensual, laughing faces express pleasure, further tying enjoyment to the process of becoming-fungus. As opposed to the wicked lovers, the mushroom men have no visages, but they laugh all the same. This defacement, alongside their impossible cackles of pleasure, turns them into figurations of the anonymous, impersonal libidinal energies driving the material forces of production and consumption. Theirs is not merely the psychotic laughter of insanity but that of the capitalistic enjoyment of excess—whether of sex, luxury, or drugs—that is always on the side of decadence.

Murai escapes the den and pilots the repaired yacht until his rescue at sea. Concluding the flashback, Honda cuts from a shot of the boat to Murai, his back to the camera, inside his cell in the psychiatric ward. He laments that he was saved, as he is now "condemned as insane," and wishes that he had eaten the mushrooms with Akiko to "become one" with her. Explaining that he was suffering from starvation, confusion, and the loss of his fiancée, Murai exclaims that he too consumed mushrooms. In the midst of this revelation, Murai turns toward his auditors, and Koizumi's camera zooms in on his face, which is covered with fungal encrustations. When a psychiatrist chides that he should be thankful for being rescued, Murai responds: "Do you think so? Tokyo is not so different from that island. People in cities are cruel, aren't they? They're becoming inhuman. It's all the same. I would be happier living on that island than in this city." The camera then pans toward the window to rest on the neon-tinged cityscape. Brothers and Kotz note the pessimism (if not nihilism) of this ending, with the former critic attributing it to screenwriter Kimura's dismal view of human nature (221). The dark twist at end of the film, which discourages reading *Matango* as a simple moral allegory inveighing against 60s decadence, is especially bleak given the cosmic absurdity of Murai's fate. Of the entire group, he holds out the longest against the temptations of the fungus, yet he survives only to become the film's most hideous monster. Arrested in a liminal state, Murai is undoubtedly no longer human, yet he cannot consummate the transformation into a mushroom man. Accordingly, Murai does not consider himself to have survived his own narrative. The mutation visited on his body outwardly reflects the inward distortion of his psychology and identity, recalling the film's concerns with the effects that material conditions exert upon subjectivity. Worse yet, the living thing once known as Murai is held captive—perhaps by his own former colleagues, much to his humiliation—under the auspices of medical care. Yet the singularity of his condition, as well as a forward tracking shot through the bars of his cell, suggest that he is not a patient in the eyes of the psychiatrists as much as a science experiment or sideshow freak.

The conclusion of the film, with its emphasis on liminality, betrays the influence of Hodgson's "The Voice in the Night," which rehearses the perplexities of attempting to think and discourse about a living thing that, by virtue of its hybridity, cannot even so much as be named. Struggling to account for what he and his fiancée have become, John can only muster: "we who had been human, became—Well, it matters less each day" (23). Nevertheless, Honda's film departs from Hodgson's tale in two crucial ways. While the short story features solely corporeal transformations that inflict no physical pain, Honda's film is deeply concerned with fluctuating psychological states and questions of pleasure, especially as they pertain to society. Thus the conclusion of the film may best be interpreted in light of these issues. At the start of *Matango*, supremely healthy in body and mind, Murai is a paragon of humanity that prizes human society and shuns the mushroom men. By the end of the film, his brain and body have degenerated into the very epitome of monstrosity, and he has come to desire the mushroom men and revile human society. These reversals underscore that *Matango* is about Murai getting all *mixed-up*: becoming half-man and half-fungus; a part of human society and the fungal mass; and a defender of values and a besotted spectacle of degeneration. Little wonder, then, that he considers himself to be dead in the wake of these changes. Yet these reversals perform another crucial mixing-up: in reiterating the film's critical target to be 60s Japanese society, they stress the identity of the fungal and human collectives as two sides of the same social body. From this perspective, Murai's infection might be interpreted as an inevitable consequence of the inability for any individual to extricate him or herself from the larger social body in which he or she is embedded. Accordingly, any attempt to read Murai as the virtuous exemplar in a straightforward moral allegory breaks down, as the distance between the good and the corrupt needed for an ethics-based critique collapses. This feeling of being ensnared by society conveys the ambivalence Honda and Kimura felt toward 60s Japan's boom, which heralded both attractive material success and repulsive moral turpitude. Here, what *Matango* implies about human nature is truly nothing short of horrifying: that we are creatures whose material realities and noxious enjoyments perpetually ruin our ideals—and we are all the more monstrous for it.

Notes

1. The 63-year period in Japan's history known as the Showa era begins in 1926, when Hirohito ascends the Chrysanthemum Throne to become emperor, and ends with his

death on January 7, 1989. For a detailed, personal recollection of the momentous political and social changes of this era, see Hans Brickmann, *Showa Japan* (2008).

2. Web source. See Works Cited.

3. See Bruce for a biography of Hodgson and bibliography of his work. Hodgson lived a short but colorful life in which he distinguished himself as a sailor, martial artist, bodybuilder, amateur photographer, gymnasium owner, soldier, and of course, fiction writer. He was killed by an artillery shell at Ypres on April 17, 1918.

4. All subsequent references to Hodgson's story by page number, cited parenthetically.

5. All subsequent references to this work by page number, cited parenthetically.

6. Fungal fictions constitute a distinct tradition in Weird horror literature. While not as emblematic of the genre as the tentacle, which is pervasively associated with the Weird due to H.P. Lovecraft's cephalopod-like horror, Cthulhu, the fungus is nevertheless a popular antagonist among practitioners of the Weird tale such as Arthur Machen, Brian Lumley, and Jeff VanderMeer.

7. This, of course, is not intended to imply that all films in the "body horror" subgenre are simple. Such a claim would be preposterous in light of the work of David Cronenberg and, in Japanese cinema, Shinya Tsukamoto. Like *Matango*, the "body horror" films of these directors investigate the myriad relationships between corporeality, psychology, identity, and the larger social body.

8. All subsequent references to this work by page number, cited parenthetically.

9. It is likely that Hodgson named the ship the *Albatross* in order to allude to Samuel Taylor Coleridge's famous poem, *The Rime of the Ancient Mariner* (1798; revised 1817). The Mariner incurs his curse by shooting an albatross with his crossbow. In terms of both content and the manner in which it is related, John's tale recalls the Mariner's narrative.

10. So desirable was this position, Allinson writes that blue-collar workers began to sport the white shirts and ties of the *sararii-man* during their railway commutes to and from work (111).

11. Brothers notes that Tsuburaya used an Oxberry 1900 Optical Printer to create this uncanny shot (221). The printer could superimpose up to five composites, obviating costly hand-painted mattes and glass shots.

12. In the noxious and degrading milieus of *Matango*, we discern early predecessors of the biomechanical environments that pathologically transform (if not engulf) the protagonists of late-eighties and early-nineties Japanese cyberpunk films. Like *Matango*, such works—which include Shinya Tsukamoto's *Tetsuo, the Iron Man* (*Tetsuo*; 1989), Shozin Fukui's *Screams of Blasphemy* (*964 Pinocchio*; 1991), and Kei Fujiwara's *Organ* (*Orugan*; 1996)—skillfully blend science fiction and body horror in order to chart, more often than not with a nihilistic sense of exhilaration, the dehumanizing transformations wrought by technological advancement.

13. Quoted in "Japan's 'Laughing Mushrooms,'" by James H. Sanford (174). All subsequent references by page number, cited parenthetically.

14. Quoted from Honda's autobiography. Brothers reports the title of Honda's book, which was published in 1994 and has yet to be translated into English, as *Ishiro Honda— Godzilla and My Movie Life* (437).

15. See Brothers for a detailed chapter on Honda's career as a soldier in WWII. He undertook multiple tours of duty through China, which often disrupted his movie-making schedule.

16 All subsequent references to this work by page number, cited parenthetically.

Works Cited

Ainsworth, G.C. *Introduction to the History of Mycology*. Cambridge: Cambridge University Press, 1976. Print.
Allinson, Gary D. *Japan's Postwar History*. Ithaca: Cornell University Press, 2004. Print.
Brothers, Peter H. *Mushroom Clouds and Mushroom Men: The Fantastic Cinema of Ishiro Honda*. Scotts Valley, CA: CreateSpace, 2009. Print.
Brickmann, Hans. *Showa Japan*. Rutland, VT: Tuttle, 2008. Print.
Bruce, Samuel W. "William Hope Hodgson." *British Fantasy and Science-Fiction Writers Before World War I*. Ed. Darren Harris-Fain. Detroit: Gale Research, 1997. 121–31. Print.
Galbraith IV, Stuart. *Japanese Science Fiction, Fantasy, and Horror Films*. Jefferson, NC: McFarland, 1994. 84–7. Print.
Gordon, Andrew. *A Modern History of Japan*. Oxford: Oxford University Press, 2009. Print.
Hodgson, William Hope. "The Voice in the Night." *Adrift on the Haunted Seas*. Ed. Douglas A. Anderson. Cold Spring Harbor, NY: Cold Spring Press, 2005. 15–24. Print.
Kotz, Sean. "A More Interesting Reality Than Ours: A Close Look at *Matango*." *SciFi Japan* (2007). Web. 8 Aug. 2014.
Rolfe, R.T. and F.W. *The Romance of the Fungus World*. Mineola, NY: Dover, 1974. 7–38. Print.
Sanford, James H. "Japan's 'Laughing Mushrooms.'" *Economic Botany* 26.2 (April–June 1972): 174–181. Print.

Part II

Monstrous Violations
of Private Life

Through the Eyes of the Monster
Angela Carter's "The Lady of the House of Love"

JAMEELA F. DALLIS

"The Lady of the House of Love" is a part of Angela Carter's *The Bloody Chamber* (1979), a renowned collection of reimagined, erotically charged, often feminist fairytales.[1] In this short story, Carter alludes to "Sleeping Beauty" and "Jack and the Beanstalk" while invoking and revising the aesthetics of well-known Gothic texts, such as Bram Stoker's *Dracula*, with a Transylvanian highlands castle and mysterious preternatural occupant. Yet, "The Lady of the House of Love" brims with tension created by what lies beneath, or somewhat beyond, the surface of the text. Carter posits, "All writing of any kind, in fact, exists on a number of different levels.... If you read the tale carefully, the tale tells you more than the writer knows ... tells you, in all innocence, what its writer thinks is important, who she or he thinks is important and, above all, why" (*Expletives* 3). Hence, Carter's narratives beckon the exhumation of buried meaning. As she is known for crafting stories that render no simple analyses—texts that pull from the literary, the esoteric, and the sensual—it is no surprise that this palimpsest narrative features the Tarot, which ultimately reveals a breadth of connections: from a thirteenth-century heretical sect to Gérard de Nerval's poem "El Desdichado" (1853, 1854).

In Carter's narrative, a monstrous, yet beautiful, disenchanted vampire Countess, and her unsuspecting hero, a virginal bicycle-riding English World War I officer, dovetails with established readings of Gothic monsters—especially vampires. It reflects early twentieth-century Western European anxieties about foreignness, contagion, and unbridled desire associated with Eastern Europe and beyond since monstrous alterity is most often "cultural, political, racial, economic, sexual" (Cohen 7). Carter's vampire represents all five. And, through the revision of traditional fairytale narratives Carter reverses and complicates the familiar invasion narrative as she introduces the rational hero into the threatening, sequestered, domestic space of the Countess. Carter's narrative invites an analysis that acknowledges what Jeffery Cohen argues in *Monster Culture* (1996): "[E]very monster is in its way a double narrative, two living stories: one that describes how the monster came to be and another, its testimony, detailing what cultural use the monster serves" (13). To discover such testimony, we recognize the monster as "pure culture" and "nothing of itself" and consider Cohen's claim that, because of this, the "monster can be read only *through*" (21; emphasis in original). Reading *through* the Countess and the diegetic space of the text reveals her testimony by interrogating the more-than-ancillary presence of the Tarot in the text. The Countess consults the cards repeatedly and references to them appear on half of the narrative's sixteen pages.

Through the Tarot, the Countess is searching for something more than her fated existence provides. She seeks plasticity and pushes against her ancestral habitat that is devoid of villagers, where only dark formless shadows remain (93). Each one of her dreadful, vicious ancestors project a sinister, incorporeal influence and the peasants driven away by troublesome revenants would rather the Countess remain caged (93). If we must read through monsters, we must read through the Countess, and what is left is the Tarot laid out before her, something critics, to my knowledge, have yet to do.[2] Carter's narrative elucidates that despite the repression and exclusion of what dominant forces consider non-rational or threatening to the order of the regimes they establish, the peoples and ideas they seek to silence and contain—abject, monstrous things—remain at the root of what they strive to keep pure and unadulterated. Reading through Carter's monster reveals the radical nature of less visible truths or other ways of knowing and being-in-the-world. Recognizing such meaning—and here it is specifically othered, polyvalent truths—provide a way to critique and revise established beliefs about purity and sacredness and ultimately subvert institutions that police borders and limit difference.

The Monstrous Tarot

If we acknowledge that Gothic texts, as Jacqueline Howard aptly argues, draw upon or transform established literary and socio-cultural "discursive structures"—"fragments of 'the already said,' both literary and non-literary"

(16)—then Carter's incorporation of the Tarot is apropos. The Tarot also invokes "the already said" while it allows new configurations of meaning, as interpretation incorporates the voices of the querent and reader, along with recognized meanings of the cards, the result of multiple and on-going revisions due to changing discursive and socio-cultural regimes.[3] The Tarot as we know it is distinctly European, but its conception originates in playing cards, brought to Europe from the Islamic world during the last quarter of the fourteenth century, and in the "trick-taking games" introduced in the same period from Persia and India (Dummett 4). The "gypsies" (who are associated with Romania, but have roots in India) are often credited with introducing Tarot cards, but David Parlett explains playing cards appeared in Europe in 1371 while gypsies appear in 1411 (39). The origins of the Tarot are still contested, and it is clear that the Tarot is inherently heterogeneous. For example, Catherine Perry Hargrave notes the prominence of the numbers seven and thirteen. Seven is associated with the magic of "old [European] fairy tales" and has been "from time immemorial" the "mystic number of the East" (223). The number thirteen, Hargrave argues, is "invariably Death" and retains its "early Eastern significance of misfortune" in early and modern-day Tarot cards (223). She concludes, "Whether they were brought by merchants or travelers, by soldiers or wandering fortune-telling gypsies, no one knows, but strange emblematic cards appeared, with a very evident allegorical significance and with a distinctly Eastern symbolism" (223).

The contemporary association of the Tarot with the occult arrives in the second half of the eighteenth century within "masonic and illuminist circles," particularly with Antoine Court de Gébelin who linked the cards to ancient Egyptian priests who purportedly concealed "symbolic instruction in their religious doctrines in the guise of an instrument of play" (Dummett 3). Michael Dummett maintains that before this period, the cards were "unquestionably invented to play a particular type of game," and until de Gébelin's claims were accepted by French fortune-tellers and occultists, the Tarot was "never used for any other purpose" (3). Yet, from the beginning, the cards were despised by many church officials due to their association with gaming (3). Hargrave asserts that the Church officials' attacks on the cards led to the "very early" appearance of "Le Pape" and "La Papesse" (223). Indeed, these two cards, the modern-day Pope or Hierophant and his counterpart the Popess or High Priestess, are a part of the earliest deck to correspond with the modern Tarot pack, the Visconti-Sforza Tarot, a deck of hand-painted playing cards commissioned by newlyweds Bianca Maria Visconti and Francesco Sforza in approximately 1450 bearing emblems of both families (Newman 182). There is no doubt that the Tarot's Eastern and Middle-Eastern playing card origins (and the imperial and religious differences of those origins) also represented a threat to the power and influence of the Catholic Church.

The Tarot is monstrous in the same sense as the Gothic text. Drawing from disparate discourses and systems of meaning, Tarot cards and Gothic texts are fecund—they engender many interpretations and applications. By the simple virtue of their convoluted histories, the two are excessive in nature in addition to being farraginous forms of art. For occultist readers and querents, the Tarot reveals hidden, repressed truths and warns of future occurrences through its imagery (Walker 18–21). In this way, we read the Tarot as we read the monster's body—deciphering the significance of its separate origins congealed into one card, one (monstrous) body. The Tarot requires our attention because if we accept that monsters do embody our anxieties, fears, and fantasies and are essentially abjected parts of ourselves while taking into account that, etymologically, monsters are things that reveal or warn, how do we read a monster, Carter's Countess, who resorts to her Tarot without fail?[4] How do we understand this phenomenon given that her Tarot also *reveals and warns* and thus becomes monstrous in its own right?

In "The Lady of the House of Love," the first reference to the Tarot is in the story's second paragraph. Alone in her darkness, the Countess, the beautiful vampire queen, wears an old bridal gown while she "counts out the Tarot cards, ceaselessly construing a constellation of possibilities" as if the cards' random fall on her red, lush tablecloth could deliver her from her cold, closed room into a country of endless summer and

Figure 1. The Papesse (La Papessa/The Popess) holds a holy text which attests to her wisdom and spiritual discernment. Some decks identify the text as the Torah. This card is now more commonly titled The High Priestess.

eradicate the "perennial sadness" of her existence as both "death and the maiden" (93). It is quite remarkable that the Tarot, something academics often relegate to the occult, and thus oftentimes view as unworthy of serious critical inquiry, is the very tool the Countess uses in her endeavor to "evade" her destiny (94). Because of its association with the occult—a type of othered truth—its importance has been overlooked. In fact, the Countess is uninterested in her power and likens it to a dream. In this dream, the Countess would like to be human, but she is unsure of this possibility. The Tarot cards always reveal the same configuration: "La Papesse, La Mort, La Tour Abolie,

Left: Figure 2. This example of La Mort (Death) is nameless, which is common in some versions of the Marseille Tarot deck and many others. *Right:* Figure 3. La Maison Dieu (The House of God) depicts divine fire breaking apart a lofty, man-made structure. This structure is sometimes associated with the Old Testament's Tower of Babel; hence, the card's more common title is The Tower or Carter's name for the card, La Tour Abolie.

wisdom, death, dissolution" (95; see Figs. 1, 2, 3). Thus, Carter's monstrous, Gothic Countess is more than an embodied repository of cultural anxieties because her inherent unease and ennui haunt her. And, in her haunted, anxious state, she seeks escape and solace in the Tarot. She "resorts to the magic comfort of the Tarot" and relentlessly constructs "hypotheses" about an "irreversible" future (95). There is a doubling here, an element so prevalent in Gothic literature, in the notion that those who read Gothic texts often approach them as an escape from the ordered, sometimes confining nature of their own conditions. In essence, the Gothic text, albeit often unsettling and incongruent with the lives readers may want for themselves, provides a type of magical comfort because readers enter into an alternate world for a moment and are free to return to their own. In a similar way, the Countess consults the Tarot—something that holds the potential for revealing a life different than her own. And in those moments of shuffling the cards, she is free to ponder the possibility of an alternate reality.

The Lady of the House of Love and the Unsuspecting Hero

The Countess is soulless. Descriptive language exaggerates reality and pushes at the limits of representation as we are invited to imagine hair that falls "down like tears" as the narrator explains that her excess of beauty renders her unnatural; it is abnormal—it is a "deformity" because she is bereft of features that convey the "touching imperfections" that affirm the imperfect nature of human life (94). This early description of the Countess calcifies conceptions of monstrosity as something that deviates from "natural or conventional order" ("Monstrous," def. 1a). Further separating her from a comfortably defined existence, while at the same time evoking sympathy, the Countess is likened to a "haunted house," terrorized by ancestors who sometimes gaze out from her own eyes, and is forced to inhabit interstitial space as she drifts between "life and death, sleeping and waking" (103). Despite her desire to do otherwise and, perhaps, become fully human, the Countess is powerless, fated to carry out her hereditary crimes by seducing, drinking the blood of, and ultimately killing young men who initially can hardly believe their good fortune when she leads them to her bedchamber (93). The Transylvanian Countess also represents an old order, one beholden to blood and land and magic in the midst of a changing world at war. It is a world in which nations seek to expand their empires through imperialism and rampant militarism and alliances between nations create varying degrees of fragile entanglements. The narrator's mention that the Countess is the heir of Nosferatu, who was killed by an Orthodox priest, exposes Stoker's latent influence on the text and, in the same stroke, introduces a telling anachronism (95).

This anachronism is a sort of postmodern relic; it divulges Carter's self-conscious use of both fiction and the Gothic mode.[5] As the Gothic is almost always about a confrontation of perceived opposites—of past and present, or male and female, of noble and peasant, the rational and non-rational—this particular reference to Nosferatu does the same action. Reading through this anachronism reveals post–World War I Western Europe's anxieties toward

> "Mitteleuropa" and its eastern flank: the Slav peoples in general and those of the Balkans in particular, a world the Germanic west had for centuries studied with fascinating antipathy. And Mitteleuropa also encompassed "the Pale"—the home territories of the eastern Jews whom the collapse of the Austro-Hungarian Empire in 1918 had forces to move westwards [Elsaesser n. pag.].

The monster "Nosferatu" translates as "undead" in Romanian, is modeled on Dracula, and reveals Western Europe's fears about the return of ethnic, racial, and religious others—the "citizens of 'Fortress Europe'" who "harbour their own nightmare visions of history's undead heading west from the 'land beyond the trees' and beyond" (Elsaesser n. pag.). Of course, this tension and apprehension echoes the world in which the Tarot was birthed—as the Middle Ages gave way to the Renaissance and an ever-expanding and increasingly connected world in which Europeans also encounter ethnic, racial, and religious others from the Middle East and the Far East through exploration, mercantilism, and burgeoning colonization.

Monstrosity, especially in the Gothic mode, exploits diegetic space as it conveys meaning through extravagance and excess, and this meaning, whatever it may be, exists contentiously between two (supposed) oppositional realms be they the rational and the non-rational, the noble and the peasant, or the beautiful and the horrible. Thus, the Gothic functions as a form that troubles convention, disrupts boundaries, and exposes the repressed realm of the marginal, the in-between, and that which is perceived by dominant powers as monstrous—something that breaks with "natural or conventional order." As signifiers of the contemporary human condition, the "oppressed and excluded" monsters of the Gothic text, such as the vampire Countess, reveal "the monstrosity of the systems of power and normalization" of this world to which we are subjected (Botting 15). Cohen argues,

> Through the body of the monster fantasies of aggression, domination, and inversion are allowed safe expression in a clearly delimited and permanently liminal space. Escapist delight gives way to horror only when the monster threatens to

overstep these boundaries, to destroy or deconstruct the thin walls of category and culture [17].

Is Carter's Countess permanently imprisoned by her fate, beholden to her heritage? No. The Countess "threatens to overstep" boundaries by reading the Tarot. Her relentless use of the Tarot, despite the cards' repetitive arrangement, demands recognition of the monster's desire to know what exists beyond the liminal space created for her. In this monster's narrative the Tarot is a venue imbued with the potential to transform her fate through its excess of meaning—through its potential to reveal and warn, reflect and predict a future outside even the boundaries provided by the text. The narrator claims more than once that the Countess's future is "irreversible," yet the Countess, unable to be comforted by anything her existence allows, returns continuously to the magical solace the Tarot provides (95). For some time, the weight of the vampires' eternity, both "timeless" and "Gothic" (97)—a space created by humans for our safe enjoyment—does threaten to close off the transformative potential of the cards. It is only when boundaries are threatened that transformation may occur.

Until this point, the Countess has lived off small animals, shepherd boys, and young gypsy men who are either reckless or unaware of the danger the Countess's realm holds within and stop to wash their feet in the estate's fountain. Then something different happens in the text, and "Jack and the Beanstalk" is invoked: "Fee fie fo fum / I smell the blood of an Englishman" (96). The narrator introduces the young English officer who, while visiting with friends in Vienna, decides to spend the remainder of his holiday bicycling the ancient cart-cut trails of the mysterious Romanian highlands— "the land of the vampires" (97). He has the "special quality of virginity" (97). Virginity is described as a condition possessing both the most and least ambiguity as within it exists both ignorance, "power in potentia," and "unknowingness," which the narrator asserts is different from ignorance. Thus, the officer is "more than he knows" and has the aura of a generation for whom "history has already prepared a special, exemplary fate in the trenches of France" (97). This hero is "rooted in change and time" and is on a course to "collide" with the "timeless Gothic eternity" of vampires, beings whose cards always reveal the same fate (97). In this passage, the narrator anachronistically mentions the officer's fate referring to the outcome of the war and then complicates the usual pattern of both Gothic and fairy tales as virginity is associated with young women. Awakening to sexual knowledge by choice or most often force or the threat of force is often the climax that leads to the misfortune or death of the heroine in such tales. However, in *The Bloody Chamber* virginity can provide protection.⁶ Of course, Carter's use of the power of virginity harps on religious and social groups' valorization of female virgins and brings to mind the complications such praise invites. Here, Carter complicates our expectations of a female virgin and, again, we are reminded that the Countess's future is always the same. Yet, with the allusion to the "Sleeping Beauty" fairytale and the sole kiss that revives her in the woods, the impossible happens: the Countess turns over the card, Les Amoureux, or The Lovers (97). Therein lies the germ of revolution: the Countess has never "cast herself a fate involving love" (97; ellipsis in original, see Fig. 4). When the Countess sees the new card, she shudders with excitement, she closes her eyes, and they flit nervously as she attempts to assimilate this impossible occurrence (97). Through the cards, she at last nears the subversion of the time and space assigned to her. She now bears the potential to break through into the daylight of an alternate way-of-being-in-the-world.

With his arrival, Carter reverses the gender roles and spatial relations of the familiar invasion narrative often found in fairytales. The "unacknowledged pentacle" of the soldier's virginity encloses, protects, and allows him to enter the Countess's domain without shivering from a rush of air so cold it was as if it issued forth from an open grave. Then, still unafraid, he watches his bicycle—a "symbol of rationality" and a common mode of transportation during the war—disappear into the unfathomable darkness of the mansion (99). Here, the bicycle represents the hero's rationality and Western Europe's banner of reason (against Eastern European aggression and its traditional association with invaders from the East) as the

Figure 4. L' Amoureux (Les Amoureux/The Lovers) depicts a marriage. Some versions of the card do not include an officiant while in others Cupid is not represented.

narrator claims the simple act of riding a bicycle provides protection against superstition and fear (97). The "hero" (103) is set against the non-rational, supernatural realm of the vampires—the inscrutable Transylvanian highlands viewed as home to dark powers, such as Dracula—that threaten to infiltrate, contaminate, and bring discord to Western Europe. The officer's arrival announces a change of fate that gives the Countess the faintest idea that he, this hero, this light of reason, as it were, may be able to "irradiate" her darkness (103).

After she invites the officer into her château, silently, she admires his attractive throat and perceives all around him the "golden light" of a "summer's day," which she has never known. She fancies he has stepped out of the card, Les Amoureux, which had just erupted from the Tarot deck's "tumbling chaos of imagery" (103). In terms of World War I, we can read the passage in a way that privileges the progress and reason the Western allies represent over the radical, irrational Eastern axis—that the fair Englishman will triumph over the dark Slav. But this is a racist, xenophobic reading that does not reflect Carter's mien. Even the embedded "Jack and the Beanstalk" fairytale, in which the Englishman enters the forbidden monster's (the giant's) abode only to return to his home with what the monster has taken from his people, is complicated by the conclusion of Carter's narrative, which I discuss below. Although the officer's arrival ultimately pronounces the Countess's fate—while disrobing to complete her ritual of seduction, feeding, and murder, the Countess drops her eyeglasses (that protect her from light), cuts herself on their shards, receives a comforting kiss from the naïve officer, becomes human, and dies—we should not read the narrative as one that praises the rational over the non-rational (105–106). After all, it is the *non-rational* Tarot that predicts the young hero's arrival through the card, Les Amoureux.

Reading Through the Monster[7]

It is important to note that the same configuration of Tarot cards shows up so often that some readers may dismiss them as meaningless. Yet, even though Carter's text is not illustrated, Tarot imagery haunts its core, and it is clear that the cards should be understood as real artifacts of the text.[8] The Countess reads La Papesse (often referred to as The High Priestess in contemporary decks and La Papessa in the Visconti-Sforza deck), as "wisdom" (95; Fig. 1). Wisdom, often gendered female, denotes not only knowledge, but the "capacity of judging rightly in matters relating to life and conduct" ("Wisdom," def. 1a). This card suggests a wise woman, or a woman who proclaims to know in excess of what dominant powers approve. Unfortunately, throughout the Western, Christian world such wisdom is often perceived as dangerous, aberrant, or monstrous. Indeed, La Papesse had long been associated with the legendary Pope Joan until Gertrude Moakley linked the card to Umiliati nun Maifreda da Pirovano in 1966 (Newman 182). The Pope Joan association mocks "female ambition" and deviates from other female popes of the Tarot who serve as wives to the Pope and provide critique of Papal corruption (Moakley 72). Maifreda was cousin to Matteo Visconti, an ancestor of Bianca Maria Visconti, heiress to the Duke of Milan, the same Visconti who commissioned the Visconti-Sforza deck (Newman 182). Guglielma, from whom the Gugliemites took their name, was Princess Blažena Vilemína, daughter of King Přemysl Ottokar I of Bohemia.

According to Barbara Newman, Guglielma most likely arrived in Milan in the 1260s as a quinquagenarian widow, but there is no account of what happened to her husband. Purported to have been born on Pentecost, and a recipient of invisible stigmata, she "established herself as a freelance holy woman ... gradually gaining the reputation of a healer and miracle worker" (185). Guglielma's foreignness raised her above the rivalry between the Torriani and Visconti factions (185). After her death in 1281, Maifreda received visions revealing that Guglielma was an incarnation of the Holy Spirit, and she would rise from the dead like Christ (187–188). In the meantime, Maifreda was to be "the new Peter," the new Pope (188). After twenty years "of priestly duties," including "celebrat[ing] Mass and consecrate[ing] hosts over Guglielma's grave" (14), Maifreda celebrated mass on Easter 1300 and went on to repeat the mass on Pentecost when the Holy Spirit incarnate in Guglielma "would rise from the dead and confer blessings on her people" (182). Instead of witnessing a resurrection, Inquisitors following up on previous investigations of 1284 and 1296 arrived, took them into custody, and later burned Maifreda and at least two of her followers at the stake (182).

Taking the Maifreda/La Papessa narrative into account enhances our understanding of the Countess's card. This card holds a feeling of secret, alternative, even forbidden ways of living in, moving in, and knowing the world—especially in terms of inhabiting the space of womanhood and pushing beyond boundaries medieval woman encountered. La Papesse holds the narrative of Maifreda and Guglielma who proclaimed a direct relationship with and connection to divinity in a period when only Church officials could make such claims with impunity. The card bears the trace of radical defiance of order—of some entity or belief that threatens to unbalance and disturb what has been established as sacred and proper. The Visconti memorialize their ancestor in the coded language of the Tarot; the Papesse card becomes a requiem for a group of inspired people who were harassed, ostracized, and executed by the Catholic Church, who viewed them as a dangerous, non-rational, heretical sect. It is a powerful invasion narrative, indeed. Carter's Countess is like La Papesse, pregnant with the wisdom of forbidden things, unearthly things. And like the woman on her Tarot card—the robed female who encompasses the legendary Pope Joan, Guglielma, Maifreda, or other female popes—the Countess has the ambition to go beyond her assigned fate. We are told that everything about the beautiful and frightening Countess—this queen of night and terror—is as it should be except for her utter aversion for the role (95). Instead of murdering the men who happen upon her abode, she wants to stroke their cheeks and run her fingers through their unkempt hair (96)—it appears she would rather *love*. Thus, she endures her reality as represented by the Tarot cards (i.e., La Papesse, La Mort, and La Tour Abolie), but she also subverts the boundaries created for her through Tarot because she reads her cards with the faith that her fate can change.

Although contemporary cartomancers often interpret La Mort, or Death as a total external transformation at the end of a cycle in lieu of physical death (Walker 104–105), the Countess's card portrays a "grisly" image of a "capering skeleton" which certainly brings mortality to mind (101; Fig. 2). The Tarot descends from a time in Europe when death was everywhere; people lived through the threat of plague, lost family members and friends, and were encouraged to become acquainted with and accustomed to death (Farley 73–74). For Carter's narrative, La Mort takes on a literal and extended meaning. The Countess represents the old death—the death of disease and rampant contamination that not even the nobility can escape. As a member of the living-dead, the Countess also becomes the personification of the fact that life can never be separated from death. She is the grisly skeleton waiting for her living prey. In her realm, she lives as long as men live and find their way to her. In the third paragraph of the text, her voice seems full of resonances from elsewhere as she repeats the phrase, "now you are at the place of annihilation" (93); later, the intonation repeats before she leads the officer into her bedroom (104). Although the officer survives his encounter, we know that death still awaits him in the trenches of France (e.g., 97, 104, 108). The officer must meet a new death born from the burgeoning entanglements and political interests of the twentieth century.

At last, Carter's nominative choice of La Tour Abolie leads me to Nerval. In "Notes on the Gothic Mode" (1975), Carter is concerned with "verbal structures as things-in-themselves as well as transmitters of meaning," though she adds, "meaning ... always tends to dominate structure" (133). I argue that these factors, along with her self-proclaimed continuous engagement with "fiction absolutely self-conscious of itself," underlie her use of "La Tour Abolie," which reveals itself as yet another sort of poignant anachronism (133). Readers familiar with Tarot and French will know that La Tour Abolie is not categorically a Tarot card but will read the card as The Abolished Tower and make a connection to The Tower card. The Tower card has had many names over the years: from Fire to La Casa del Diavolo (The Devil's House) to La Maison Dieu (The House of God).[9] "La Tour Abolie" originates in the second line of Nerval's 1853 and 1854 sonnets "El Desdichado" or "The Disinherited": "Je suis le ténébreux,—le veuf,—l'inconsolé, / Le Prince d'Aquitaine à la tour abolie" (1–2; Fig. 3).[10] Both versions tell of a man once noble who has lost love and wealth, and, as a result, he has been disinherited of tradition, of happiness (Kristeva 144). In general, the poem's overwhelming feeling of loss, and its images of crumbling edifices and deprivation bring to mind the sad state of the Countess and her dilapidated lair where dark red wallpaper is distressed and marred by rain that seeps in through a derelict roof leaving foreboding stains like the ones left on her sheets by deceased lovers (94). Although the gender roles are reversed when we consider the poem and Carter's narrative together, sections of the poem retain uncanny similarity to the plot of the short story and the Countess's translation of her card, "dissolution." The Countess and what she represents has, in effect, been disinherited by the world the officer represents. Her castle is in ruin—a state of perpetual disintegration. Her realm and Nerval's poem resemble a requiem, a literary dirge to the many ruins of the conditions of life, society, and the disavowal of what falls outside the easily contained. The officer's innocent curiosity speaks to a subconscious longing to encounter the non-rational.

(Failed) Seduction

Referencing "Sleeping Beauty" once more and reminding us that only one kiss woke the Sleeping Beauty, the narrator sets the scene for (and complicates our expectations of) the soldier's seduction (103). The officer sees her nails, which are "birdlike" and "predatory," and something shifts; uncanniness overcomes him (103). Here, he fully encounters the Countess-as-monster; he is unable to comprehend what his eyes see in front of him, and to find some comfort he thinks perhaps even if certain things are indeed true, people should not believe them to actually be possible (103–104). Yet, Les Amoureux is the card that shifts the fate of the Countess and that of her presumed prey (Fig. 4). For contemporary readers, this card denotes an important decision concerning a relationship or other life-changing event and the need for careful discretion and guidance in making the choice, as the result of one's decision will most often significantly affect the course of one's life. Historically, the card depicts either two lovers and Cupid or two lovers, Cupid, and an official. In the early Italian decks, the card is called "L'amore" (Love) and shows a blindfolded Cupid (Dummett 112). Moakley addresses the blindfold citing Erwin Panofsky who argues it is "because love is inferior to the intellect," and Edgar Wind who argues it is "because love is superior" (77). I believe the latter is true in relation to Carter's narrative. Her Countess is, after all, the lady of the house of love. Moakley also notes that the love represented in Les Amoureux breaks from the cold, rigid courtly love tradition (77) and, thus, I argue it depicts the love between two people who open fully to an other and enter the vulnerable space of love. Until Les Amoureux appears, the "house of love" has been a house of subterfuge, of hereditary wanton desire. Deep, romantic love has no place in the Countess's domain. Nevertheless, her persistent desire to evade her fate by way of the Tarot proves triumphant, which is apropos as the ancestral names of the Tarot are trionfi, triumphi, or triumphs.[11]

In her bedroom, her familiar place of seduction and murder, the Countess shakes badly as she moves to unhook the clasp of her mother's wedding gown, but her eyes become tearful as she realizes she cannot remove the dress before removing her tinted glasses. Alas, she has botched the ritual, and it ceases to be "inexorable" (105). In the next moment, the Countess's glasses fall and crash into shards against the tiled floor. Because there is no space for novelty in her ritual, the "unexpected, mundane" sound of the crashing glass "breaks the wicked spell in the room, entirely" (106). She reaches down to retrieve the shards in "awed fascination" as she has never seen her "*own* blood" (106; emphasis in original). Instead of taking advantage of her vulnerability in a sexual manner, as would most certainly happen in a typical Gothic tale, the virginal officer brings the "innocent remedies of the nursery," and through his very presence becomes an "exorcism" and kisses the Countess's wound as her mother would have, had she been alive (106). This action is too much. She wakes to life like Sleeping Beauty, and the ancestors immortalized in portraiture grind their fangs and look away—how can the Countess endure the pain that is becoming mortal, being human, wonders the narrator, for the "end of exile" is the "end of being" (106). In this moment it is love— the opening to alterity, the relinquishing of boundaries, the loosening of restrictive histories—that triumphs. Love triumphs in the fraction of time in which the soldier is no longer prey, no longer a soldier, but caretaker. Love triumphs when the Countess is no longer a strange, othered monster, but an injured being in need of compassion.[12]

After sleeping on the floor the morning following the failed seduction, the officer awakes alone and finds a lightly blood-stained negligée and a rose he believes to be from the "fierce bushes" creeping in through the open window (106). Earlier, we learn that the roses, originally planted by the Countess's mother, are "almost too luxuriant," "obscene," intoxicating, and excessive (98). These roses both permeate and define boundaries—they shield the Countess's realm from the outside world (incarcerating the Countess [95]) and fearlessly enter the space where the rational hero, the virginal soldier remains. Eventually, he finds the Countess sitting in her white dress at her round table with Tarot cards laid out in front of her. The cards are so dirty, fingered, and worn due to habitual shuffling that he is unable to discern any of their arcane images (107). In death, the Countess looks older, less beautiful, and fully human. In death, the cards' faces are blank. (Could this suggest that it is the Countess's faith—arguably the ultimate acknowledgement of the non-rational—that engineers her release?) The Countess's last words are prosopopeial: she will "vanish in the morning light" because she was only an "invention of darkness"; she leaves as a souvenir the "dark, fanged rose" she has taken from between her thighs, "like a flower laid on a grave" (107). The Countess may no longer be a monstrous vampire, but she is in no way conquered. But, rather, she is free. Her desire has been fulfilled.

It seems monsters always escape utter annihilation and are reborn as something else, and when they come back, Cohen writes, "they bring not just a fuller knowledge of our place in history and the history of knowing our place, but they bear self-knowledge, *human* knowledge—and a discourse all the more sacred as it arises from the outside" (20). The officer, the hero, the emblem of rationality, who comes, in effect, to *exorcise* the archaic, and triumph over the non-rational, still clings to the material of the past. Or rather, this othered rose and all it represents is discovered at the root of the hero's person. For, in the narrative's final paragraphs, the officer returns to his regiment's barracks and finds a rose tucked in his cycling jacket's breast pocket—near his heart, his core—and realizes that despite the long journey from Romania, the flower was not altogether dead. And because the Countess had been so beautiful and her death so sudden and sad, capriciously, he decides to "resurrect her rose" (107). Sometime later, he finds his room profuse with the intoxicating perfume of a flower—plush, monstrous, radiant—whose petals are once more resilient and blooming in their "corrupt, brilliant, baleful splendour" (108).

Of course, the rose is a well-known, multifaceted symbol. Secrecy, love, fertility, passion, purity, death, and life all fall under the symbol of the rose.[13] It is an excessive, even monstrous, symbol apt to represent the Countess. By resurrecting the Countess's rose, the officer calls attention to the fact that our boundaries are often not as neat as they seem. Indeed, this profane, beautiful, and sublimely unnatural rose expels its essence in a purported bastion of rationality and order—a barracks. The final sentence of the short story reveals the officer's fate: "Next day, his regiment embarked for France" (108). Yet, beyond the diegetic space of the text, we may surmise the Countess's rose endures (108).

Ultimately, "The Lady of the House of Love" suggests that reading through our monsters reveals more monstrosity by way of acknowledging othered, repressed, and polyvalent ways of knowing.[14] Carter's inclusion of the Tarot calls for recognition of esoteric forms, forms of the non-rational that leave us with more than one answer, more than one reference. Carter maintains the Gothic mode is one that "retains a singular moral function: that of provoking unease" while asserting, "I think that it is immoral to read simply for pleasure"; thus, it becomes difficult for readers and critics to disregard the conspicuous Arcana ("Notes" 133). The Countess's preternatural rose, this emblem of the monsters we have created, calls for us to embrace the monstrous alterity that pushes at the limits of our realities, our truths, our discursive regimes, and to resurrect it, invite it in, and allow its fragrance to perfume the barracks of our lives.

Acknowledgments

This essay has undergone many transformations, and I give special thanks to the editors Sharla Hutchison and Rebecca A. Brown for their interest in bringing this publication to light. I also thank the reviewers for their thoughtful questions and insights throughout publication process. I thank advisors, colleagues, and friends—especially Heather Branstetter, María DeGuzmán, Shayne Legassie, and Rebecca Nesvet—who read and commented on various versions of this work. Finally, I offer very special thanks to Lisa D. Chàvez, whose English 412 course introduced me to Angela Carter and inspired me to write the first version of this essay in 2006.

Notes

1. "The Lady of the House of Love" is inspired by Carter's 1976 radio play *Vampirella*, which, in turn, is inspired by the sound of a pencil running across a radiator that Carter says, "made a metallic, almost musical rattle ... the noise that a long, pointed fingernail might make if it were run along the bars of a birdcage" (Carter qtd. in Hennard 217). We see this image in the short story on p. 93. See Martine Hennard Dutheil de la Rochère's excellent book *Reading, Translating, Rewriting: Angela Carter's Translational*

Poetics (Detroit: Wayne State University Press, 2013) for a thorough discussion of the radio and play and its relationship to the short story (pp. 209–225).

2. See, for example, Merja Mankinen's "Angela Carter's *The Bloody Chamber* and the Decolonization of Feminine Sexuality," *Feminist Review* 42, Feminist Fictions (1992): 2–15; Sarah Sceats' "Oral Sex: Vampiric Transgression and the Writing of Angela Carter," *Tulsa Studies in Women's Literature* 20.1 (2001): 107–121. Hennard does note "a series of Tarot readings that always present the same configuration of cards" in her study, but does not name or interpret the cards (209).

3. Barbara Walker comments, "Like the Bible, the Tarot passed through the hands of many interpreters who kept revising its 'canonical' meanings. The process still goes on today. Part of the charm of Tarot cards lies in their fluid adaptability to any creative exposition, verbal or symbolic" (19).

4. The word "monster" is two-spirited in that it combines the Old French and Latin words for revealing or displaying and through its revelation comes a warning (Bissonette 112). In "Teaching the Monster: *Frankenstein* and Critical Thinking," *College Literature* 37.3 (2010): 106–120. Melissa Bloom Bissonette writes, "The monster can reveal something internal, as the longings of its mother during gestation, or the sin of its conception, or village or nation. The monster might also be a warning, the prophetic embodiment of a nightmare of progress, the visual emblem of momentous change" (112).

5. F. W. Murnau's film *Nosferatu*, based on Stoker's *Dracula*, appeared in 1922, four years after the end of World War I. For further reading about the making and subsequent copyright violations of the film, see Elsaesser. It is of interest that an anachronism brought the authenticity of the first edition of Horace Walpole's *The Castle of Otranto* into question. See E. J. Clery's notes to the novel in the 2008 Oxford World's Classics Edition edited by W. S. Lewis.

6. See "The Tiger's Bride" (e.g., 63) and "The Company of Wolves" (e.g., 113–114) in Carter's *The Bloody Chamber*.

7. I have been a cartomancer for nearly half my life. For this reason, some contemporary interpretations of the cards lack a secondary source. However, in addition to various sources I cite, I suggest further reading in Sally Gearhart and Susan Rennie's *A Feminist Tarot*, Watertown, MA: Persephone Press, 1981; A. E. Waite's well-known *The Pictorial Key to the Tarot* originally published in 1910; and Walker's *The Secrets of the Tarot* listed in my works cited.

8. I include images from the French Tarot de Marseille (ca. 1650) as it was and remains a widely popular deck on which many other decks are based. And also because the Countess's cards are French and the narrator reveals she speaks French: "the adopted language of the Romanian aristocracy" (100). See Dummett and Moakley for images of the Visconti-Sforza deck.

9. There is a fascinating history of this card's name much too long for this essay. Farley argues that in the case of the Visconti-Sforza Tarot, The Tower is representative of the della Torres, bitter rivals of the Viscontis who eventually came to ruin. The della Torres's coats-of-arms often depicted towers similar to the one on The Tower card. The fire from heaven could be interpreted as divine intervention leading to the collapse of della Torres power (Farley 88). See also Dummett 6–7, Farley 84–88, Moakley 99.

10. "La Tour Abolie" is mentioned in line 429 of the last stanza of T.S. Eliot's poem "The Waste Land": "*Le Prince d'Aquitaine à la tour abolie*." This reference led me to Nerval.

11. See, for example, Parlett 240–241.

12. The third stanza of "El Desdichado"—specifically line 10, "Mon front est rouge encor du baiser de la reine"—evokes Les Amoureux and the preceding scenes of "The Lady of the House of Love" (although the gender roles are reversed).

13. For an interesting history of the rose as a symbol, see "A Brief Study of the Rose Cross Symbol" by Fra. Thomas D. Worrel, VII°, "A Brief Study of the Rose Cross Symbol" available here: http://www.sricf-ca.org/paper3.htm.
14. This translation is Julia Kristeva's as found in *Black Sun* (140–141). Gerard de Nerval's poem "El Desdichado" ("The Disinherited"), 1854 version:

> Français:
>
> Je suis le ténébreux,—le veuf,—l'inconsolé,
> Le Prince d'Aquitaine à la tour abolie:
> Ma seule *étoile* est morte,—et mon luth constellé
> Porte le *Soleil noir* de la *Mélancolie*.
>
> Dans la nuit du tombeau, toi qui m'a consolé,
> Rends-moi le Pausilippe et la mer d'Italie,
> La *fleur* qui plaisait tant à mon cœur désolé,
> Et la treille où le pampre à la rose s'allie.
>
> Suis-je Amour ou Phébus? ... Lusignan ou Byron?
> Mon front est rouge encor du baiser de la reine;
> J'ai rêvé dans la grotte où nage la sirène....
>
> Et j'ai deux fois vainqueur traversé l'Achéron :
> Modulant tour à tour sur la lyre d'Orphée
> Les soupirs de la sainte et les cris de la fée.
>
> English:
>
> I am the saturnine—bereft—disconsolate,
> The Prince of Aquitaine whose tower is destroyed:
> My only star is dead, and my constellated lute
> Bears the *Black Sun* of *Melancholia*.
>
> In the night of the grave, you who brought me solace,
> Give me back Posilipo and the sea of Italy,
> The *flower* that so pleased my distressed heart,
> And the arbor where the grapevine and rose combine.
>
> Am I Cupid or Phebus? ... Lusignan or Byron?
> My brow is still red from the kiss of the queen;
> I have dreamt in the cave where the siren swims....
>
> I've twice, as a conqueror, been across the Acheron;
> Modulating by turns on Orpheus' lyre
> The sighs of saint and the screams of the fay.

Works Cited

Botting, Fred. *Gothic Romanced: Consumption, Gender, and Technology in Contemporary Fictions*. New York: Routledge, 2008. Print.
Carter, Angela. *Expletives Deleted: Selected Writings*. London: Vintage, 1992. Print.
_____. "The Lady of the House of Love." *The Bloody Chamber*. New York: Penguin, 1993. Print.
_____."Notes on the Gothic Mode." *The Iowa Review* 6.3/4 (1975): 132–134. Print.
Cohen, Jeffery Jerome, ed. *Monster Theory: Reading Culture*. Minneapolis: University of Minnesota Press, 1996. Print.
de Nerval, Gerard. "El Desdichado." In *Black Sun: Depression and Melancholia*. Trans. Leon S. Roudiez. New York: Columbia University Press, 1989. 140–141. Print.

Dummett, Michael. *The Visconti-Sforza Tarot Cards*. New York: George Braziller, 1986. Print.

Elsaesser, Thomas. "Six Degrees of Nosferatu." *Sight and Sound* (February 2001): N. pag. Web. 16 April 2014.

Farley, Helen. *A Cultural History of the Tarot: From Entertainment to Esotericism*. London: I. B. Tauris, 2009. Print.

Hargrave, Catherine Perry. *A History of Playing Cards and a Bibliography of Cards and Gaming*. Mineola, NY: Dover, 2000. Print.

Howard, Jacqueline. *Reading Gothic Fiction: A Bakhtinian Approach*. New York: Oxford University Press, 1994. Print.

Kristeva, Julia. *Black Sun: Depression and Melancholia*. Trans. Leon S. Roudiez. New York: Columbia University Press, 1989. Print.

Moakley, Gertrude. *The Tarot Cards Painted by Bonifacio Bembo for the Visconti-Sforza Family: An Iconographic and Historical Study*. New York: New York Public Library, 1966. Print.

"Monstrous" Def. 1a. *OED Online*. December 2002. Oxford University Press. Web. 8 May 2010.

Newman, Barbara. *From Virile Woman to WomanChrist*. Philadelphia: University of Pennsylvania Press, 1995. Print.

Parlettt, David. *The Oxford Guide to Card Games*. New York: Oxford University Press, 1990. Print.

Walker, Barbara. *The Secrets of the Tarot: Origins, History, and Symbolism*. New York: HarperCollins, 1984. Print.

"Wisdom" Def. 1a. *OED Online*. December 2002. Oxford University Press. Web. 6 September 2014.

Re-Vamping the Early 1960s
Freakish Vampires and Monstrous Teens in Richard Laymon's *The Traveling Vampire Show*

REBECCA A. BROWN

Horror author Douglas Clegg glibly remarks, "If the kid who eats bugs up the street wrote horror, he would write like Richard Laymon."[1] While the proverbial "weird" neighborhood child may be considered a monster, Laymon's visceral fiction disgusts and terrifies readers through confrontations with the monstrous. Alexa Wright offers a definition of the term that resonates with the writer's narratives: "The idea of monstrousness encapsulates the impossible, dreadful, amoral, inhuman, unspeakable and even unthinkable qualities that lie at the periphery of human identity. The monstrous is the inverse or outside of what is acceptably human in any particular social or cultural context" (3). Using familiar settings, densely structured plots, and "buckets of blood," Laymon invites readers to wrestle with characters and situations that defy the good, the sane, and the normal. In highlighting the monstrous, his extensive oeuvre downplays or dispels the supernatural, frequently transforming young adults and nefarious men, instead of animalistic or hybrid creatures, into nightmares.[2]

Laymon's Bram Stoker award-winning novel, *The Traveling Vampire Show* (2000), brilliantly showcases multivalent representations of the monstrous and its related term, monstrosity. In brief, the book concerns three teenage friends, Slim (female), Rusty (male), and Dwight (male), who prepare over a single day in the summer of 1963 to see "The Traveling Vampire Show" featuring Valeria, "the one and only known VAMPIRE in captivity!" (Laymon 11). Like the consummate ringmaster toying with his audience, Laymon withholds his monsters' appearances until the final quarter of his tome, unleashing a traumatic show where violence, mayhem, and sex coalesce. His three-tiered temporal matrix—the novel's 1963 present, its retrospective time of narration, and its twenty-first century publication date—conjures a wealth of intertextual delights. The book pays homage to *Dracula* (1897), *Something Wicked This Way Comes* (1962), "freak shows," horror comics, and low-budget horror films. Simultaneously, it offers striking meditations on postwar gender roles and youth culture that are both socio-historically resonant and nostalgia tinged.

In this novel Laymon displaces "human freaks" from the center stage of traveling shows with a violent female vampire and a voracious male creature. As a result, he mobilizes the slippage between the terms freak and monster, rewriting the vampire's metaphoricity to foreground the potentially monstrous behavior of women and white, middle-class teenagers in early sixties America. The term freak, although rarely uttered in the novel, and the word vampire, which is frequently articulated, are invested with a surplus of meaning, alluding to the non-normative "freak show" bodies of the past and the hyper-sexed, violent bodies within the narrative's present. Significantly, then, *The Traveling Vampire Show* demonstrates that vampires' violence, sexuality, and rebelliousness may function as an apt metaphor for two types of popularly perceived socio-historical liminality: youth between the sixties countercultural movement and the fifties delinquency scares as well as women between the conscious-raising movements of the sixties and the "domestic containment issues of the fifties."[3]

Freak Shows and Monstrosity

The book begins on a grey summer morning when Rusty and Slim "liberat[e]" Dwight from his yard work to examine a Traveling Vampire Show poster (Laymon 10). Rusty enthuses, "We've got us a traveling *vampire* show! A real live *female* vampire, right here in Grandville! And it says she's *gorgeous*! See that? Gorgeous! Beguiling! A stunning beauty! And she's a *vampire*! Look what it says! She stalks volunteers from the audience and bites their necks! She *sups* on their blood!" (Laymon 12; italics Laymon's). The teen's exclamatory remarks convey a condensed version of the poster as well as his erotically charged enthusiasm. His stimulation derives from the hopes of confronting the monstrous feminine, which he demonstrates by gleefully intermingling words such as "gorgeous" and "beauty" that emphasize Valeria's physical attributes with verbs like "stalks," "bites," and "sups," which underscore her predatory nature. But what is perhaps most compelling about this scene is that the advertisement foregrounds Valeria's sexually alluring *absence*. Rusty commands Dwight and Slim to "See that" and "Look what it says!" His orders reveal that words rather than an image are the object of his gaze. Consequently, the youth's possession of the poster demonstrates the ways that a freak/monster cataylzes his virility and highlights his sexual frustration.

The vampire in fiction and cinema has intrinsic sexual allure, and similarly, Leslie Fiedler contends that freaks have always titillated spectators. He declares, "'all Freaks are perceived to one degree or another as erotic. Indeed abnormality arouses in some "normal" beholders a temptation to go beyond looking to knowing in the full carnal sense the ultimate other'" (qtd. in Fahy 73). Robert Bogdan, examining freakery within the context of dime museums, carnivals, circuses, and other popular forms of American entertainment, additionally foregrounds eroticism but with a different emphasis than Fiedler. He discusses two forms of presentation, underscoring that the "exotic mode" enabled "[p]romoters" and "lecturer[s]" to provide the "freak" with "an identity which appealed to people's interest in the culturally strange, the primitive, the bestial, the exotic" ("The Exhibition of Humans" 540).[4] Laymon's traveling show poster draws upon these various precedents to fashion Valeria as an erotic, ethnic "other." The advertisement positions her outside of Western society since she is "born in the wilds of Transylvania" and highlights her non-normative behavior because she "sleeps by day in her coffin" (11). These features pay homage to the vampire's folkloric and literary origins, endowing Valeria with the same background and licentious nocturnal behaviors as Dracula and his progeny. As "strange," "bestial," and "exotic," the female vampire, before she even appears, is coded as the ultimate sexual fantasy for the middle-class white teens to consume.

Laymon's novel thus instantly delves into the slipperiness of the terms freak and monster by substituting a vampire, a conventional horror creature, for a sideshow "freak," a human anomaly. Although freak shows did not showcase vampires, they did exhibit people of diverse ethnicities, races, and disabilities, casting them as monsters due to their unconventional physical characteristics and behaviors.[5] For instance, in a letter dated January 30, 1843, to Boston Museum manager Moses Kimball, P.T. Barnum writes, "I *must* have the fat boy or some other monster [or] something new *in the course of this week* so as t[o be] *sure* to put them in the General's place *next Monday*" (qtd. in Taylor 35; italics Barnum's; brackets Taylor's). Barnum's canny marketing testifies to the commodification of the human body, capitalizing on the public's visual consumption of otherness (Adams 12–13). General Tom Thumb was already established in the public eye as an "aggrandized" freak: although diminutive in height he was advertised as "a perfect man in miniature" and displayed a range of talents at Barnum's museum and other venues (Bogdan, *Freak Show* 149). However, in this sentence he is syntactically associated with the "fat boy," the exhibit that will take his place. This conventional freak's excess weight is a somatic abnormality that Barnum verbally manipulates, transforming him into a monstrosity. Drawing upon the *OED*, Fahy claims, "Not until the 1840s did *freak* refer to 'a monstrosity, an abnormally developed individual of any species; in recent use (especially in the United States) a living curiosity exhibited in a show'" (7). While twenty years after this letter both exhibitions might have been referred to as "freaks," Barnum's use of the word "monster" in this letter marks a resonant socio-cultural, scientific, and medical crossroad, alluding to the past while anticipating the future. Laymon's traveling show poster exploits these tensions, marking Valeria as beautiful, ethnic, violent, absent body upon which the terms vampire and freak can readily intermingle.

Beyond her multifaceted allure, the teens' desire to see Valeria "stalk[ing] volunteers from the audience and bit[ing] their necks!" finds especial relevance within the context of postwar entertainment. Bogdan and Fahy identify the 1910s and 1920s as the beginning of the freak show's decline. The former summarizes this transformation: "By 1940, economic hard times, technological and geographic changes, competition from other forms of entertainment, the medicalization of human differences (Szasz, 1961) and changed public taste resulted in a great decline in 'freakshows'" ("The Exhibition of Humans" 537).[6] Adams, while acknowledging these socio-historical changes, relays a different perspective which emphasizes the freak show's longevity: "freak shows never really vanished. During the period of their decline, they maintained a firm hold on the imaginations of the many Americans who had visited them in better days"; their "history and iconography [are] preserved in literature, film, the visual arts" and in twenty first century "performance art" (2). This imaginative grip was not only evident through the re-release of Tod Browning's *Freaks* (1932) in 1962 but through also birth defects caused by thalidomide in the early sixties that made their victims interchangeably monstrosities and freaks (Skal 289). As David Skal further explains, "the late fifties" witnessed the beginnings of "Monster Culture," a confluence of "Shock Theater" on television, new horror films in the theater, horror movie magazines, and other monster related ephemera (Skal 266). Mummies, invisible men, Dracula, Frankenstein's Creature, and werewolves increasingly invaded homes, ensuring interested youths'—often, but not always, boys'—domestic confrontations with (representations) of otherness.[7]

Slim, Rusty, and Dwight have not seen *Freaks* or encountered thalidomide-inflicted children, but they are avid consumers of horror films and fiction including *The Haunting* (1962), *Frankenstein* (1818, 1931), and *Dracula* (1897, 1932). A month before the Traveling Vampire Show's appearance, they eagerly attended the "All Night Shockfest," six horror movies in a row, but they were barred by their parents from staying out past midnight. Whereas science and medicine eventually intervened by the mid-twentieth century to explain the physical disabilities and abnormalities of "freaks" (Bogdan, *Freak Show* 64–67), no rational discourses can explain a vampire. Thus, the Traveling Vampire Show upstages the monstrous delights of the Shockfest by enabling them to experience a gorgeous female vampire's allure and violence, knowing that they will not be passive consumers of the spectacle in a darkened theater, but possibly active participants.

Nonetheless, the show's age restriction, ticket price, and site pose several challenges for the teens that horror films and fiction do not. Adams explains, "Freak shows were part of a broader development of mass entertainment that included amusement parks, circuses, dime museums, and vaudeville" for the middle classes and their families in the mid-nineteenth and early twentieth century (10–11). Moreover, these shows were often constructed to ensure that freaks and audiences did not "share the same social space" (Wright 90). The Traveling Vampire Show with its age restriction, single-attraction emphasis, midnight start time, and ten dollar tickets deviates from its precursors since it is marked by the poster and later by the owner, Julian Stryker, as "adult entertainment." This categorization is further reinforced by the show's site, Janks Field, where the deaf-mute young adult—Tommy Janks—killed and consumed the bodies of young women several summers prior and where the teens have experienced other frightening ventures. Positioned as a site of microcosmic trauma within Grandville's history, Janks is a repository for the monstrous that has been expelled from the town's own borders, the ideal site for a show that will undermine "good taste." Although the youths are aware of Janks' sordid history, the promise of adult entertainment, particularly sexual entertainment, proves to be too intoxicating an offer for them to ignore.

"Freakish," Monstrous Teens

Valeria's impending appearance at Janks inspires a series of events, spanning from the late-morning until just before midnight, in which the youths cast off the social mores their parents and the town impose upon them. Dwight explains the strictures that typically govern his home: "In Grandville, not only does everyone know everyone, but they figure your business is their business. Nowadays, you hear talk that 'It takes a village to raise a child.' You ask me, it takes a village to wreck a child for life. In Grandville, you felt like you were living in a nest of spies. One wrong move and everyone would know about it. Including your parents" (51). On the one hand, the teen's statement may be read within a generalized literary/socio-cultural tradition of small-town life where size precludes secrecy, particularly for teenagers seeking autonomy and privacy. On the other hand, Dwight, whose name, short hair, and conflicted morality partially entrenches him within the fifties, neatly conflates nationalistic Cold War paranoia, which encouraged neighbors to spy on neighbors, with parental paranoia that enables his relations and other adults to structure his (and often his friend's) life/behavior. Living in a small town that implicitly champions "containment," an ideology Elaine Tyler May has famous characterized as "more than merely a metaphor for the cold war on the homefront … [it] aptly describes the way in which public policy, personal behavior, and even political values were focused on the home" (xxv), Grandville's adults are literal or surrogate parents and social rebellion is suppressed for the maintenance of white middle-class social values. However, on the day of the Traveling Vampire Show, the teens' parents, particularly their fathers, are mostly absent, enabling them to subvert these rules.

It is not just the presence of the vampire and the absence of patriarchal figures that enables the youths to rebel, though. Bill Osgerby explains a socio-cultural shift from the late fifties into the early sixties wherein fears of juvenile delinquency and familial dissolution were replaced by "the ethos of hedonism and hectic consumerism central to the 'teenager' experience [that] came to set the pace for the new values and lifestyles evident among ascending sections of the middle class." As he further remarks, "With the rise of the new, middle-class 'ethic of fun,' a more liberal set of social, sexual and cultural mores came into play—an ethos that was formed in tandem with (and drew inspiration from) the developing 'teenage' realm of leisure and material gratification" (91). Despite their parents' late night curfews and upholding of repressive middle-class values/behaviors, Slim, Dwight, and Rusty are poised on the brink of change as consumers. They have some money to spend, due to allowances and work; while they primarily walk on the day of the show, Slim's car (handed down to her, but nonetheless, hers) enables them to cruise town at night or go for joyrides. However, the vampire magnifies their own desires for hedonism and consumption.[8] And although the steep price of the show, alongside their ages, prohibits their purchasing power, Dwight's sister-in-law, Lee, buys the tickets for them. Thus, the teens gain access to Valeria through middle-class prosperity at the same time that they rebel throughout the day against normative middle-class values.

Fittingly, then, Laymon establishes a symbiotic connection between the vampire and the teens through various episodes that symbolically foreground sexuality and consumption. For instance, in the early afternoon when the boys venture to Slim's house in search of her, they enter the private territory of her bedroom. Later, they surreptitiously liberate food from Rusty's refrigerator—Velvetta and Oscar Meyer wieners—without his mother's knowledge. The former event is not only a conventional precursor to intimacy and intercourse but a domestic invasion that disrupts female-coded space. The refrigerator pillaging robs a symbolic container of maternal plentitude and also connotes displacement (hotdogs for oral gratification). As the evening begins, the tensions between sex and consumption escalate. Slim and Dwight crystallize their romance by kissing at his empty house, prior to and while eating dinner. Later in the evening, at Slim's place, the female teenager arouses Dwight so much that he prematurely ejaculates. Dwight's "accident" foregrounds his body's lack of control, reinforcing that the connections between teenagers and monsters rely in large part upon uncontrollable physical as well as psycho-sexual transformations (Evans 354–355).

Whereas Slim and Dwight primarily show their affinity to Valeria through conventional teenage sexuality and consumption, Rusty, the hyper-sexed teen, and his sister Bitsy, who is in love with Dwight, additionally exhibit their connections to Valeria through transgressive desire and violence. Earlier in the afternoon, Dwight and Rusty abandon Bitsy in their search for Slim; later, Slim discovers her copy of *Dracula* has been chewed up while Dwight finds one of her mother's roses in his own bedroom. The teens assume the vampire show workers and Valeria carried out these mysterious actions. Yet, the irrational displaces the supernatural when Bitsy confesses to both antics, causing her brother to call her a "freak" (260). Rusty's use of the term "freak," the only explicit one in the novel aside from a few uses of "don't freak out," is significant. As Adams relays in her discussion of racial otherness in Carson McCullers' *The Member of the Wedding* (1946), "freak is not an innate quality, but an identity imposed on certain bodies to justify their exclusion from the privileges of normality" (103). Wright, in glossing the term "monstrosity" provides a similar definition, noting that while the word may be rooted in "corporeal irregularity" it "is never an intrinsic quality ... [monstrosity] is a narrative imposed on certain appearances or behaviors at particular times in specific social contexts" (3). Rusty verbally and behaviorally sets Bitsy apart from her family and normative society, coding her infatuation with Dwight as abnormal. Yet she is no more freakish and no more of a monstrosity than her brother who causes her to fall and rip her dress, and then stares at her inappropriately. The implications of incest in this scene and others that involve the brother and sister magnify their unconventional desires.

Their violence also assumes monstrous proportions at night. Bitsy and Rusty become nearly lethal when the former pummels Slim, ensuring that Dwight's love interest cannot attend the show; as a result, Rusty beats up his sister, leaving her in the woods hurt.

All four teens perform various iterations of freakishness and monstrosity throughout the day, demonstrating the plasticity of these terms within Laymon's novel. Fahy, drawing upon Fiedler's contentions from the first part of this essay, states that the critic "believes that desiring to know the other on sexual and intimate terms makes the viewer a type of freak" (73). Laymon thus continually marks the teens, not just Bitsy, as freaks through their longing for "sexual or intimate" knowledge of Valeria. However, by revealing the teens' yearning to attend the show at all costs, using any means necessary, no matter how dishonest or poorly they behave to parents, siblings, and even each other, infuses their freakery with the harmful and destructive behavior so often aligned with the monstrous.[9]

Sex, Blood and Performance

At the Traveling Vampire Show, Laymon elaborates his medley of freakery, monstrosity, and the monstrous when the teens finally experience the carnal wonders of Valeria. Rusty, Dwight, and Lee sit in the bleachers with several other Grandville inhabitants as owner Julian Stryker opens the midnight entertainment. He verbally capitalizes on the "exotic mode of presentation," extending Valeria's backstory to make her "A DIRECT DESCENDANT OF THE GREAT COUNT DRACULA HIMSELF" and detailing her capture in Transylvania (314–315; ellipses Laymon's). Notably, Stryker underscores her violence, linking it to her ethnic otherness, declaring that these qualities preclude her from American assimilation: "UNFORTUNATELY, DUE TO HER BLOOD-THIRSTY NATURE, VALERIA IS NOT A WELCOME GUEST IN OUR LAND. LIKE THE WANDERING JEW, SHE MUST FOREVER CONTINUE HER TRAVELS … NEVER FINDING A HOME" (315). In addition to resonating with Cold War anxieties about foreigners and racial otherness within America, his vampire is dangerously sexual. Styrker relays how "OVERWHELMED" he was by her beauty; alluding to Stoker's novel, he contends, "WITH THE AID OF A WISE MAN WELL VERSED IN THE ARTS OF MESMERISM, I GAINED CONTROL OVER VALERIA'S MIND AND THUS ENSLAVED HER TO MY WILL" (315). The monster's enslavement posits her as definitively under patriarchal rule, augmenting her status as "THE WORLD'S ONLY LIVING VAMPIRE IN CAPTIVITY!" (315). In this sense, she initially appears as little more than a subjugated beautiful woman, whose sexuality has been contained and whose autonomy has been mastered. Yet Valeria's impending performance and corporeality complicate these notions.

When Stryker reveals his monster, Dwight, Rusty, and Lee not only gain affirmation of Valeria's physical existence but additionally discover that her sexuality surpasses the poster's promises. Dwight claims,

> I gazed at Valeria, stunned.
> Gazed at her amazing, beautiful face.
> Gazed at her deep cleavage.
> Gazed at the magnificent globes of her leather-encased breasts.
> Gazed at her flat belly and the swell of her hips and her
> smooth, solid-looking thighs [317].

Laymon's use of anaphora highlights Dwight's overwhelming reaction to the vampire. Sheathed in a red leather bra, red skirt, and red boots the entirety of her body is placed on display for male and female viewing pleasure and further eroticized by the color of her accoutrements. Dwight visually consumes each part of her hyper-sexualized body from top to bottom, indicating that she is "well-over 6 feet tall" (317) and moves with ethereal mobility (323). Valeria's body does not include the classic "freak" physical distortions of excessive giantness, dwarfism, or extra hair, nor does any aspect of her body gesture towards disability. Nonetheless, her figure reinforces Adams' contention that "the centrality of the body remains a constant and determining feature of the freak's identity" (6) because it resonates with the 1950s fetish for "freakishly" voluptuous female physiques, demonstrated by Marilyn Monroe, Jane Mansfield, and early *Playboy* centerfolds. By 1963, these female forms were poised to become obsolete, overtaken by the Twiggy-mod type and within a few years by the girlish hippie body. Anticipating the equally curvy, scantily-clad female comic book vampire, Vampirella, Valeria's body encompasses several narratives of corporeal female monstrosity—past and present—which are enhanced by her unconventional behavior.

Valeria's job as the star and only attraction of the Show challenges the "important cultural work" freak shows accomplished in the nineteenth and early twentieth centuries (Adams 2). Stryker announces that audience members have the opportunity to battle the vampire in the cage and will win $500 if they endure five minutes. If they fail, his monster will take her evening nourishment from their bodies. The night's entertainment, then, consists of Valeria fighting and ultimately defeating four socially representative males in her cage—a Marine, a middle-aged "codger" (327), a Wild One wanna-be, and Rusty. She exhibits her physical strength and cunning when she brutally tackles and is tackled, in turn, by each of these contenders. Although two of them physically violate her, one whips her with his belt, and three of her adversaries deprive her of her clothing, she demonstrates her physical superiority to them, concluding each fight by sucking blood from their necks, stomachs, or arms, symbolically draining them of their lives. She thus transgresses the lines between spectacle and realism, ensuring that the audience does not just passively objectify the show, but rather becomes a part of it. "[F]reak shows … allow[ed] ordinary people to confront, and master, the most extreme and terrifying forms of Otherness they could imagine" but this confrontation, while taking place in public, was primarily visual rather than physical (Adams 2). The vampire's contestants, who not only represent the inhabitants of Grandville and its surrounding environs but also signify varying degrees of patriarchal authority, are unable to "master" Valeria through their gaze, their voice, and their bodies. Moreover, the audience visually consuming the spectacle shifts much of its verbal support from the contestants to the vampire. In overturning these power dynamics, the female monster becomes unconventionally empowered within the context of the freak show.

The vampire's unconventional empowerment also has significant bearing on women's gender roles within Cold War America. Dwight reveals towards the end of the sanctioned show, "Valeria obviously wasn't a vampire, after all. Just a beautiful woman with a very strange and dangerous job" (348). Although Dwight's mother and Lee work, they are domesticated through marriage and hold traditional female occupations since they are English teachers; Slim's mother is employed as a waitress and her husband has "gone south," but she nonetheless lives in an upper-middle-class neighborhood and dates men. These fictional women, albeit minor characters in the novel, do not embody the "contradictory" gendered politics of the 1950s and implicitly the early 1960s that Joanne Meyerowitz discovers in "postwar mass culture" where "domestic ideals coexisted in ongoing tension with an ethos of individual achievement that celebrated nondomestic activity, individual striving, public service, and public success" (231). Conversely, Valeria is advertised as "in captivity"—her sexuality and violence are literally contained, yet both are simultaneously infectious. As a female vampire she is liberated from the roles of wife, mother, lover, and even political aspirant, crafting her own form of unconventional "public success." She earns her own money through an occupation that relies on her physical strength, transgressiveness, and non-reproductive sexuality, which marks her as a social aberration/outcast within Grandville and, by extension, a popular perception of America at this time. Thus, what Valeria ultimately reveals is that the freak and the female vampire align because of the performative nature of these roles.

Adams contends in her discussion of freak photography, "freakishness is a historically variable quality, derived less from particular physical attributes than the spectacle of the extraordinary body swathed in theatrical props, promoted by advertising and performative fanfare" (5). While Valeria demonstrates during the performance how the poster, pre-show lecture, her costume, cage, coffin, and her fights transform her into an empowered spectacle, after the show, she oversteps additional social and sexual boundaries, revealing why, like all monsters, she "must be exiled or destroyed" (Cohen 16). When the theatrics conclude early due to a storm, Stryker offers Lee the chance to retrieve Rusty's body if she fights Valeria in the cage. Although Lee is initially an adequate adversary for the vampire, the monster overpowers her and begins to sexually violate her. Dwight rushes to his sister-in-law's aid; the vampire, in turn, offers Dwight the chance to sexually explore her body before she kills him, but he refuses. The monster's performance in this post-show confrontation engages with two forms of socio-culturally deviant sexuality. Donna Penn explains, "Whereas the prostitute had historically served as the symbol of female wantonness and degeneracy, during the postwar years the lesbian, in the popular culture, joined her in filling that role. As such, this association helped make publicly visible those who formerly went undetected and thereby helped define the parameters of the normal and acceptable" (360). Valeria thus becomes a performative embodiment of cultural anxieties, in short, a body which makes manifest the recognizably transgressive attributes of female vampires within fiction, film, and folklore.[10]

Appropriately, given the novel's emphasis on youthful monstrosity and rebelliousness, Valeria is not defeated by a paternal figure, but rather by Slim, whose nightmarish familial past and literary knowledge mark her as the ideal vampire slayer. The teen, an archery expert, creeps into the Show with her bow and quiver of arrows, and then shoots Valeria three times. Even though the vampire has been exposed as a dangerous female performer, these injuries—in the eye, in the breast, and in the heart—pay homage to the literary and folkloric origins of the vampire, maintaining the emphasis on "production," "fabrication," and spectacle that Bogdan claims has always been essential to the freak show's success (*Freak Show* 95). The shot in the eye nullifies the vampire's mesmeric gaze; the shot in the breast disfigures one of the most sexualized parts of her female body as well as a part of the body that literary and filmic vampires feed from. And significantly, the shot in the heart, the site of all important blood flow, kills her like a stake. Living up to the gender ambiguity of her nickname, Slim steps into a masculine-coded role with Western (cinematic) undertones, ultimately orchestrating their escape from the Traveling Vampire show crew. The teenager, whose sexuality has already become an enticing danger to Dwight, and whose brutal tactics eliminate most of the post-show perils, out performs the hyper-sexed, vicious human vampire.[11] Although this performance is sanctioned by the show's site and the vampire's threat, Slim, at this point in the novel, nonetheless reinforces the potent monstrosity and potential monstrousness of youth.

Sideshow Gaff: The "Real" Vampire?

Although Dwight, Lee, and Rusty view the legitimate vampire show, and Dwight, Lee, and Slim endure its unsanctioned aftermath, Laymon reserves an unexpectedly climactic performance for his characters. Adams briefly remarks, "Sideshows typically end with a gaff, a hidden attraction that can only be viewed for an extra price. Those gullible enough to pay are almost always disappointed by what they find when the final curtain is parted" (21). Bogdan, in discussing the gaff, does not position it as the sideshow climax or conclusion; however, he does relay reasons for the audience's potential disappointment. The critic claims that gaffs are "fakes who pretended to be born with anomalies." They do not bear the marks of so-called authentic fakery that "self-made freaks," such as "tattooed people," "Circassian beauties," "sword-swallowers," "snake charmers" possess (Bogdan, *Freak Show* 235). Laymon reserves a "hidden attraction" for his surviving characters, one who does not disappoint and appears authentic. The novel thus reframes Jeffrey Jerome Cohen's contention that "the monster is always coming back, always at the verge of irruption" (20) by substituting the demise of one monster (Valeria) for a significantly different lively one.

After the trio leaves Janks in the mysterious hearse, a thump in the back of the vehicle piques their curiosity, ensuring that they confront the Traveling Vampire Show's ultimate horror. Dwight explains, "We all gazed in. The volunteers who'd gone up against Valeria in the cage were there.... They were all naked. They were all in pieces, piled up next to the casket within easy reach of ... *its occupant*" (387; second italics Laymon's). Whereas earlier the youth objectified Valeria's sexualized body, the unnamed resident sits amongst the pieces of the female vampire's contenders. Their nudity connotes vulnerability, figuring as an ironic inversion of their attempts to disrobe her. Dwight goes on to relay that the occupant is "an obese, legless, hairless man ... [who] looked like a bloated sack of slippery white skin. Except the skin was mostly scarlet with blood. His bulgy eyes looked like a pair of bloodshot golf balls. Clutched in both hands, upside-down just under his chin, was Rusty's head" (387). Here, the creature bears the physical marks of a sideshow "freak," since its hairlessness implies sexual/gender otherness while its leglessness and obesity presents the image of "real" physical disfigurement. Furthermore, his behavior suggests a cross between the cannibal and the "'gloaming geek,'" the latter "a wild man who, as part of his presentation, would bite the heads off of rats, chickens, and snakes" (Bogdan, *Freak Show* 262). This creature does not resemble Dwight, Rusty, Slim, or Lee's preconceived notions of a vampire, particularly since he bears no marks of corporeal beauty and eroticism; his potential ethnic/racial ambiguity appears quite literally whitewashed due to his coating in blood. Gnawing on the ultimate symbol of human rationality, a head, this vampire upstages Valeria's and the teens' violent antics to represent "the impossible, dreadful, amoral, inhuman, and unspeakable" (Wright 3).

Gothic critic Fred Botting, drawing upon Ann Radcliffe's classic formulations of horror and terror while adding a Lacanian inflection, provides an apt context for the teens' confrontation. Botting writes,

> Unbearable horror finds an object that turns it into terror. Neither inside nor outside human linguistic bodies, horror connotes an experience of some Thing that is "extimate," an uncanny and confounding interior exteriority. Horror nonetheless is also made to function within systems of morality as a limit to desire, while the gap it discloses in those systems serves as a screen for the projection of fantasy and the assuaging of anxieties, for the constructions of objects of horror—monsters, vampires, demons, terminators: these figures turn horror into terror, invigorating the imaginative energy of expulsion [144].

In contextualizing physical and intellectual responses to horror, Botting also states, "Without an object, horror delivers only bodily paralysis and mental chaos" (144). When Dwight explains the group's reaction to this monster, he demonstrates the transformation of horror into terror: "What we saw in there ... it knocked out whatever remained of our brains and guts. I have vague memories of noises coming from us. Things like '*Whoa!*' and '*Yahh!*' and '*Eeee!*' as we backed away from the rear of the hearse.... And then we were running down the middle of the dirt road as if we have the boogey-man after us" (388; first ellipses Laymon's; italics Laymon's). The idea that the vampire "knocked out whatever remained of our brains and guts" suggests a confrontation with otherness that initially results in paralysis. However, Dwight, Lee, and Slim's subsequent somatic reaction reveals that this entity ignites terror, ensuring a physical action—in this case, fleeing. These reactions have significant bearing on Laymon's doubling of monsters within the *Traveling Vampire Show*.

Taking Botting's notions into consideration alongside this particular scene leads to some startling conclusions towards the novel's end. Valeria, the performative vampire, is not an object of horror. Instead, she is an erotic simulacra who latently inspires terror, arousing Lee, Dwight, and Slim to mentally and physically fight. Conversely, the thing in the back of the hearse is an embodiment of vampiric, ghoulish, and freakish monstrosity and the monstrous. Its grotesque body and relentless action give representation to the unrepresentable—horror itself which, as Botting explains by drawing upon Victor Sage, might be likened to a "'black hole'" (144)—because it threatens complete and utter annihilation of the self, community, and culture through uncontrolled consumption. Whereas Valeria symbolizes sociocultural, gendered anxieties, this creature figures as an object of transhistorical horror, the ever-looming threat of the boogeyman. Amidst the impending annihilation of the nuclear age, something freakish, hybrid, and not quite human, pushed to the margins of culture—yet preserved—still resides within it. This monster, more frightening than Valeria, the teens, or its freak show predecessors, surfaces as part and parcel of an established form of American entertainment with a lengthy history of exhibiting the marginalized for profit, to scare to death and destroy bodies and through them societies simultaneously from without and from within.

Unlike Valeria, then, this monster cannot be destroyed or expelled, even though a confrontation with its body inspires action. Nonetheless, Slim, Lee, and Dwight return to Janks in the early morning hours, cast as the proverbial Crew of Light seeking to eradicate this threat, displacing active Gothic paternalism with empowered femininity and youthful masculinity. Yet the hearse, the creature, and every other sign of the show have vanished. Slim sums up this mystifying scene by quoting the final lines of Henry Wadsworth Longfellow's poem "The Day Is Done" (1844), a work that eloquently celebrates poetry's power to comfort and enchant its listener. In Longfellow's piece, the speaker, seeing "the lights of the village" (line 5) from a distance in the night, calls upon an unnamed addressee to read "some humbler poet['s]" writing (25) rather than the "grand old masters" (17) or "the bards sublime" (18), to "soothe this restless feeling, / And banish the thoughts of day" (15–16). Such a poet's works will have a powerful effect:

> [T]he night shall be filled with music,
> And the cares, that infest the day,
> Shall fold their tents, like the Arabs,
> And as silently steal away [41–44].

Slim decontextualizes the final lines two lines of Longfellow's poem to allude to the Vampire Show's befuddling disappearances, implicitly associating the "exotic" Arabs with the monster(s) and their show. But unlike the speaker who seeks the poet's words to articulate his emotions and provide comfort, under the slowly rising sun, there can be no poetry or words penned by a humble poet or a "grand master" to quell the three survivors. Comforting paternalism cannot be reinstated, even when Dwight's father, a stalwart figure of power, a police chief, launches an investigation of the vanished show. Instead, Slim, Lee, and Dwight will be plagued by the horror, embodied in the show and its monsters, ensuring that the creature will haunt their remaining days. Dwight's narrative becomes, like *The Strange Case of Dr. Jekyll and Mr. Hyde* (1886), *Dracula*, and *The Beetle* (1897), a testimony to a horror that, once glimpsed, cannot be emotionally and psychically expelled.

Horror as Truly Horrifying

Dwight provides a Stokerian epilogue at the novel's end. He recounts that he and Slim begin to officially date, and Slim finally replaces her gender-ambiguous moniker for a feminine nickname (Fran), short for her real name (Frances). Lee gives birth to a child. However, these affirmations of domesticity and heteronormativity are merely a smokescreen: Rusty's death, Bitsy's disappearance, and the aftermath thereof still haunt the three characters. Dwight's final lines tell readers to "stay away from" the Traveling Vampire Show, "for God's sake," should they hear that it's "coming to ... [their] town" (391). While the word monster etymologically means to warn, here the teen's words act as a powerful warning in place of monstrous bodies. Dwight's evocation of a divine, paternal force in the novel's closing statement implies a sense of utter powerlessness in the face of Traveling Vampire Show, imbuing it with horrific potency, and perhaps even implying its status as a symbolic harbinger of change within a tumultuous era.

By enabling his monsters and the show they are a part of to maintain such a powerful impact upon his last man and women standing, Laymon foregrounds the visibility and potential horrors of freak shows during a time of their cultural transformation. He also highlights the slippages between freak and monster to show that while the overt violence, sexuality, and rebelliousness of vampires serves as an apt metaphor for middle-class youth and women, the potential power of that metaphor can be easily overshadowed by the unbridled, the monstrous, the consuming, unnamable evil that is both inside and outside of culture. Significantly, then, from the perspective of the book's publication date, Laymon's novel functions as an anathema for Botting's millennial concerns about Gothic horror: "Horror, so it seems, has passed beyond the capacity and comfort of anything vaguely resembling Gothic presentation." As Botting laments, the late-twentieth century's over-proliferation, repetition, and recycling of objects of horror, particularly in film and television, has evacuated the genre of its Gothic overtones (139). Retrospectively returning to the early sixties, a less remote past than Ann Radcliffe's and Matthew "Monk" Lewis', Laymon recaptures much of the potency of Gothic horror by catalyzing the socially repressed, marginalized, and monstrous in his own inimitably bloody, violent, erotic way.

Notes

1. Clegg's remarks appear in opening of Laymon's autobiography, *A Writer's Tale*, and thus there is no page number. See Works Cited for full citation.

2. In Laymon's forty or so published novels, corporeal whiteness rather than blackness or darkness, the latter a conventional Gothic/horror monster marking that all too often refers to the collusion between racial/ethnic otherness and evil, is a signifier of the monstrous and monstrosity. See in particular the novels *Allhallows Eve* (1985), *Resurrection Dreams* (1988), *Funland* (1989), *Darkness Tell Us* (1991), and *Savage* (1993). (Publication dates are all "firsts" and obtained from *A Writer's Tale*). If one were to place Laymon's works within a classic Gothic context, one might compare him to Mrs. Carver, author of *The Horror of Oakendale Abbey* (1797). Curt Herr explains that Mrs. Carver proffers the supernatural and dispels it with rationality, but unlike Anne Radcliffe, the real explanation for the supernatural is often more horrifying than what readers might have imagined since it reveals the monstrousness of human actions (159). Laymon often raises the specter of the supernatural and while occasionally he leaves these threads unexplained, more often than not, a human agent, usually a young adult or a man, is responsible for the horror. His vampire novels, though, including *The Traveling Vampire Show, The Stake* (1990), and *Bite* (1996) more frequently leave some mysterious threads for readers to chew on.

3. I use the term Cold War as the book's most appropriate historical period marker because the narrative takes place one year after the Cuban Missile Crisis, and although it conveys signs of youth rebellion, the novel implicitly coheres to the ideology of postwar "domestic containment" Elaine Tyler May examines in *Homeward Bound* (1988, reprint 1999). However, Laymon's book never *explicitly* mentions the Missile Crisis, atomic energy, space travel, scientific advancement, the rumblings of the Vietnam War, or even the important milestones in the Civil Rights movement. Instead, the vampire and her show become the symbolic markers of these social unrests and others that I directly address in the essay. I've also used the word "popularly perceived" since the countercultural movement predates the late 1960s and since Elaine Tyler May characterizes the early 1960s as a time when "Signs that the postwar consensus was beginning to crack were hardly more visible than they had been in the fifties..." (195).

4. Posters were not frequently used for advertising freaks in the nineteenth and early twentieth centuries (Bogdan, *Freak Show* 98).

5. While vampires were not, to my knowledge, exhibited in nineteenth- and twentieth-century freak shows, skeletons and mummies were. Additionally, to clarify one of the central tenets that underlies this essay, Wright claims, "A freak is, by definition, a monstrosity" (81); Elizabeth Grosz also reinforces this connection (56–58). However, Bogdan claims, "'Freak' is a frame of mind, a set of practices, a way of thinking about and presenting people. It is the enactment of a tradition, the performance of a stylized presentation" (3). Bogdan also indicates that "monsters" are one of many "imprecise terms" for freaks and that prior to the late nineteenth century, "monsters" were one of two "major categor[ies] of [freak] exhibits that" connoted a "medical term for people

born with demonstrable difference" (6). As he further elaborates, "In the last quarter of the nineteenth century the blurred distinction between species and freaks of nature became moot; all human exhibits ... fell under the generic term *freak*" (*Freak Show* 7). The exhibition of human physical abnormality for profit was particularly prominent in Renaissance fair grounds (Adams 10), especially at Bartholomew Fair (Semonin 69–77).

6. Thomas Fahy also endorses this view of the freak show, citing the beginning of its demise around the 1920s (10–12).

7. Hammer Films and American International Pictures panned their wares to enthusiastic postwar teen consumers.

8. See also Rob Lantham on post–Fordism and vampiricism in *Consuming Youth: Vampires, Cyborgs, and the Culture of Consumption* (Chicago: University of Chicago Press, 2002) 10–12.

9. As Fahy explores in his analysis of Truman Capote's *Other Voices, Other Rooms* (1948) and Carson McCullers' play *The Member of the Wedding* (1950), "Freaks," both the conventional performers on midways in these narratives as well as the sexually nonnormative adult characters, "possess a freedom that" the teenager characters do not have. He maintains, "For adult characters, freaks represent the social marginalization that comes with a nonheterosexual lifestyle, but sexually conflicted teenagers feel an affinity for these performers" (111). In contrast, Laymon's teens are coded as excessively heteronormative; the teenagers, immersed in their own hormone-laden conflicts, nonetheless "feel an affinity for" Valeria, but it seems to have little to do with the specific type of sexual and gendered identification Fahy examines.

10. Carol Senf discusses three central attributes of the female vampire—"bloodsucking, rebellious behavior, and overt eroticism"—all of which embody "everything traditional women were not supposed to be" (200). Valeria surpasses these attributes.

11. In my mind, this scene is one of Laymon's most explicit allusions to Bradbury's *Something Wicked This Way Comes*, since he rewrites/restages Will Holloway's deft, yet ultimately non-lethal bow and arrow shooting of the Witch (in balloon form) from his rooftop. Substituting a female teenager for a male one in handling weapons and saving the proverbial day in some respects undermines the misogynistic overtones of Bradbury's scene and foreshadows the more fluid gender politics on the horizon wherein a male can be the "damsel" in distress, saved by a female.

Works Cited

Adams, Rachel. *Sideshow U.S.A.: Freaks and the America Cultural Imagination*. Chicago: University of Chicago Press, 2001. Print.

Bogdan, Robert. "The Exhibition of Humans with Differences for Amusement and Profit." *Policy Studies Journal* 15.3 (March 1987): 537–550. *Academic Search Premier*. Web. 15 Oct. 2012.

_____. *Freak Show: Presenting Human Oddities for Amusement and Profit*. Chicago: University of Chicago Press, 1990. Print.

Botting, Fred. "Future Horror (the Redundancy of Gothic)." *Gothic Studies* 1.2 (1999): 139–155. *MLA Bibliography*. Web. 4 Aug. 2014.

Cohen, Jeffrey Jerome. "Monster Culture (Seven Theses)." *Monster Theory: Reading Culture*. Ed. Jeffrey Jerome Cohen. Minneapolis: University of Minnesota Press, 1996. 3–25. Print.

Evans, Walter. "Monster Movies: A Sexual Theory." *Journal of Popular Film* 2.4 (1973): 353–365. *Taylor & Francis Online*. Web. 18 Nov. 2013.

Fahy, Thomas. *Freak Shows and the Modern American Imagination: Constructing the Damaged Body from Willa Cather to Truman Capote*. New York: Palgrave Macmillan, 2006. Print.

Grosz, Elizabeth. "Intolerable Ambiguity: Freaks as/at the Limit." *Freakery: Cultural Spectacles of the Extraordinary Body*. Ed. Rosemarie Garland Thomson. New York: New York University Press, 1996. 55–66. Print.

Herr, Curt. "Introduction." *The Horrors of Oakendale Abbey*. Crestline, CA: Zittaw Press, 2006. Print.

Laymon, Richard. *The Traveling Vampire Show*. New York: Leisure Books, 2001. Print.

_____. *A Writer's Tale*. Los Gatos, CA: Deadline Press, 1998. Print.

Lewis, Robert M., ed. *From Traveling Show to Vaudeville: Theatrical Spectacle in America, 1830–1910*. Baltimore: John Hopkins University Press, 2007. Print.

Longfellow, Henry Wadsworth. "The Day is Done." *Poetry Foundation*. Web. 9 Sept. 2014.

May, Elaine Tyler. *Homeward Bound: American Families in the Cold War Era*. 1988. New York: Basic Books, 1999. Print.

Meyerowitz, Joanne. "Beyond the Feminine Mystique: A Reassessment of Postwar Mass Culture, 1946–1958." *Not June Cleaver: Woman and Gender in Postwar America, 1945–1960*. Ed. Joanne Meyerowitz. Philadelphia: Temple University Press, 1994. 229–262. Print.

Osgerby, Bill. *Playboys in Paradise: Masculinity, Youth and Leisure-Style in Modern America*. Oxford: Berg, 2001. Print.

Penn, Donna. "The Sexualized Woman: The Lesbian, the Prostitute, and the Containment of Female Sexuality in Postwar America." *Not June Cleaver: Woman and Gender in Postwar America, 1945–1960*. Ed. Joanne Meyerowitz. Philadelphia: Temple University Press, 1994. 358–381. Print.

Semonin, Paul. "Monsters in the Marketplace: The Exhibition of Human Oddities in Early Modern England." *Freakery: Cultural Spectacles of the Extraordinary Body*. Ed. Rosemarie Garland Thomson. New York: New York University Press, 1996. 69–81. Print.

Senf, Carol A. "Daughters of Lilith: Women Vampires in Popular Literature." *Blood Is the Life: Vampires in Literature*. Ed. Leonard G. Heldreth and Mary Pharr. Bowling Green: Bowling Green State University Popular Press, 1999. 199–216. Print.

Skal, David J. *The Monster Show: A Cultural History of Horror*. New York: Penguin, 1993. Print.

Wright, Alexa. *Monstrosity: The Human Monster in Visual Culture*. London: I.B. Tauris, 2013. Print.

Gothic Commodification of the Body and the Modern Literary Serial Killer in Child of God and American Psycho

CHRISTOPHER COUGHLIN

The titular figures of Cormac McCarthy's *Child of God* (1973) and Bret Easton Ellis's *American Psycho* (1991) hail from starkly different socioeconomic backgrounds, but their respective authors address monstrosity in similar ways. McCarthy's Lester Ballard and Ellis's Patrick Bateman give the physical impression of humanity, but they are monsters who live in plain sight. McCarthy addresses his audience directly, commenting that Ballard is "[a] child of God much like yourself perhaps" (McCarthy 4). He poses this suggestion to the reader before Ballard's journey into homicidal madness, yet the nominal phrase echoes in the reader's mind even when Ballard is at his most horrifying. On the other hand, Ellis devotes many passages to Patrick Bateman's slipping grip on his own humanity. The most haunting of these passages comes during a long weekend away from the comforts of Wall Street that leaves him particularly anxious and unhinged: "I had all the characteristics of a human being—flesh, blood, skin, hair—but my depersonalization was so intense, had gone so deep, that the normal ability to feel compassion had been eradicated, the victim of a slow, purposeful erasure" (Ellis 282). Initially defined by human characteristics, each character evolves into a monster within the capitalist machinations of their respective societies. McCarthy and Ellis excise the old economy of property and marriage traditional to the early Gothic novel and replace them with women's bodies as mass goods in an era of late-capitalism that is defined by commodity fetishism and the hyper-exchange of goods. The exploitation of women's bodies allows these serial killers to exert control within capitalist structures that make them feel powerless.

The Serial Killer and Gothic Economies

In order to exact a clear definition of monstrosity in relation to Ballard and Bateman, the actions and media portrayal of true life serial killer Ted Bundy serve as an apt illustration. Bundy terrorized seven states over the course of the 1960s and 1970s when he abducted, raped, and murdered at least 30 women. He was a handsome and charismatic young man who used his charm to lure his victims. This makes his actions seem all the more horrific because he was so *ordinary*. The true horror of Bundy as a cultural figure is that he seemed so normal in media portrayal to the point that he gained a substantial female following in a similar manner as a culturally significant celebrity (Wright 148–49). Alexa Wright's recent work on monstrosity and image takes a deep look at Bundy's motivations and peculiar appeal to the masses: "If Bundy's personal anguish was what led him to carry out so many devastating murders, perhaps his monstrous actions can be read as a sign of the self-centered alienation of a late twentieth-century capitalist society" (Wright 158). Wright notes that Bundy may have been scorned by the dissolution of his long-term relationship and the emotional trauma led him to victimize women who looked similar to her. Lester Ballard and Patrick Bateman share a common bond with Bundy's brand of monstrosity; both of these literary figures are motivated by different brands of isolation in their given communities which lead them to act out in a manner that commodifies their victims. Bundy targeted women who shared similar physical characteristics as his estranged girlfriend, grouping all women who looked like her into one group of scornful girlfriends whom he deemed worthy of his hyper-violent wrath. Bundy redirected his rage toward an entire population of women, twisting the darkly handsome masculine image into one of distorted horror. Similarly, McCarthy and Ellis take seemingly ordinary men and twist them into horrifying literary monsters who grotesquely begrudge the machinations of their respective capitalist societies.

McCarthy's assertion that Ballard is simply another child of God and Ellis's narration of Bateman as an interchangeable figure within Wall Street yuppie culture establishes the distinctly ordinary qualities of these killers. There is nothing visibly monstrous about either of them; their horror comes from their actions. In each instance, the modern Gothic serial killer is stripped of its supernatural aspects in order to produce a more sinister figure:

somebody that the reader can relate to on a very basic level. Karen Halttunen notes this aspect of humanity in her examination of popular culture's engagement with "true-crime" tales, including Bundy's story:

> [True-crime stories] suggest that evil is not entirely alien to the hearts and minds of true-crime readers. For if the killer is so deeply alien to us, why must we repeatedly imagine ourselves walking in his footsteps, accompanying him to the crime, witnessing his murderous violence, revisiting the scene, examining his weapons, gazing upon his victims? Our fascination with the "monster" betrays our uneasy sense that our intense interest implicates us, if only as voyeurs, in the crime, however much we assert the inhumanity of the murderer [Halttunen 245–246].

Whether intentionally or not, McCarthy and Ellis's human monsters exploit a Gothic anxiety in the reader that they have the potential to become one of these monsters. Simply, Ballard and Bateman are driven by different senses of isolation in their given communities, which lead them to extremes of Gothic commodification. Yet, as grotesque and brutal as these two serial killers become, their authors do not completely detach them from their human aspects. In his chapter on *American Psycho* in *The Spaces of Violence*, James Giles notes that Ballard and Bateman are similar in that even though the characters who surround them refuse to acknowledge their existence, monsters like them do in fact exist in the world (Giles 173). Visibility is crucial to both of these figures—Ballard just wants to be a member of the community that shuns him while Bateman is such an active participant in his community that he is often mistaken for his peers, even by his fiancée. Ballard's severe detachment and Bateman's over-immersion causes a heightened materialism that goes to horrifying depths. Their emotional disconnection causes them to relate to women by collecting their physical bodies and using them as a display of their interactions with capitalist society.

Women as Dolls in Child of God

Lester Ballard is a problematic figure in a closely-knit community in the Appalachians. His father's suicide and mother's abandonment are traumatic events that stand outside of his control. However, these events define him and make the townspeople look at him with fear and suspicion. His family's property is taken away from him, so he squats in one of the abandoned houses that cover the ruinous landscape of Frog Mountain. One morning, Ballard encounters a homeless woman sleeping in the trees near the shack where he is squatting:

> He could see her heavy breasts sprawled under the thin stuff of her nightdress and he could see the dark thatch of hair under her belly. He knelt and touched her. Her slack mouth twisted. Her eyes opened. They seemed to open downward by the underlids like a bird's and her eyeballs were gorged with blood. She sat up suddenly, a sweet ferment of whiskey and rot coming off her. Her lips drew back in a cat's snarl [McCarthy 41–42].

Their verbal conflict becomes physical when Ballard pulls off the nameless woman's flimsy nightgown and leaves her naked under the trees as she screams at him. Due to their similar socioeconomic dilemmas, these two characters are in direct competition with each other for what amounts to territory, just like animals. Ballard disarms her by shaming her through exposure. This action is a bizarrely cryptic precursor to Ballard's madness that will unfold throughout the narrative. Their altercation is brief, primeval, and animalistic; the situation leads the woman to go to the authorities to accuse Ballard of raping her, which creates an even larger rift between Ballard and the community.

Many different animals and creatures are used by McCarthy to describe Ballard over the course of the novel; he makes a point to show that Ballard's humanity is drained from him by building him into a mythically horrifying creature. Critic Andrew Bartlett notes this progression:

> We see the animality of Ballard: a protohuman simian creature, an ape.... The text also sees Ballard as gnome, troll, ghoul, monster, hermit—as an anti-pastoral demonic figure who takes, loves, and treasures female corpses, who threatens all enlightened common sense and lives in a fearful, pagan, fantastic realm. It is the subtle power of the condensation in McCarthy's archaeological vision that both permits and produces the terribly haunted discourse of these irreconcilable traces—traces of a Christian spirituality, of a wasting Appalachian society, of a bewildered and deprived animal nature, and of a strange pagan enigma [Bartlett 13–14].

Ballard is terrifying because he is so enigmatically different. The citizens of Sevier County, in rejecting Ballard, have created a legend that exists to be a demonic threat to the town. Early in the novel when Ballard tries to attend a church service, he is seen as a threat to the sanctity of the experience: "Ballard had a cold and snuffled loudly through the service but nobody expected he would stop if God himself looked back askance so no one looked" (McCarthy 32). Even before Ballard's monstrous tendencies come to light, he is seen as an affront to God—and by extension, all cultural norms that exist in this community.

Critic Ashley Craig Lancaster notes that since Ballard is a human—not an immortal vampire, not a construction of parts from other humans—his eventual monstrosity is made all the more horrific: "As one of the first mythical Gothic monsters, Frankenstein's Monster represents a less threatening version of the social outsider than Lester because the Monster's identity disconnects him from humanity and because his desire for community never reaches the height of Lester's desperation" (133–134). McCarthy fashions Ballard in such a way that he transcends Frankenstein's Creature in terms of their relations to their societies. Ballard is not a symbol for the "other," the societal outsider, he *is* the "other." He has been heavily scrutinized by the townspeople and rejected as a problem. Therefore, he is fated to be a transgressive and strange nuisance because of the stigma that comes from his mother's abandonment and father's suicide. These are all qualities that are gradually stripped from Ballard as the novel goes on.

As much as Ballard tries to integrate himself into the town, he does not make a significant human connection until he finds the bodies of a dead couple in a car on Frog Mountain. He ignores the man but is immediately smitten with the woman, pocketing her underwear and talking to her as if she were still alive before having sex with her corpse: "A crazed gymnast laboring over a cold corpse. He poured into that waxen ear everything he'd ever thought of saying to a woman. Who could say she did not hear them?" (McCarthy 88–89). His human connection is an odd hostage situation where he owns the woman's corpse in a disturbingly necrophilic fashion. He keeps her in an abandoned house he has usurped, buys her new clothes, and imitates domesticating her into his partner. He puts her body into a sitting position and admires her from outside the house. Cristina Mazzoni's study of dolls in Italian children's literature helps illuminate the grotesque impact that this dead woman plays in Ballard's life: "[T]he transfiguration of trash into treasure ... is the material representation of the reward for the selfless care that dolls demand for their owners' acquisition of a mature and loving self" (Mazzoni 251). Ballard legitimately cares for this woman as if she were a spouse that he takes care of, a desperate appeal for human interaction that becomes corrupted by his detached state of mind. His constant admiration of his domesticated home is his own recognition of social growth and status through what he perceives is a relationship. Before she has the chance to decompose completely, Ballard accidentally burns down the house where he keeps her. However, the trauma of losing his first "doll" and his own carelessness serves as a catalyst to quickly hunt down a replacement.

Gary Ciuba says that the first body that Ballard finds and takes in helps him to cultivate a perverse ideal woman that he takes care of and legitimately cares for. However, she is more of a trophy for him to admire almost as if she were a piece of art. Ciuba asserts that this is not an emotional connection; it is an impression of a human connection that exists outside of humanity:

> After [Ballard] buys a red dress for the first of his dead women, brushes her hair, and applies lipstick, he places her in various positions and then goes outside his shack to view her through the window. Ballard makes this doll his model female, a dummy who does not share, respond, demand, or challenge. In valuing the likeness of a woman over a woman herself, he loses sexual desire in mimetic desire: he seeks erotic fulfillment not with a person but with a gussied-up pretense of femininity. Whereas the Girardian subject imitates the desires of the model, Ballard desires nothing but the kind of store-window model that he poses and makes subject to his own desires. He does not so much simulate sexual intercourse as make love to mimesis [Ciuba 178].

On an unconscious level, Ballard desires human connection because he sees that the rest of Sevier County desires this as well. This society exists in an isolated and crumbling ruin that is as lonely as Ballard's cave. Ballard takes the women from town, all of whom are presumably "above" him socially. He relates to them by mimicking a genuine human relationship before his progressive isolation-induced madness perverts this bond into a desperate need to become these women. He connects to the social norm by grotesquely absorbing it.

Mazzoni also indirectly addresses Ballard's state of mind as he moves on from the first body to create a massive collection of "dolls" (female bodies) in a cave that he converts into a disturbing version of a child's play room. He does not value these bodies in the same way that he values the first body he encounters, mostly because he has to fatally shoot these women in order to collect them: "The debasement of treasures into trash, namely the placement of dolls in the garbage—whether because the doll has lost its initial monetary value, or never had any to begin with—is the result of a violence that, even as it debases its object, diminishes the humanity of the one operating the transformation" (Mazzoni 251). Ballard is desensitized by these women because he sees them as objects in a collection rather than human beings. A flash flood that destroys his cave-dwelling furthers his devolution into monstrosity; rather than mourning for the loss of his collection, he focuses on how he must replenish his makeshift family.

The main channel of power that Ballard possesses is the ability to instill fear into the townspeople by murdering its women, defiling their bodies, then disguising himself as a horrifyingly bastardized version of these women. He connects to the community forcefully by terrorizing it. Critic Vince Brewton explains:

> Ballard's obsession with corpses (bodies) and his purloining of trophies from the dead transcend the ordinary pilfering of a criminal. Having been symbolically expelled from the community, Lester feeds on the edges of communal space. Out on the margins, Ballard recreates the world from which he has been

estranged, and the corpses, clothes and ultimately the "fright-wig" itself have the talismanic quality of the souvenired trophy [Brewton 125–126].

Though Ballard believes that he is establishing a genuine human connection with his dead victims, he is also terrorizing his community as a retaliation for their rejection. He dresses himself as a grotesque version of his victims. The superficial remains of their identities are his trophies because that is all that he has left, and the result is an almost comedically grotesque monster:

> His shuffling boot tracks trampling out the prints of lesser life. Where mice had gone, or foxes hunting in the night. The dovelike imprimatur of a stooping owl.
> He'd long been wearing the underclothes of his female victims but now he took to appearing in their outerwear as well. A gothic doll in illfit clothes, its carmine mouth floating detached and bright in the white landscape [McCarthy 140].

Since Ballard exists in a natural setting outside of Sevier County, his commodification of these women is a horrifying caricature of their former selves. He is a "gothic doll" in that his imitation of his victims is sloppily put together and serves to terrify the status quo. Ballard places himself somewhere between human and perverse imitation of human. McCarthy rarely describes Ballard's human qualities and by the end of the novel any semblance of humanity has dissipated, just like his history.

Traditional Gothic spaces tend to be expansive, dark castles and mansions. Keeping with Lancaster's connection between Ballard and Frankenstein's Creature, their physical movement throughout their stories are vaguely similar; simply, they go from having a physical place to having no place. Frankenstein's Creature felt rejected from humanity when his creator refused to make a companion for him, killed Frankenstein's loved ones, then headed to the Arctic. Ballard, losing his connection to humanity, retreats to the fringes of Sevier County and ends up taking refuge deep in a cave that resembles "the innards of some great beast" and serves as a shrine "where dead people lay like saints" (McCarthy 134–135). Later on, Ballard recognizes that he does not have a place, "going across the face of the mountain to review the country he once inhabited" (169). This leads to an emotional breakdown that is juxtaposed with a scene in the cave where Ballard thinks he hears his dead father whistling. At this point he is disturbing nature by staying in the cave, and he is disturbing the town with his destructive actions. He mocks societal convention by taking from the town forcibly. Ballard shows up to the town's fair and wins a variety of large stuffed animals and basks in the attention—both positive and negative—that this gives him: "Ballard loaded up his bears and the tiger and started off through the crowd. They lord look at what all he's won, said a woman. Ballard smiled tightly. Young girls' faces floated past, bland and smooth as cream. Some eyed his toys" (McCarthy 65). Dianne Luce connects this scene to Ballard's monstrous actions:

> From this society in which the weak are dispossessed, Lester learns to take possession of others forcibly. Moreover, his feat at the shooting gallery parodies the worker's endeavor in capitalist society: he converts his time and skill into prizes or rewards until he becomes burdened down by these goods, the giant stuffed tiger and bears with which he peoples his cabin. Lester's shooting and hoarding his human victims is an extension of the same impulse: he expends his talents and efforts in amassing material goods—much like ourselves, perhaps. The quarry and the dump with their dead machinery are merely less covert versions of Lester's boneyard [Luce 162].

In observing and copying the everyday life of Sevier County's citizens, Ballard picks up on the misery that lies underneath their grasp at a "normal" existence. The used industrial machinery and dilapidated structures are represented in Ballard's perverse cave, though the rot of his collection progresses at a more rapid rate. His collection burdens him in the same way that the ruins of Sevier County burdens the townspeople, and they both seek to fill their respective voids with material possession. McCarthy mocks the capitalist structure by setting a monster loose in the ashes of a society that struggles to thrive.

Ballard's terrorism of Sevier County is too much for the community to take, and soon he realizes that he cannot get away with these actions. He voluntarily submits himself to a mental institution where he is placed into the care of the state. This is a warped version of the sort of connection to society that Ballard wanted, but this is the best that he can hope for if he hopes to redeem himself in any way. Critic Georg Guillemin explains,

> The strange form this reintegration takes is his institutionalization and the postmortem. Yet this minimal redemption is anything but incidental or ironic. Lester's body is used for scientific procedures that are detailed as barbaric but are socially sanctioned.... The function of this turn of events is to confirm that the entire collective is informed by violence of varying degrees. It serves to address the patent ambiguity of "normality" in the context of a latent systemic violence [Guillemin 44].

Ballard is a monster in a society that is defined by violence, yet McCarthy gives him a clinical end. He dies of pneumonia in a mental hospital, before his body is shipped to a medical school in Memphis for research purposes. His body parts are unceremoniously removed and placed into an anonymous system to be utilized in a productive manner: "He was laid out on a slab and flayed, eviscerated, dissected. His head was sawed open and the brains removed. His muscles were stripped from the bones. His heart was taken out. His entrails were hauled forth and delineated and the four young students who bent over him like those haruspices of old perhaps saw monsters worse to come in their configurations" (McCarthy 194). As a peculiar aside, McCarthy notes the probable indifference of these students to their subject's deeds. He is not the first monster, and he certainly will not be the last; any reflection that the students perform on Ballard's actions avoids idealization. Though grotesque in its own right, Ballard's systemic removal from the world is juxtaposed with the horrifying discovery of his cave and the many inhabitants of his ersatz community: "[t]he bodies were covered in adipocere, a pale gray cheesy mold common to corpses in damp places, and scallops of light fungus grew among them as they do on logs rotting in the forest" (196). Despite Ballard's attempts to preserve, domesticate, and humanize his collection, his attempts at control over his victims' post-mortem is futile.

Bodies as Capital in American Psycho

Patrick Bateman's apartment exists in complete isolation from the rest of the world and serves two purposes. First, this is where the symbolic monster meticulously puts on his human disguise before he goes to Wall Street. Early in the novel the reader is introduced to his living space in a pages long paragraph that outlines the extravagant commodities that decorate his home, including "Steuben glass animals placed strategically around expensive crystal ashtrays from Fortunoff, though I don't smoke" (Ellis 25). Bateman also describes his morning routine with meticulous detail. He applies many different lotions, gels, aftershaves and the like after performing a rigorous workout whose intensity increases as the novel goes on. He spends a carefully orchestrated amount of time putting himself together in the morning, but he cannot deviate from this routine. At the end of the novel, he asserts that there is an idea of a Patrick Bateman, but he simply does not exist, so this routine is something he absolutely must do in order to maintain his human disguise. The other purpose of Bateman's apartment is to serve as a torture chamber for the women that he violently disembowels—a deplorable pastime that may be occurring solely in his mind. The only people besides Bateman who are allowed into his apartment throughout the novel end up dead. Bateman's apartment is like a Gothic castle because of its isolation and role as a realm to unleash his monstrous behavior. By the end of the novel, the entrails of one of his regular prostitutes will adorn his living room.

Ruth Helyer argues that Bateman's space branches out into the city streets, which he wanders when he needs to reinforce his sense of control:

> New York is represented as a desolate and dirty urban backdrop, inhabited by penniless beggars, showing the other side of the obscene wealth of the yuppie traders. The streets seem alienating and full of menace, yet ironically it is Patrick who is a threat, not the street dwellers. He delights in taunting the homeless and never gives them any money. His wealthy companions share his values and priorities, commenting facetiously that one beggar badly needs a facial. While they think nothing of spending $500 on a meal, they would never give the beggar a single dollar [Helyer 738].

Whereas Lester Ballard seems to be relegated away from civilization, Bateman has full access to an ornate apartment and a desolate city to remind him that he stands far above those who fall victim to New York City's urban decay. As long as he can maintain his lifestyle and not lose his prominent position, he does not have to help anybody who is socially or economically "below" him. In contrast to Ballard, Bateman is not rejected by society. In fact, he fits in well with his peers and buys into the benefits of his socioeconomic status. However, he lives in constant fear of being rejected by the status quo. Essentially, Lester Ballard is a worthy example of who Patrick Bateman most fears becoming.

Judith/Jack Halberstam states that Gothic economy is essentially a disturbance of capitalism. She employs *Dracula* to illustrate her point; Castle Dracula is filled with currency from many countries that sits in his Gothic palace collecting dust. Dracula is an aristocrat who takes the blood of his victims but never spends the money that he amasses (Halberstam 101–102). Like a true aristocrat, he allows his capital to accrue and gain interest so that he can invest and gain property. In the 1980s, consumption is much more conspicuous and dependent on instant fulfillment. To apply this image to Patrick Bateman and his peers, they stimulate the economy by spending their earnings in two ways. First, they spend money on lavish objects and gestures that propagate the image that they are wealthy and elite. However, these gestures are empty ones that build nothing past their image: "Armstrong would still be talking about not only his vacation but what seems like the *world's* vacation in the fucking Bahamas" (Ellis 140). Like Armstrong, Bateman and his friends talk about their vacations and material possessions impersonally, as if they are brochures and advertisements for the things that they buy. They commodify themselves and each other, entering absurd competitions over who has the classiest business cards when they are essentially all white paper with black lettering. This occurs alongside the plights of countless suffering homeless people of Manhattan who Bateman and his peers victimize for their amusement.

The second use of Bateman's capital is the pursuit of his illegal habits:

cocaine and prostitutes. These are expenses that all of his Wall Street peers indulge in, creating a hedonistic underground market that deals in bodies. Bateman and friends go to clubs to get high and look at "hardbodies" then act on their desire for power by purchasing prostitutes in a symbolic meat market. The disparity between the wealthy Wall Street yuppie and most of the city's desperately poor population creates a role for determined prostitutes to put themselves into the clutches of sociopaths like Patrick Bateman to do what he wants with them. They are no longer people; they are commodities whose bodies literally splatter his apartment like his arbitrary decorations. Bateman disembowels and eats the women he kills just for the sake of exuding his financial power and to sustain his ego. Bateman is not a part of a crumbling capitalist institution so he lives hedonistically, which Ellis shows frequently through the indulgent scenes of physical torture that Bateman's prostitutes endure.

One of Bateman's regular prostitutes is Christie, a woman who fears his bizarre behavior but keeps doing business with him because she needs the money. People like Bateman are a terrifying occupational hazard for her. He continues to victimize her because he is paying her: "As a prostitute, she is a person-as-commodity; and as a commodity, she is, in Bateman's twisted imagination, his to do with so long as he pays for her. In this case it means killing and eating her. His act of cannibalism is capitalist consumerism reductio ad absurdum" (Heise 147). Ellis preposterously mocks the capitalist system through grotesque episodes that literally use bodies as a form of exchange. Bateman has no boundaries with these prostitutes because he is paying them enough money to presumably degrade them in whatever way he sees fit. During his first encounter with Christie and fellow prostitute Sabrina, he moves them around like automatons to achieve his perfect impulsive sexual fantasy: "I push Sabrina off my cock and lay her on her back, her head at the foot of the futon. Then I lay Christie over her, placing the two in a sixty-nine position..." (Ellis 175). There are no words exchanged between the three at this moment aside from crass sexual dialogue that actors in pornography use to enhance their arousal for the audience. Bateman physically moves them rather than dictates what he wants from them. They are toys on which he can vent his dark psychosexual impulses and desires. In this initial transaction, the narrative also cuts away while Bateman physically abuses them for an hour after their menage-a-trois. The next time Bateman purchases Christie and yet another prostitute, toward the end of the novel, he graphically disembowels them. The morning after this he notes all the body parts and viscera that now decorate his apartment: "I have to open the venetian blinds, which are splattered with burnt fat from when Christie's breasts burst apart, electrocuting her..." (290), and "[h]er left hand, chopped off at the wrist, lies clenched on top of the island in the kitchen, in its own small pool of blood" (291). Bateman lists the aftermath of his elaborate torture scenes in the same manner that he lists the expensive decorations for his apartment or his exhaustively detailed morning routine.

Bateman fantasizes about owning women who are similar to the ones he sees in the videos that he rents: "Last night I had dreams that were lit like pornography and in them I fucked girls made of cardboard" (200). Equally pornographic to Bateman is his exhaustive use of women's bodies before and after he has killed them. It is not until the final explosive encounters that he details consuming their bodies. There is a significant disparity between his meals at Manhattan restaurants and his frenetic and frantic acts of cannibalism: "I'm kneeling on the floor beside a corpse, eating the girl's brain, gobbling it down, spreading Grey Poupon over hunks of the pink, fleshy meat" (328). Ellis blatantly uses this deplorable (and possibly imagined) action to speak to the emptiness of Bateman's lifestyle. The rotting moral structure of Wall Street frays his well-being from excess to profound sadness: "Maggots already writhe across the human sausage, the drool pouring from my lips dribbles over them, and still I can't tell if I'm cooking any of this correctly, because I'm crying too hard and I have never really cooked anything before" (346). He does not know how to properly cook his meal because this is the only one that he attempts to prepare. Everything else is provided for him; the ease of his life has led to a basic misunderstanding of the way that the world functions.

Bateman's fiancée, Evelyn, is a problematic figure whose toxic relationship with him amplifies a total culture of consumption that deals in bodies. They are on the same economic level and blatantly use each other with the same motive: to maintain and further cultivate their yuppie images for their peers. Though they are engaged, there is a distinct emotional disconnect between the two; she never enters his apartment and often talks over him on dates—he refers to their conversations as "monologue[s]" (Ellis 123). Evelyn also illustrates the complete immersion into yuppie culture that the characters of this novel experience. Wealth and traditional attractiveness are so commonplace for Evelyn that they are almost passé:

"*Everybody's* rich," [Evelyn] says, concentrating on the TV screen.
"[Price is] good looking," I tell her.
"*Everybody's* good looking, Patrick," she says remotely.
"He has a great body," I say.
"*Everybody* has a great body now," she says [Ellis 23].

Evelyn's playful cluelessness bothers Bateman but makes her safe to him. He can cheat on and belittle her openly with no real consequences because she just wants to be married to Bateman or somebody similar to him. This is mutually beneficial to uphold their yuppie credentials toward their peers. When Bateman and Evelyn part ways for the evening, his masturbatory practice is telling: "I masturbate, thinking about first Evelyn, then Courtney, then Vanden and then Evelyn again, but right before I come—a weak orgasm—about a near-naked model in a halter top I saw today in a Calvin Klein advertisement" (24). "Real" women involved in Bateman's life flash through his head in quick succession, but what makes him finally ejaculate is a generic model. Bateman and Evelyn clearly commodify each other for the sake of image preservation to reinforce that they are powerful partners in Wall Street culture.

Patrick Shaw asserts that calling Bateman a monster is banal and misses the point of Ellis's satire: "[B]ecause his sadism is imagined, we can convict Bateman of nothing that ordinary, everyday, good citizens are not guilty of. Bateman, like all of us, is free to imagine any horror that he chooses" (Shaw 196). Bateman is a participant in a collectively repugnant social circle that thrives on excess. This world is predictable and empty to the point that he has to fantasize about owning more than just *things* and eating the conventional fancy dinners; he needs to collect human capital. Evelyn, to a much less visceral degree, has the same thoughts in mind for Bateman. Once he has fully realized his innate monstrosity, they go on the novel's final date at the new Chinese restaurant, Luke. Bateman seeks to torture Evelyn by presenting her with a urinal cake that he coated with chocolate and placed in a Godiva box. This scene brings together and satirizes all of the aspects of commodification that define Bateman's character. His devotion to brand names is usurped by his cruelty and need to control Evelyn by sadistically watching her eat the cake. Perhaps the irony of successfully repurposing a Godiva box to fool Evelyn is lost on him, but he has a sudden moment of self-realization during the scene:

> Even though I marveled at her eating that thing, it also makes me sad and suddenly I'm reminded that no matter how satisfying it was to see Evelyn eating something I, and countless others, had pissed on, in the end the displeasure it caused her was at *my* expense—it's an anticlimax, a futile excuse to put up with her for three hours [Ellis 337].

They both share the same goal to physically own each other. Evelyn is complicit in this because she will gladly be a prop for Bateman. Since she does not see him as a person with feelings or a personality, she does not see his innate darkness. Bateman also seeks to uphold the image of normalcy by marrying Evelyn, but he exerts control in bizarre and abusive ways. Since she wants to own him as well, this causes him to turn his resentment into sadness.

This self-awareness also causes him to realize that Evelyn is commodifying him: "For the first time I notice that she has been eyeing me for the last two years not with adoration but with something closer to greed" (338). Essentially, Bateman and Evelyn are each others' props, and since he cannot control her in the same way that he can control somebody like Christie, he feels weak and empty. Evelyn has no self-awareness so she has no fear of Bateman. She also has the rare position for a women in this novel to hold a vague power over her fiancé's reputation amongst his friends. Evelyn is happy to be commodified as a trophy housewife for Bateman, which bothers him because he can hardly take any forceful power over her that is not childish and petty.

Bateman's simultaneous hatred of Wall Street cultural mores and dependence on its trappings creates an intense internal conflict that leads him to break off his engagement with Evelyn and consider acting on his interest in his secretary, Jean. She exists outside of Bateman's world and regards him with sarcastic yielding that he mistakes for "almost total devotion" (66). As he begins to know her better and realizes that she does have interest in him other than his yuppie exterior, he notes the hopelessness of his situation:

> I see Jean as uninhibited; she seems stronger, less controllable, wanting to take me into a new and unfamiliar land—the dreaded uncertainty of a totally different world. I sense she wants to rearrange my life in a significant way—her eyes tell me this and though I see truth in them, I also know that one day, sometime very soon, she too will be locked in the rhythm of my insanity [378].

Bateman believes that Jean will either become Evelyn—a marriage-hungry automaton—or worse, one of the "hardbodies" that he objectifies and disembowels just so he can feel a sense of free will. The novel ends almost exactly how it begins. Bateman recycles the same conversation about cavemen consuming more fiber than them while dining in one of the many fancy restaurants that he haunts with his interchangeable peers.

Concluding Thoughts

Through the lens of Gothic monstrosity, the anxiety of capitalism is exploited by the disturbing but parodic commodification of human bodies. Lester Ballard and Patrick Bateman are the most prime examples, but the horror genre continues to engage with the use of victims' bodies as material goods. In *The Silence of the Lambs* (1991), FBI trainee Clarice Starling enlists the help of cannibalistic serial killer Hannibal Lecter in order to apprehend Buffalo Bill, a Gothic monster who abducts overweight women and uses their skin to craft a suit. When pontificating about the origin of human monstrosity, Lecter vehemently suggests that monsters covet what is most familiar to them. In the case of Lester Ballard and Patrick Bateman, as well as the monstrous figures in *The Silence of the Lambs*, they covet power over their victims even after they are dead. The inspiration for Buffalo Bill's character, Ed Gein, has also been augmented to fit horror icons like Norman Bates and Leatherface. These are characters who also commodify human bodies in order to further their desires. Gothic commodification is a true indicator of monstrosity because it exploits the disconnect between genuine human connection and the need to control every aspect of the human victim—particularly the body after death.

Works Cited

Bartlett, Andrew. "From Voyeurism to Archaeology: Cormac McCarthy's *Child of God.*" *The Southern Literary Journal* 24.1 (1991): 3–15. *JSTOR*. Web. 22 March 2013.
Brewton, Vince. "The Changing Landscape of Violence in Cormac McCarthy's Early American Novels." *The Southern Literary Journal* 37.1 (2004): 121–143. *Project MUSE*. Web. 22 March 2013.
Ciuba, Gary M. *Desire, Violence, and Divinity in Modern Southern Fiction*. Baton Rouge: Louisiana State University Press. 2010. Print.
Ellis, Bret Easton. *American Psycho*. New York: Vintage, 1991. Print.
Giles, James. *The Spaces of Violence*. Tuscaloosa: University of Alabama Press, 2006. Print.
Guillemin, Georg. *The Pastoral Vision of Cormac McCarthy*. College Station: Texas A&M University Press, 2004. Print.
Halberstam, Judith. *Skin Shows: Gothic Horror and the Technology of Monsters*. Durham: Duke University Press, 1995. Print.
Halttunen, Karen. *Murder Most Foul: The Killer and the American Gothic Imagination*. Cambridge: Harvard University Press, 1998. Print.
Heise, Thomas. "*American Psycho*: Neoliberal Fantasies and the Death of Downtown." *Arizona Quarterly* 67.1 (2011): 135–160. *JSTOR*. Web. 3 May 2012.
Helyer, Ruth. "Parodied to Death: The Postmodern Gothic of *American Psycho.*" *Modern Fiction Studies* 46.3 (2000): 725–746. *Project MUSE*. Web. 3 May 2012.
Lancaster, Ashley Craig. "From Frankenstein's Monster to Lester Ballard: The Evolving Gothic Monster." *The Midwest Quarterly* 49.2 (2000): 132–148. *JSTOR*. Web. 22 March 2013.
Luce, Dianne C. *Reading the World: Cormac McCarthy's Tennessee Period*. Columbia: University of South Carolina Press, 2009. Print.
Mazzoni, Cristina. "Treasure to Trash, Trash to Treasure: Dolls and Waste in Italian Children's Literature." *Children's Literature Association Quarterly* 37.3 (2012): 250–265. *Project MUSE*. Web. 14 Sept. 2014.
McCarthy, Cormac. *Child of God*. New York: Vintage, 1993. Print.
Shaw, Patrick W. *The Modern American Novel of Violence*. Troy, NY: The Whitson Publishing Company, 2000. Print.
Wright, Alexa. *Monstrosity: The Human Monster in Visual Culture*. London: I.B.Tauris, 2013. Print.

Rocking and Reeling through the Doors of Miscreation
Disequilibrium in Shirley Jackson's *The Haunting of Hill House*

Susan Poznar

Reminiscent of the riven fabric of the castle in Horace Walpole's *The Castle of Otranto* (1764) and the twice-fallen tower of William Beckford's Gothic folly Fonthill Abbey, edifices in American and British Gothic tend either to collapse, moulder away (like Anne Brontë's Wildfell Hall) or vanish in flames (as with du Maurier's Manderley in *Rebecca* [1938] or Charlotte Brontë's Thornfield Hall in *Jane Eyre* [1847]). Scholars of the Gothic traditionally link these ill-fated habitations to the ruined fortunes of an etiolated, decadent, or irresponsible aristocracy and its historically diminishing power, to anti–Catholic sentiment, or to more generalized mistrust of antiquated religious institutions that presumably wield a moribund but still menacing power. Almost always, as in Poe's "House of Usher" (1839) or C. P. Shiel's "Vaila" (1896), architectural instability or aberration represents dynastic weakness, vice, tragedy, or crime and is therefore intelligible. Such famed monstrous Gothic edifices are "demonstrative": they enact a sadomasochistic dance with readers, gesturing towards an abysmal mysterium that yields eventually to the reader's analytic logic. The prescriptive dark castles with unfathomable histories, enigmatic inhabitants, and inexpungible crimes that proliferate during 19th and 20th century supernatural fiction, in which characters and readers typically revisit and even reenact the physical and emotional site of trauma, almost invariably unveil occluded motivations to subsume the spectral within a cogent historical pattern.

Hill House's haunting resists such unveilings. During the first night at Hill House, Theodora asks Dr. Montague, "What's here? What really frightens people so?" No reader of the Gothic will expect any other immediate response than his "I will not put a name to what has no name" (Jackson 74). Aficionados of the Gothic mode know they won't name the monster, the origins of the paranormal disturbance, before penetrating the labyrinth, enduring a hermeneutic dance of misdirection, shocks and surprises, and ponderable clues. Usually, at the last gasp, identifying the abysmal site of trauma either reclaims the haunted house's habitability or triggers its salutary obliteration.

Yet in *Hill House* no one ever labels this nameless force. At the end, Jackson's monstrous Gothic "power house" is empty and unredeemed, seething with still unfathomed energies, the ghost-hunting experiment abandoned without ever disclosing the locus of peril. Hill House's architectonics and the novel's narrative properties are not mere standard props calculated to thrill and chill before satisfying the hermeneutic drive.[1] Jackson practices an art of cunning disorientation and opacity, short-circuiting the typical Gothic dynamic of prolonged mystification, yielding to a final, spasmodic elucidation. She injects distortion, instability, and uncertainty into the dynamics, not only of Hill House, but of the reading experience itself. Characters and readers experience parallel vertiginous reactions of dis-ease. Hill House's physical disproportions, decentered and self-enclosing construction, and daemonic midnight "dances" literally and figuratively throw inhabitants and readers off balance. To do justice to Jackson's masterly deferrals of closure, then, my approach will strenuously resist the urge to stabilize the novel's meanings. This essay will combine several earlier exegeses to demonstrate the workings of Jackson's unstable brew and to suggest how Jackson's art deftly evades clarification and exceeds interpretive limits, creating tantalizingly liminal spaces that we struggle to label or map.

Trying to Map Hill House's Labyrinthine "uncharted wastes"

Admittedly, a barely contained physical, mental, and spiritual confusion are by no means unusual in the Gothic. In his "Introduction" to *Spectral Readings,* David Punter comments,

> Just as Gothic castles from Udolpho to Gormenghast *exist in a world where there are no maps,* where halls, corridors and stairways go on forever, where rooms that were there in the night have vanished by morning, so *Gothic itself challenges that very process of map-making by means of which we might hope to reduce the world to manageable proportions*; while, of course, it remains constantly fascinated by the very impossibility which it so convincingly propounds [4, my emphasis].

Romantically tenebrous descriptions of Gothic sites usually explicitly challenge the protagonist and reader's cognitive processing. Ironically (and unusually), Jackson *does* from the outset offer maps to give the sense—which increasingly proves delusory—that we can master the layout of the house, the logic of the haunting. Simultaneously and self-reflexively, the narrative thematizes our own increasing conviction that drawing maps, formulating plausible theories, and even intuiting connections, are not enough. To instance a rather mundane illustration, Dr. Montague's driving directions, sent to protagonist Eleanor Vance, are impeccably accurate, but they bring her to a gate that only evokes her question "Why am I here?" (28). Montague later declares smugly that he has studied a map of the house (63), but even he gets lost in what he facetiously calls the "uncharted wastes" of the mansion (64), and the characters suggest posting signs and arrows for future guidance through the domestic maze. Jackson likewise obligingly offers convincing rationales for Hill House's malaise when Montague explains the main floor's confusing layout of concentric rings of rooms and suggests that any optical delusions or disorientating effects are due to deliberate defects of construction: wrong angles, off-center doorways, and other slight "aberrations" that create cognitive dissonance in the house's occupants (105–6). Such precise, rational mappings of the apparently irrational provide an illusion of mastery, both to characters and readers, whose continuing unease is therefore all the more potent. Just as the characters feel that they *ought not* to get lost, *ought* to adjust to architectural eccentricity, *ought* to keep doors and sightlines open, so we feel that we *ought* to follow narrative clues to neat epiphanies.

However, the narrative, like the house, is a "masterpiece of architectural misdirection" (106), or, more precisely, of contradictory imperatives. Montague posits that Hill House creates mental conflicts in its indwellers: "We have grown to trust blindly in our senses of balance and reason, and I can see where the mind might fight wildly to preserve its own familiar stable patterns against all evidence that it was leaning sideways" (107).

Resisting Traditional Gothic Maps

Similarly, the reader tries to apply familiar, stable Gothic paradigms to the novel, but it actively thwarts this effort. Indeed, the narrative self-reflexively undermines such reassurance when, during the first evening, Theo not only mentions Dracula, but light-heartedly plays with Gothic clichés: "Mrs. Dudley is probably the only true surviving member of the family to whom Hill House *really* belongs. *I* think she is only waiting until all the Sanderson heirs—that's you, Luke—die off in various horrible ways, and then she gets the house and the fortune in jewels buried in the cellar." When Dr. Montague assures her that Hill House possesses none of these devices (66), the author is being elaborately disingenuous for, in fact, the first description of Hill House not only invites but refutes familiar Gothic traditions, while presenting the site as unanalyzable:

> No human eye can isolate the unhappy coincidence of line and place which suggests evil in the face of a house, and yet somehow a maniac juxtaposition, a badly turned angle, some chance meeting of roof and sky, turned Hill House into a place of despair, more frightening because the face of Hill House seemed awake, with a watchfulness from the blank windows and a touch of glee in the eyebrow of a cornice [34].

The facade is at once canny and uncanny, somehow governed at once by chance and by an indeterminate malignity, possessing panoptical power but confounding human vision. It awakens emotional apprehension while eluding intellectual apprehension: Dr. Montague points out that Hill House continually misleads its inhabitants (105). Hill House is a sublime tease, seducing and withholding, alerting attentive readers to the possibility of their eventual frustration.

Jackson, indeed, parodies the readerly need for explanation and causation by satirizing Mrs. Montague and Arthur, whose prefabricated, stale theories about the haunting parody the tidy, sensational solutions of late 18th century Gothic romance. Their motifs of nuns buried alive and treasures buried in cellars evoke completely inapropos 18th century precursors. This haunting, Jackson implies, is no updated variant of traditional literary hauntings and their familiar formulae. To underline this point, I would cite Christine Berthin's summation of traditional trans-generational Gothic as a mode in which family or community secrets concern repressed guilt, shame, and unresolved traumas (4); she adds that this trauma almost invariably involves issues of inheritance, legitimacy and illegitimacy. In fact, *none* of these issues arise in Hill House, and the latest relative, Luke Sanderson, is the least affected by the haunting. There is no family curse, no disputed inheritance, no bastard child to undermine family polity. Hill House itself seems almost to know and mock these formulae: after the first episode of violent banging, suggesting that the house will self-destruct in the time-honored tradition of Poe's House of Usher, Eleanor anticlimactically notes that the seemingly violent assaults the house made on its own fabric have no visible results (133). In this and various other ways, Jackson jolts us out of a sense of mastery of the text and any controlled reading experience yields to vertigo.

A Haunting Without Origins or Moral "Ownership"

More profoundly instantiating this interpretive limbo, the reader can never securely attribute the evil of Hill House to family conflict, identifiable supernatural agencies, or specific causal events. One of the most obvious diegetic lacunae is that none of the characters ever tries to explain the supernatural manifestations. If the Gothic is obsessed with assigning responsibility and punishing transgression, then Jackson defies that tradition by leading the reader into a maze without moral center or metaphysical exits. There are no discrete apparitions, no revelations. Dr. Montague's exposition of the House's history contains a possibly accidental death (builder Hugh Crain's wife crashed against a tree), an apparent suicide (the sister's companion hanged herself in the tower), and a possible case of death hastened by neglect (the companion might have neglected the sister). His account, however, of all these events is sketchy. Moreover, none of the manifestations appears to issue from any of these victims: the hollow banging has no identifiable source, nor do the words scrawled in the hall. The voice Eleanor hears at night is a child's, but there is no evidence that the Crain children (or any others) were victims or perpetrators of any crime. Theodora flippantly conjectures that the companion may be searching for a companion of her own by destroying Eleanor, and certainly Eleanor has affinities with her and nearly reiterates her suicide. However, Theo trails away before completing her suggestion; nothing suggests that the haunting speaks for this companion; and no other character (not even the pedantic Montague) can lucidly theorize the haunting. Long before the ghost-hunters leave, they give up taking notes and forming conjectures. In many ghost stories—both canonical fiction by such authors as Henry James and popular Gothic by Barbara Michaels, for instance—such scenes are a staple, but Jackson foregoes them entirely.[2] Significantly, aside from the puritanical scrapbook that Hugh Crain created for his daughters out of other men's cannibalized works, no words, no voice of any of the house's dead inhabitants survive to enlighten us. Like Eleanor gazing at the house, the reader is "fruitlessly endeavoring to locate the badness..." (35).

Our first glimpse of Hill House, indeed, compromises any plausible theorization of the haunting, confusing causality, endlessly displacing responsibility, shifting Gothic guilt away from the human realm:

> This house, which seemed somehow to have formed itself, flying together into its own powerful pattern under the hands of its builders, fitting itself into its own construction of lines and angles, reared its great head back against the sky without concession to humanity. It was a place without kindness, never meant to be lived in, not a fit place for people or for love or for hope [35].

This disintegrative impulse informs Jackson's narrative as well. Flagrantly insisting on its own irreconcilable contradictions, the novel juxtaposes its own drive towards anthropomorphism (evident in the above descriptions) with the house's own resistance to, and freedom from, any human influence. It's significant that the narrative characterizes Eleanor's initial reactions as "inadequate" (36): no reaction to this "unfit" domain is adequate or fitting. Ultimately, the haunting demonstrates that efforts to source human culpability, human motivation, humanly understandable origins, are futile here. Hugh Crain, though he was evidently cruel and authoritarian, was apparently no villain; indeed, the house itself seems the only destructive force. If so, there is no imaginable revenge or just outcome available to inhabitants besides destroying the house. If there is no comprehensible ghost, just enigmatic manifestations, then there can be no appeasement or exorcism. And if there was no originary crime, then there is no hidden truth to disclose.[3]

Indeed, the reader traverses the novel's complexities only to arrive at repeated impasses. Kahane notes that in the Gothic "confusions—its misleading clues, postponements of discovery, excessive digressions—are inscribed in the narrative structure itself" (334). Readers, then, can only judge what elements are digressive or irrelevant or misleading when they know the outcome. We cannot perform such discriminations at the close of Jackson's narrative, however, since the text forever defers the meaning of the haunting. The author instead inscribes our perpetual uncertainty by elaborating promising frames that really enclose nothing or whose "contents" never materialize. One such emblematic moment marks an early stage of Eleanor's journey, when she passes ruined stone gateways that open onto an empty property enclosed by rows of poisonous oleander trees. Eleanor immediately wonders what was there or was planned but never materialized and fills the space with her own impromptu fairytales (19). The narrative itself frames the haunting repeatedly but defers our complete penetration into its murky spaces, just as the eerie cold spot resists scientific measurement. The narrative likewise invests much textual energy in ceremonious entrances, such as Eleanor's prolonged and reluctant arrival at Hill House and the doctor's dramatic exposition of its history, but they ultimately lead only to question marks. And Hill House's interior boasts a baroque profusion, simultaneously cozy and oppressive, that only emphasizes its inner desolation.

Slippery Identities and Tenuous Bonds

Moreover, contradictory imperatives invade other aspects of this text. Hill House reflects and magnifies its builder Hugh Crain's unbalanced yet seductive matrix of religion and sublimated sexuality. An extension of its maker's hatred of female sexuality, it either arrests young female inhabitants in a sexless childhood, as with the Crain daughters, or regresses sexually mature women like Eleanor and fellow ghost-hunter, Theodora, into a zestful but anxious limbo of insecure girlhood, dooming any adult homosexual or heterosexual bonds within the transient community of ghost-seekers. Eleanor and Theo compare their first moments at Hill House with the first days at summer camp or boarding school and bond rather desperately against the menace of the house. Like children, they run outside to plan a picnic and trade lighthearted jokes about their girlhood, with Theo concluding that they must be related (53). But their relationship, like all those in Hill House, is erratic and tenuous, registering the terrifying unpredictability and insidious pressures of the haunting itself, which first instigates defensive efforts at intimacy—mocked-up facsimiles of a family circle—and then relentlessly undermines those bonds.

Tricia Lootens claims that "the characters are trapped within a nightmare embodiment of the nuclear family, an insidious Home Sweet Home that will not allow its victims to belong or to be happy, but will not let them go" (157). At first, Hill House offers its guests illusions of plenitude, inviting them to reinvent themselves and regress endlessly into childhood fantasy and plasticity. It encourages identification with its history, its ghosts, its very architectural fabric—all under the apparent sign of unity, rebirth, wholeness. The first few mornings of their sojourn find all of the ghost-hunters exhilarated, purposeful, and energetic, instantly addicted to a heightened sense of living in the moment. Their research promises to be the apotheosis of Dr. Montague's career and provides the sense of belonging and purpose that Eleanor has craved; it vaguely promises all of them romance and self-discovery.

Yet Hill House also relentlessly isolates and frustrates, not only revealing all bonds as factitious and groundless, but literally disorienting and shaking up its guests by eroding individual identities. Eleanor and Theo draw closer during the first manifestation (the nocturnal banging), but Dr. Montague points out that this event also separated the women from the men, and, immediately afterward, we see that they "gave one another fast, hidden, little curious glances, each of them wondering what secret terror had been tapped in the others, what changes might show in face or gesture, what unguarded weakness might have opened the way to ruin" (133). Usually, hauntings that test intrepid teams confronting the monstrous ultimately empower and regenerate them, as with the vampire-hunters in Bram Stoker's *Dracula* [1897]or Sheridan Le Fanu's *Carmilla* [1872]. In Hill House, every scene of bonding that mimes group solidarity collapses after a paranormal shock. The first literal writing on the wall, which drives a wedge between Eleanor and Theo, follows their heady collective abandonment to hyperbole and laughter. Again, a few pages later, Eleanor and Theo, suggestively completing each other's sentences, indulge in escalating parodies of cliché messages, but a deeper antipathy surfaces when they confront Theo's bloodstained room. The house undermines the very unity it inspires. Indeed, since the characters usually "bond" most easily through collective fabulation, their intimacy seems peculiarly hollow. Jackson underlines the fragility of such fabrications by demonstrating that even the characters' half-conscious roles fluctuate oddly: Theodora, for instance, sometimes plays Eleanor's "cousin," her "sister," her would-be lover, and her mother, and these roles shift and overlap unpredictably. Claire Kahane points out that "compelled ostensibly by the house to share the same bed, the same room, the same clothes as Theodora, Eleanor both fears and delights in their confusion of identity" (341). Ironically, Hill House, that oppressively substantial construct, promotes ever eliding, ambivalent relations between its inhabitants.

Moreover, the narrative deliberately ambiguates these relations: character motivations and purposes are extraordinarily hard to grasp, in part because Jackson begins many scenes *in media res*, omitting necessary preliminary clues. After an abortive private conversation between Luke and Eleanor in the summerhouse, Theo teases/chastises Eleanor, and it is impossible to tell whether lesbian jealousy, friendly concern, or a selfish desire to be the center of attention drive her remarks, and the mystery deepens when she and Eleanor wander outside, filled with conflicting emotions: "Each was so bent upon her own despair that escape into darkness was vital…" (173). Eleanor's despair with her life is only too obvious to the reader, but Theo's despair remains obscure.

Just as the characters, particularly Eleanor, experience intensified oscillations between attraction and repulsion towards both each other and the house, so Eleanor fails to acknowledge, much less negotiate, other mutually exclusive urges. She refers to her route to Hill House as "that magic thread of road Dr. Montague had chosen for her, out of all the roads in the world, to bring her safely to him and to Hill House; no other road could lead her from where she was to where she wanted to be. Dr. Montague was confirmed, made infallible, under the sign which pointed the way…" (17–18). Although Eleanor savors her freedom, almost automatically she translates her actions into necessity, invoking an ineluctable destiny under the auspices of a male authority for whose protection and guidance she is grateful, mythologizing herself as a female Theseus guided through the labyrinth by a paternal figure. She does not even realize that her incompatible desires doom her journey. In a bizarre paradox, this adventure both represents Eleanor's first steps as an adult and leads, as argued above, to regression. When she imagines different futures settled in chaste solitude in chance dwellings noticed en route, it is hard to tell whether these fantasies represent a desire for mature autonomy or a childish retreat. Clearly, struggling between opposite imperatives, she doesn't know yet what she really wants, though she imagines different possible futures for herself.

Gaps, Conflicts and Fragmentation in Female Experience

Of course, we cannot deny that literary hauntings are often troubled by the interplay of antitheses. Susanne Becker claims that "the gothic has always thrived on the connectedness of extremes" and the "clashing disharmony" (38) of Hill House unleashes contrary but equally irresistible urges for integration and dis-integration, power and submission, psychic enhancement and psychic dispersal, without ever resolving them; it embodies and releases those mutually exclusive desires and energies that haunt both Jackson's life and her writing.[4] Maggie Kilgour notes that recent criticism of the Gothic has "focused on the gothic's fragmentation as a response to bourgeois models of personal, sexual, and textual identity, seeing it as a Frankensteinian deconstruction of modern identity" (6). From this angle, Julie Nash rightly insists that *Hill House* is "more than a great ghost story; it's a great *woman's* ghost story, and belongs in a long tradition of women writers who use the supernatural as a vehicle for exploring feminist concerns" (174). Bernice Murphy mentions "Jackson's desire to resist imprisonment within the ideological norm, and a willful eccentricity and defiance that characterizes many of her finest fictional creations" (13). However, this is only half of the story. Biographer Judy Oppenheimer tells us that Jackson, while largely contemptuous of the average American housewife, "couldn't help but feel she was being judged by these women and was coming up wanting, and this was something she was acutely sensitive about" (159). Living during the height of American bourgeois conformism, and instinctively skeptical of available suburban models of maturation, Jackson herself anxiously registered the lure of that "well-adjusted" and "well-balanced" individual espoused by midcentury psychology, yet deliberately cultivated the variety and contrariety of her temperament. Oppenheimer's biography documents Jackson's anxieties about not fulfilling her mother's conventional expectations and not fitting into small town Vermont life or the faculty wife role imposed on her. At the same time, her life evidences deliberate and consistent attempts to thumb her nose at the norms as can be seen with, her obsession with the occult and the magical. Oppenheimer amply demonstrates that "a part of Shirley ... leaned to the conventional" (108), and Jackson herself describes "a human and not very rational order struggling inadequately to keep in check forces of great destruction" (qtd. in Hoeveler 268). Oppenheimer notes that Jackson acknowledged "several different personalities, all jostling against each other" (162), but concludes, "she would not be cubbyholed" (139). Her writing registers the continuing shock and scandal of irrevocably antipathetic urges, of a split that amplifies and Gothicizes a tension experienced by many women in post–World War II America, and which Jackson, although no feminist, repeatedly represented. Her writing reveals that no will, no energy, no theory can fill in the chasm between these antipathetic forces.[5]

Hill House reflects this sense that authentic, consistent, and independent being is impossible, and this is exacerbated by the disturbing permeability and mutual infiltration—the uncanny fusions and diffusions—of the characters' individual psyches. In her first minutes in Hill House, Eleanor begins to lose control of her thought processes and merges momentarily (and proleptically) with the house as she thinks that she feels like a tiny creature engulfed by the monstrous house, which senses her movements (42). Somewhat later, she suspects that the guests are all psychologically linked: "Perhaps she was to be allowed to speak occasionally for all of them, so that, quieting her, they quieted themselves..." (98). Jodey Castricano persuasively argues that Jackson challenges classical models of consciousness by suggesting "an uncanny circulation of thought" (92) that challenges "the division between mind and matter so that the question of 'whose' is endlessly deferred, especially with regards [to] reading and interpretation" (90). She notes, moreover, that "Eleanor's thoughts often seem to merge with the narrator's observations..." (95).[6] Hill House's consciousness invades Eleanor's, Eleanor's invades the narrator's, and Jackson's unsettling use of free indirect discourse draws the reader likewise into this equivocal zone.

The otherwise bogus séance towards the end emblematizes this bewildering elision of consciousness as Mrs. Montague and Arthur read from the planchette's script. Their earliest lines obviously issue from either their own unconscious or their imaginations, but then a seemingly "real" spirit announces itself as "Nell" and evidently describes Eleanor's existential situation: it wants to be "home," is waiting for something, and its motivation is "mother," but it cannot be helped and is "lost." But who drives the planchette? Perhaps it is Eleanor's unconscious, but she is distant from the séance scene, and never calls herself "Nell." The telepathic Theo has conferred that nickname on her—perhaps her perceptions of Eleanor dictated these messages. Or perhaps Hill

House itself, having tapped into Eleanor's psyche, is driving the planchette. Conceivably, all three sources are somehow mysteriously complicit. Confusion about identity boundaries abounds: during their playful first dinner conversation Luke jokes, "Now that I know which of us is me…" and a few lines later absurdly concludes, "That makes me Dr. Montague…" (61). Moreover, on a deeper, less obvious level Jackson implies that the residents and the haunting are sharing impulses. During the first terrifying nocturnal door-banging episode, we see Eleanor giggling hysterically and "rocking a little" with the noise; moments later the haunting emits a "thin little giggle … a little mad rising laugh … a little gloating laugh" (131). The next morning all the guests laugh with "giggling burst[s]" that "rocked Hill House" (143). Several nights later, Eleanor, believing she is holding Theo's hand in the dark, hears a wild laughter that turns into a "moan of wild sadness" followed by a "wild shrieking voice she had never heard before and yet knew she had heard always in her nightmares." Its words—"Go away! Please don't hurt me. Please let me go home"—apparently issue from a child ghost who speaks also for Eleanor's own deepest needs and fears (161-62).

Slippery Causalities

If conscious and unconscious forces inexplicably circulate, like Eleanor dancing elusively through Hill House's spaces, then the sourcing of agency and assignment of responsibility is, again, obfuscated throughout the haunting. Jackson raises questions of agency and causality on nearly every page. Early in the novel, Dr. Montague queries whether nature or nurture poisoned Hill House, but the origins, motivations and operations of its malevolence are alike elusive. Just possibly, the ghost-hunters, driving Eleanor away, ostensibly for her own good, are not really saving her but in fact colluding, unconsciously or half-consciously, with the house's own apparent desire to destroy and consume her. Jackson complicates the issue of agency and free will further by suspending causality repeatedly. When Eleanor first glimpses the house, she brakes involuntarily and words ("The house is vile") inexplicably traverse her mind (33)—who is stalling the car and whence the warning words? Likewise, Eleanor's past implies not only a paranormal loss of control but bewilderment about the causes of this loss. When her father died, showers of stones assaulted her home; most commentators theorize that Eleanor caused the disturbance, and indeed she is miserable when dominated by her mother and sister and later fantasizes about stoning Theo (158). Nevertheless, Jackson undercuts any theory that either sister was the cause when she wraps up the incident by noting that both Eleanor and her sister had forgotten the event, each presuming that the other was somehow responsible for it (7). Perhaps there was a true poltergeist, or perhaps Mrs. Vance was right in contending that hostile neighbors caused the weird occurrence—Jackson leaves this wide open. Similarly and more importantly, Downey and Jones point out that "The manifestations themselves, their multifarious natures ... all imply an amorphous malevolent force, without origin or motive" (226). The final and best example is Eleanor's death: is it suicide? Is it escape from others' insensitivity and defiance of their rejection? Is it murder by ghost? Who is steering the car into the tree? Agency slides away perpetually in another constant, dizzying dance.

Hill House's elusive evil, moreover, as the author obliquely suggests, does not end at its gates. Generally, once the Gothic narrative identifies transgressor, transgression, and consequences, it thus implies that evil is containable, but Jackson's narrative withholds this tacit solace. Since Jackson intimates that nearby Hillsdale's bleak and miasmatic lethargy emanates from Hill House, the house presumably embodies larger collective frustrations and pressures. A key specific textual instability emerges in Eleanor Vance's literal, figurative, and absolute homelessness while she half-voluntarily merges with Hill House, which dramatizes the irreconcilable alternatives that society offers an insecure personality like hers. She must either yield to its imperatives, be subsumed within its roles, and submit to its established (though insane) patterns, or she must accept alienation and invisibility. Thus, the house exposes the non-negotiable, deadly paradox of hegemonic social scripting, which ostensibly rewards conformity with acceptance, yet ultimately engenders the endless anxiety, self-scrutiny, and inner destitution that haunt an Eleanor Vance.

Hill House as Transgendered Site

Another deadly paradox, a continuing and ungovernable ambiguity in this shifty text, concerns the gender of Hill House. Generally speaking, intimidating Gothic edifices are ostentatiously masculine, representing and enforcing patriarchal powers. However, scholars such as Claire Kahane, Tricia Lootens, Judie Newman, Andrew Smith, and Roberta Rubenstein read Hill House as "the original womb/tomb" (Lootens 176), which infantilizes its guests into a pre-Oedipal fusion with an overpowering maternality by provoking sinister "familial and erotic" intimacies (Lootens 167). I would argue that, paradoxically, Hill House operates not only as an insidiously inviting "mother house," but as an oppressive "father house."

On one hand, Eleanor's flight to Hill House defies the "dead hand" of a selfish, petty, autocratic mother, a tyranny perpetuated by Eleanor's married sister. Eleanor significantly finds the very first phase of her flight temporarily delayed by a nameless old lady, who evidently is another disappointed grasper of life's sad leftovers and thus also a forewarning of Eleanor's own potentially impoverished future. This encounter figures Eleanor's ambivalence towards suffocating maternal figures. Eager as she is to begin her adventure, she is cowed by and abjectly apologetic toward the little old lady and must propitiate her, indicating a deeper desire for maternal support (she is relieved when the old lady finally blesses her and sends her on her way). Contrastingly, in her fantasies during her drive, Eleanor concocts a fairy tale in which an idealized mother welcomes home a peripatetic princess. Roberta Rubenstein shrewdly argues that Hill House "functions figuratively as the externalized maternal body" (135) and that Eleanor "is destroyed by her own ambivalent submission to maternal domination" (137). And Claire Kahane notes that "Eleanor surrenders to the house, surrenders her illusory new autonomy to remain the child, dependent on the maternal..." (342). The knocker on Hill House's front door is a child's face, reflecting Eleanor's entrance into a simultaneously blissful and horrifying regression. When she first enters the dim, oppressive hallway, she speaks to Mrs. Dudley like an adult guest, but silently she imagines herself breaking into childish sobs (37). Hill House lures its guests into a cozy, convoluted space over-furnished with a feminized late Victorian décor: as Luke observes, "It's all so motherly.... Everything so soft. Everything so padded. Great embracing chairs and sofas which turn out to be hard and unwelcome ... and reject you at once" (209). We are reminded that Hugh Crain's three wives all died tragically, leaving him alone with his children. True motherhood seems doomed in Hill House, and Eleanor's unvoiced desire to be mothered is hopeless. In Lacanian terms, then, Eleanor retreats into an alluring Imaginary realm of fusion with the "mother-house" that is as illusory as her bond with her real, dead mother. As James Egan puts it, "For Eleanor, attempts to establish normal or surrogate familial relationships end the same way, in rejection and alienation" (20). It is notable that Dr. Montague describes Hill House as "unclean" and "sick" (70), epithets that link it to a specific mother: Eleanor's mother who died after a prolonged illness and whose personal care often disgusted Eleanor.

Ultimately, however, Hill House offers itself as father as well. Eleanor is installed in the blue room and her reflexive reference to "Sister Anne" (38) invokes the Bluebeard whose castle was a prison, a site of masculine prohibition and murderous, unjustifiable punishment. Anne Williams points out that "the Gothic castle also concretely represents what many poststructuralist critics, following Lacan, refer to as 'the Symbolic'—'le nom du père,' the Law of the Father" (46). It is noteworthy that her own father's death preceded Eleanor's first supernatural experience, that she flirtatiously pretends to invite Hugh Crain's statue to a dance, that she treats Dr. Montague as a surrogate father, and that the tower that she associates with her mother is also unmistakably phallic, as is the tree she ultimately crashes into. Dr. Montague, who constitutes himself as guide and protector of the group, immediately, if humorously, presents himself as the father of three spoiled children (69). Hill House—designed by an arrogant New England patriarch whose misbegotten creation apparently killed his first wife before she entered to take possession and whose hellfire religion terrorized his daughters—simultaneously represents the violence of Symbolic patriarchal impositions and deploys a destructive "supernaturalized" masculine potency. Lootens, indeed, describing Jackson's drafts, points out that "Hill House has become more phallic with each rewriting" (158).

Hill House thus fuses an overpowering maternality and paternality that are equally insanely possessive and unloving. It further reproduces in its prey earlier phases of psychosexual development to foreclose Eleanor's maturation and devour her, not to mention foreclosing our own urge to assign a clear sexual identity to the haunting.

Eroticized Hauntings and Eroticized Readings

Not only is the haunting transgendered, it—and our reading of it—are insistently if subtly eroticized. Near the climax of the novel, when Eleanor is about to yield herself to Hill House, the haunting caresses the door protecting the ghost-hunters, then batters it before, as Theo later puts it, "Hill House went dancing ... taking us along on a mad midnight fling..." (205). The female characters' physical reactions exemplify this equivocal dynamic: one moment they are "reeling" ecstatically (a recurrent verb in the novel) with excitement; the next they reel back, cringing, from a spectral onslaught. The haunting teases, seduces, and overpowers.

Regressing and seemingly liberating its occupants by detaching them from fixed roles and identities, Hill House provides an undeniably erotic stimulus. When the guests first indulge in self-mythologizing, Eleanor presents herself as an artist's model leading a "mad, abandoned" life (62), eerily foreshadowing her later insane abandonment of self to the house and hinting at pent-up sexual desires. While it's hardly surprising that this adventure offers an erotic outlet for the deprived Eleanor, it stimulates the other three guests as well, none of whom appears otherwise inhibited. This erotic influence is so powerful that it affects even Eleanor's relatives in Boston, as her trip triggers prurient speculations in her sister about nameless deviant experiments that the doctor might involve his unmarried female guests in.

Consider, similarly, Dr. Montague's erotic, emotional investment in this dubious experiment. Montague has rented the mansion for the traditional honeymoon period of three months, and he resembles a patient and possessive lover seeking his *beau ideal* ... or his *belle dame sans merci*: "He had been looking for an honestly haunted house all his life ... he was not the man to let go of Hill House once he had found it" (4). He expects his ghost-hunt to produce consummate proof of the supernatural as well as his mastery of seemingly unmanageable forces. This becomes clearer when we meet his wife, a Thurberish ball-crusher, who seems to have imbibed Hugh Crain's domineering, angry, puritanical righteousness. Of course, Hill House cheats him: his experiment there is incomplete, and the resultant publication receives a disdainful reception that prompts his retirement from teaching (246). Evidently, Montague's attempt to reclaim his stifled manhood by mapping Hill House has been defeated by the house itself.

Of course, the Gothic is infamous for fusing the spectral and the sexy, but usually in more overt and predictable fashion, building a crescendo of titillating snatches of intimacy and dodgy glimpses of the spectral towards a thrilling consummation of the love plot and revelation of the ghost plot. In Judith Hawkes' superb *Julian's House* (1989), for example, in the first climax (in both senses) the heretofore impotent male parapsychologist, momentarily possessed by the unconsummated desire of the male ghost, makes love to his wife, and in the final climax, fully possessed, welcomes her home with a kiss. In Stephen King–style Gothic, an extravagant gore-fest will often accompany sexual climaxes.

Hill House: Sexual Tease and Withholding Lover

Admittedly, Jackson seems to follow formula by mounting a series of violently erotic, intensified episodes climaxing with a phallic penetration in which the haunting assaults its victim—unusually, however, this violence does not result in a full disclosure of secrets that defuses its dangers. Beyond this obvious escalation of effect, though, Hill House exudes and arouses a polymorphous, veiled, subtilized desire, always deflected, never satisfied.

Theo's gently titillating painting of Eleanor's toenails is characteristic of both human and spectral seductions in the novel, epitomizing overtures that are never fulfilled. While Hill House is capable of direct threat, of its own weird shock and awe, Jackson's eroticism is often far more diffuse and delicate, its excitation turning the ladies into, as Theo puts it, "two blooming, fresh young lovelies" (137) and involving the men as well in an intoxicating sharpening of the senses. Hill House's seductive stimulus not only rejuvenates the ghost-hunters, but it stimulates their sensuality. The haunting entices its inhabitants into rituals of sensual assertion and self-abandonment through eerie convolutions of affinity and antipathy. When Eleanor literally loses her balance gazing up at the fatal, phallic tower, imagining someone (herself?) preparing to hang herself, Luke catches her in a tango-like dip before she falls backward. Eleanor is dizzy, "staggered," as he holds her and the world rocks around her (113). Although she tentatively tries later to reach Luke, she fails, and this embrace again is a tease, an unconsummated preliminary. Or we could instance the aforementioned scene when Eleanor, clutching Theo in her bed for warmth, hears that insane little spectral giggle along her back, a suggestively seductive touch—which suddenly vanishes. The house instigates such brief, tantalizing encounters, sexy *frissons* that lead nowhere. During the second episode of midnight banging (here, particularly, I use the word advisedly), the haunting uses the same intimate, "caressing" touch, "patting and fondling the doorframe," which then "was attacked without sound, seeming almost to be pulling away from its hinges, almost ready to buckle and go down, leaving them exposed" (201). Moments later, Eleanor decides to succumb to the haunting and that assault on a shaken but not broken door seems to represent her near-rape, leaving Eleanor's hymen intact, but seducing her into capitulating in every other sense. Eleanor, who is averse to being physically touched and vulnerable, and who confuses foolishness and wickedness (as Theo perceptively notes) (117), will never succumb to a human lover. Rather, the only completed seduction in the novel occurs in a quasi-romantic scene of rapt dancing as Eleanor both possesses and is possessed by the house.

Pervasive Un-Consummation

This rapture of possessing and being possessed is delusive, however. The House lures Eleanor, only to cheat her in the end. At first, under the aegis of Hill House and bonding with Theo, Eleanor savors an ecstasy of enhanced autonomy, as if Hill House is helping her establish her personal boundaries (83). Already, however, we sense the fragility of her assertions, since she defines herself only by trivial traits like disliking lobster. As I've tried to show, though, Hill House very quickly, in fact, undermines Eleanor's efforts. The morning after that first midnight banging, Eleanor experiences an ecstasy that is, indeed, mad and abandoned, both erotically powerful and submissive: "Suddenly, without reason, laughter trembled inside Eleanor; she wanted to reel, chanting, across the stretches of the lawn, she wanted to sing and to shout and to fling her arms and move in great emphatic, possessing circles around the rooms of Hill House…" (141). During her last living nights in Hill House, Eleanor feels sensuously merged with the house, her senses intensified, so that she can hear everything in the house as she "disappear[s] inch by inch into this house" (201), as if the house is a human lover whom she is acutely aware of. Her fusion with it is figured as a romantic and erotic union: "I will relinquish my possession of this self of mine, abdicate, give over willingly what I never wanted at all; whatever it wants of me it can have" (204). Nell begins spying on the others as if in league with the house; she hears phantom calls and thinks, "Don't let me go" and sees "vacant footsteps" outside that move "slowly and caressingly up and over the hill" (215). Inside, and increasingly detached from the ordinary human activities around her, she senses someone invisible in the center of the room walking and singing a playful melody, including the line "Go forth and face your lover." The invisible presence is spookily delicious: "The voice was light, perhaps only a child's voice, singing sweetly and thinly … She heard the little melody fade, and felt the slight movement of air as the footsteps came close to her, and something almost brushed her face…" (226). Her entropic ecstasy intensifies when she dances uncannily into a liminal psychic space between the human and the ghostly, symbolically taking possession of the nighttime realm, in a scene that merges childhood games of evasion with semi-mystical, semi-erotic self-abandonment. Wandering the house alone later, Eleanor finds the cold spot gone, and she pounds doors, laughs and dances as if complicit with the haunting, finding Hill House both comforting and amorous: she dances with the status of Hugh Crain and feels him take her hands; she enters the tower sensing herself embraced by the house; the tower is suddenly warm and "[u]nder her feet the stone floor moved caressingly, rubbing itself against the soles of her feet, and all around her the soft air touched her, stirring her hair, drifting against her fingers, coming in a light breath across her mouth, and she danced in circles." She thinks, "I have broken the spell of Hill House and somehow come inside" (231–232).

I would insist that such passages romance the reader as well, so that we share in Eleanor's bliss, enticed by Jackson's incantatory style. Jackson unsettles readers by drawing us into this unpredictable rhythm, encouraging us to indulge (like Eleanor's relatives) in erotic imaginations (for example, when her introduction to Luke Sanderson implies that he is his aunt's elderly friends' boy toy): this allurement may be perhaps the most subtly unnerving tactic that Jackson utilizes. Unlike such popular writers as Barbara Michaels or Kate Morton, Jackson does not create erotically charged mysteries merely to exploit their affective value. In a refusal of readerly distanciation, Jackson entrances and unsettles readers with her suggestive and incantatory style. Jackson's narrative beguiles readers into dwelling on its suggestive specificity as, like an unpredictable demon lover, it delicately touches and toys, then suddenly batters at our defenses, but without offering satisfying consummations, either for the bedazed Eleanor or the discomfited reader.

This entrancing ambiance deludes and cheats; and Jackson's handling of sublime affect in her anomalous ending reveals this cheat. Like Becker above, Marshall Brown contends that "the essence, the true sublimity, of the gothic ... lies in its play with un-reconciled antinomies" and its "lingering uncertainties" (14). Classic Gothic maintains such tensions precariously until the last gasp, when order just barely triumphs, although the alluring lost wildness lingers as a poignant tang—the echo of vanished vampire footsteps in Le Fanu's *Carmilla*, or Desiderio's memory of Albertina in Carter's *The Infernal Desire Machines of Doctor Hoffman* (1972). As I have maintained, however, Hill House forever defers resolution, explanation, closure. Jack Voller's theory of the radical sublime helps us highlight the significance of this failure when he reminds us, "The conventional sublime, at the moment of 'arrest and expansion,'" creates "a sense of transcendent achievement and metaphysical plenitude." But the "*radical* supernatural sublime" (my emphasis), as he terms it, "foregrounds this moment and unmasks the helplessness and unfulfillment" that inhere in the sublime (29–30).

Helplessness and unfulfillment mark the anomalous finale of the novel. The unendurable truth that rocks its last sentence is that even yielding oneself to an incorporeal corporate, like the haunting, does not bring community or loving union; surrendering one's individuality will not assuage irrevocable solitariness: "whatever walked there, walked alone" (246).[7] Eleanor, yielding to Hill House, expected the plenitude and timeless expansion of a true home, true parents, and a true lover, but Hill House suckers her and us.[8] This shocking epiphany betrays, again, that just as Hill House malevolently refuses to accommodate either the living or its dead victims, so Hill House's truths, its experiences, its traumas, resist all efforts of assimilation. Like Susan Hill's Eel Marsh House (in *The Woman in Black* [1983]), Hill House stands unyielding after the ghost-hunters' project fails and before they can validate coherent theories of the haunting. Like the doors in Hill House that eerily close when one tries to prop them open, the narrative will not permit easy analytical ingress or egress but continually opens and closes doors to alluring and plausible discursive pathways through its labyrinthine interior.

Inferentially, Jackson involves readers in Eleanor's endlessly suspended gratification, for the narrative creates another gap between Eleanor's last words, demanding why no one is stopping her, and the denouement, "Mrs. Sanderson was enormously relieved to hear that Dr. Montague and his party had left Hill House..." (246). Cheated, we witness neither Eleanor's death nor the characters' departures. Essentially, like Eleanor, we remain trapped in an ambiguous space, neither penetrating fully nor exiting Hill House, victims of Hill House's "insistent hospitality" (67), yet aware, indeed, that the novel's perverse charm inheres in its dance of offering while forever withholding answers. Hill House and *Hill House* alike release a pleasurable and tantalizing surplus of meaning, promising readerly *jouissance* (in Roland Barthes' term), while revealing the futility of our efforts to furnish this deranged house with stable meanings.

Concurrent with writing this essay, I read Kate Morton's *The Forgotten Garden* (2008), which sharply illuminated for me Jackson's postmodern radicalism. Morton's novel focuses on a female protagonist figuratively (not literally) haunted by a mysterious legacy and the family secrets it conveys. By exploring the histories of two eerie spaces—a long uninhabited Cornish cottage and its walled-off garden—she gradually uncovers the answers to a mysterious disappearance and untimely death, with their attendant complications of uncertain parentage, illegitimate births, and transgressive desires. She ascertains her own true identity when she finds the long-lost body and fully comprehends the chain of past events; simultaneously, she is united with her destined love. What surprised me was how disappointed I was by the tidy resolution of all these problems, which reminded me that the crimes ultimately disclosed in Gothic resolutions so rarely "live up to" the sinister adumbrations, the suspenseful shivers, of the body of the narrative.

Much more powerful and perversely gratifying is Hill House's tantalizing mystique of balance and "wholeness"—architectural, supernatural, or psychological—ever dissolving before the characters' and readers' intuition that losing control is both deeply frustrating and deeply pleasurable, ever beguiling our secret assent to Gothic submission and disintegration.

Notes

1. This is not to say, however, that Hill House does not conform in some respects to the traditions of Gothic habitations. David Punter's succinct summary of the haunted castle applies well to Hill House: "[T]he image of the castle is multifaceted: it is the

established world conceived as enclosure and bondage, it is the retreat of the mind tortured by chaos, it is the sign of the failure of human aspiration, and it is the locale for the persistence of primal fear" (122).

2. I think of the debates between the governess and housekeeper in Henry James' *The Turn of the Screw* (1898), the ongoing theorization between the parapsychologists in Judith Hawkes' *Julian's House*, and the group discussions in Barbara Michaels' *The Crying Child* (1971) and *Ammie Come Home* (1968).

3. Joshi is "forced to admit that the supernatural manifestations ... in many cases seem random, unmotivated and unexplained" and the psychic laws involved "are never specified nor are the psychic events ... ever plausibly accounted for or harmonized within the overall scheme of the novel." I argue that this is an intrinsic part of Jackson's aim and not a weakness or failure. I disagree with Joshi's assertion that the supernatural incidents merely "enhance the atmosphere of weirdness" (20).

4. Oppenheimer's biography emphasizes that Jackson never felt "whole" and was aware of many gaps in her life as, for instance, between herself and her mother. Her disingenuous letters to her mother were "in part a vain attempt to bridge the unbridgeable—the gap between her parents' life and her own" (136). In reference to her fascination with the occult, Oppenheimer comments, "She was simultaneously believer and debunker, psychic traveler and removed, amused onlooker. It was the same duality that made it easy for her to move between humor and fear in her work. She would not cut any of her options; she would not be cubbyholed..." (139).

5. Hague tells us that "[s]uffering from what her psychiatrist diagnosed as 'acute anxiety' and agoraphobia near the end of her life, she revealed: 'Insecure, uncontrolled, I wrote of neuroses and fear and I think all my books laid end to end would be one long documentation of anxiety.' But her characters' anxieties have a larger context than Jackson's own personal problems ... with the result that her fiction pervasively reflects the repression and fears of the Age of Anxiety" (76).

This deliberate refusal, to integrate or rationalize antipodal impulses emerged five years earlier in *The Bird's Nest*, in which the psychoanalyst somehow "cures" Elizabeth R.'s "disintegrated personality" during a crucial textual hiatus (199). After failing to coalesce her four disparate personalities, Dr. Wright compares himself to a Dr. Frankenstein "patching and tacking" psychic fragments together (276). Ultimately, however, he neither integrates nor salvages these clashing personalities. This therapeutic failure underlines Jackson's tendency to document psychic "warfare" without allowing resolution, compromise, or truce.

Like Elizabeth R., Eleanor Vance is an empty vessel whose family and sequestered life cloistered her emotionally. She seeks to shore up a tenuous identity with fantasies furnished with the impedimenta of others' lives and with tentative relations with Dr. Montague's guests. But only Hill House itself, monstrously, can pretend to fill the gaps in Eleanor's life and psyche.

6. Kahane also discusses this phenomenon: "Jackson dislocates me in typical Gothic fashion by locating me in Eleanor's point of view, confusing outside and inside, reality and illusion, so that I cannot clearly discern the acts of the house—the supernatural—from Eleanor's own disorder acts—the natural" (341).

7. Jackson wrote privately, "We are afraid of being someone else and doing the things someone else wants us to do and of being taken and used by someone else, some other guilt-ridden conscience that lives on and on in our minds, something we build ourselves and never recognize..." (qtd. in Oppenheimer 233).

8. Fred Botting discusses "the sacrificial violence by which Gothic forms reconstitute a sacred sense of self from the undead and spectral figures of humanist narratives" (179). Hill House claims its sacrificial victim, but is anything reconstituted?

Works Cited

Berthin, Christine. *Gothic Hauntings: Melancholy Crypts and Textual Ghosts.* Basingstoke: Palgrave Macmillan, 2010. Print.
Botting, Fred. *Gothic.* New York: Routledge, 1996. Print.
Brown, Marshall. *The Gothic Text.* Stanford: Stanford University Press, 2009. Print.
Caminero-Santangelo, Marta. "Multiple Personality and the Postmodern Subject: Theorizing Agency." *Shirley Jackson: Essays on the Literary Legacy.* Ed. Bernice M. Murphy. Jefferson, NC: McFarland, 2005. 52–80. Print.
Carpenter, Lynette, and Wendy K. Colmar. *Haunting the House of Fiction: Feminist Perspectives on Ghost Stories by American Women.* Knoxville: University of Tennessee Press, 1991. Print.
Carter, Angela. *The Infernal Desire Machines of Doctor Hoffman.* New York: Penguin, 1986. Print.
Castricano, Jodey. "Shirley Jackson's *The Haunting of Hill House* and the Strange Question of Trans-Subjectivity." *Gothic Studies* 7/1 (2005): 81–101. Print.
Egan, James. "Sanctuary: Shirley Jackson's Domestic and Fantastic Parables." *Studies in Weird Fiction* 6 (Fall 1989): 15–24. Print.
Hague, Angela. "'A Faithful Anatomy of Our Times': Reassessing Shirley Jackson." *Frontiers* 26.2 (2005): 73–96. Web. 7 Aug. 2014.
Hansen, Clare. *Hysterical Fictions: The "Woman's Novel" in the Twentieth Century.* Basingstoke: Palgrave Macmillan, 2000. Print.
Hattenhauer, Darryl. *Shirley Jackson's American Gothic.* Albany: State University of New York Press, 2003. Print.
Hawkes, Judith. *Julian's House.* New York: Ticknor & Fields, 1989. Print.
Jackson, Shirley. *The Bird's Nest.* New York: Penguin, 2014. Print.
_____. *The Haunting of Hill House.* New York: Penguin, 1984. Print.
Johnson, Anthony. "Gaps and Gothic Sensibility: Walpole, Lewis, Mary Shelley, And Maturin." *Exhibited by Candlelight: Sources and Developments in The Gothic Tradition.* Ed. Valeria Tinkler-Villani and Peter Davidson. Atlanta: Rodolpi, 1995. 7–24. Print.
Joshi, S. T. "Shirley Jackson: Domestic Horror." *Shirley Jackson: Essays on the Literary Legacy.* Ed. Bernice M. Murphy. Jefferson, NC: McFarland, 2005. 183–198. Print.
Kahane, Claire. "The Gothic Mirror." *The (M)other Tongue: Essays in Feminist Psychoanalytic Interpretation.* Ed. Shirley Nelson Garner, Claire Kahane and Madelon Sprengnether. Ithaca: Cornell University Press, 1985. 334–351. Print.
Kilgour, Maggie. *The Rise of the Gothic Novel.* New York: Routledge, 1995. Print.
Lamont, Claire. "Jane Austen's Gothic Architecture." *Exhibited by Candlelight: Sources and Developments in the Gothic Tradition.* Ed. Valeria Tinkler-Villani and Peter Davidson. Atlanta: Rodopi, 1995. 107–15. Print.
Le Fanu, Sheridan. *Carmilla and Twelve Other Classic Tales of Mystery.* Ed. Leonard Wolf. New York: Signet Classic, 1996. Print.
Lootens, Tricia. "'Whose Hand Was I Holding?' Familial and Sexual Politics." *Haunting the House of Fiction: Feminist Perspectives on Ghost Stories by American Women.* Ed. Lynette Carpenter and Wendy K. Kolmar. Knoxville: University of Tennessee Press, 1991. 166–192. Print.
Mighall, Robert. *A Geography of Victorian Gothic Fiction.* Oxford: Oxford University Press, 1999. Print.
Murphy, Bernice M., ed. "Introduction." *Shirley Jackson: Essays on the Literary Legacy.* Jefferson, NC: McFarland, 2005. Print.
Nash, Julie. "'Whatever Walked There, Walked Alone': The Feminist Supernatural in

Charlotte Perkins Gilman, Shirley Jackson, and Fay Weldon." *Paradoxa* 20 (2006): 173–184. Print.

Newman, Judie. "Shirley Jackson and the Reproduction of Mothering." *American Horror Fiction from Brockden Brown to Stephen King*. Ed. Brian Docherty. New York: St. Martin's Press, 1990. 120–134. Print.

Oppenheimer, Judy. *Private Demons: The Life of Shirley Jackson*. New York: G. P. Putnam's Sons, 1988. Print.

Parks, John G. "Chambers of Yearning: Shirley Jackson's Use of the Gothic." *Twentieth Century Literature* 30.1 (Spring 1984): 15–29. Print.

Punter, David. *The Literature of Terror: The Modern Gothic*. Vol. 2. 2d ed. New York: Longmans, 1996. Print.

_____. and Glennis Byron, eds. *Spectral Readings: Towards a Gothic Geography*. Basingstoke: Palgrave Macmillan, 1999. Print.

Rubenstein, Roberta. "House Mothers and Haunted Daughters: Shirley Jackson and The Female Gothic." *Shirley Jackson: Essays on the Literary Legacy*. Ed. Bernice M. Murphy. Jefferson, NC: McFarland, 1995. 127–149. Print.

Shapiro, Gavriel, ed. *Nabokov at Cornell*. Ithaca: Cornell University Press, 2003. Print.

Smith, Andrew. "Children of the Night: Shirley Jackson's Domestic Gothic." *The Female Gothic: New Directions*. Ed. Diana Wallace and Andrew Smith. Basingstoke: Palgrave Macmillan, 2009. 152–165. Print.

Stoker, Bram. *Dracula*. New York: W.W. Norton, 1997. Print.

Tinkler-Villani, Valeria, and Peter Davidson, eds. *Exhibited by Candlelight: Sources and Developments in the Gothic Tradition*. Atlanta: Rodopi, 1995. Print.

Voller, Jack G. *The Supernatural Sublime: The Metaphysics of Terror in Anglo-American Romanticism*. De Kalb: Northern Illinois University Press, 1994. Print.

Williams, Anne. *Art of Darkness: A Poetics of Gothic*. Chicago: University of Chicago Press, 1995. Print.

Part III
Millennial Monsters

"I think I am a monster"
Helen Oyeyemi's *White Is for Witching* and the Postmodern Gothic

Bianca Tredennick

In her introduction to *The Female Gothic,* Juliann Fleenor suggests that narrative complexity and instability are distinctive traits of the Gothic, especially as written by women:

> The narrative structure is usually one of multiple narrators. Epistolary novels or narration within narration are used.... Even in choosing the narrative structure Gothic writers, and in particular Female Gothic writers, choose one which by its nature undermines its validity. The struggle with the absolute is so threatening that even the narration must be questionable [12].

Narrative complexity and indeterminacy are also, of course, associated with postmodernism where such protean forms merge into self-referentiality, self-consciousness, and metafiction. Catherine Spooner has described Gothic's self-consciousness as a "cannibalistic ... consuming [of] the dead body of its own tradition," a metaphor which is both an apt description of the self-consuming, self-consumed nature of Gothic and the postmodern, and representative of the content of much that is Gothic (10).

Beyond the structural and narrative issues, parallels between the Gothic and postmodernism are too numerous to comprehensively catalog, but they can certainly include destabilized identities, perilously insecure settings, epistemological and ontological uncertainties, concern with the uncertainty of the real/unreal and self/other binaries, and complication of the center/margin dichotomy. Attempting to articulate a definition of Gothic postmodernism can be slippery business, given the famously versatile nature of each of these terms. David Punter locates the overlap between Gothic and postmodernism in the shared concern with "narrative that is never sure or reliable" (53). He goes on to explain, "the distortion of perspective which is a constant hallmark of Gothic fiction finds a further 'home' in the postmodern" (53). Maria Beville, tackling the same definition challenge, argues that the similar epistemological and ontological uncertainties of the Gothic and the postmodern combine in the Gothic postmodern to form a "literary monster" (16). Both quotations here are felicitous for this essay as I will examine a text that is both postmodern and Gothic, the novel *White Is for Witching* (2009), and argue that the effect of Helen Oyeyemi's narrative structure is to turn the Gothic postmodern novel itself into a monster, the haunted house of fiction. A comprehensive examination of this claim would require more space than I am allotted here, so I will focus my attention on the novel's paratexts and two of its four narrators.

Criticism on the novel has focused on social evils, seeing the novel as a postcolonial Gothic. Working in this mode, critics have noted the way in which the novel's concern with the monstrous other becomes a means of commentary on the monsters within society, including racism and anti-immigrant violence. In "Helen Oyeyemi and the Yoruba Gothic," for instance, Helen Cousins argues that the novel, like *Dracula*, explores reverse colonization, the fear that the English will be consumed by the foreign outsider. However, Oyeyemi's inclusion of Yoruba motifs delineates the novel from its Victorian ancestors by undermining the insider/outsider, white/black, English/foreign binaries. Ultimately, Cousins claims, "Oyeyemi describes what is monstrous in the colonial past and its present legacies from the perspective of those that England designates as its 'others' at home" (57). Similarly, Amy K. King argues in "The Spectral Queerness of White Supremacy" that Miranda becomes a "hungry ghost that acts as an agent of racist ideology and haunts a multiethnic Britain" (59). Expanding these readings into feminist theory, Anita Harris Satkunananthan maintains that the novel's postcolonial metaphor of consumption embodies the novel's concerns with its female characters' desire to be heard, and the "connection between ... physical-yet-supernatural acts of silencing and the ... racial terrorism which occurs as a result of a xenophobic house" (52). While my own reading is concerned with motifs of consumption, with the inside/outside binary, and even with the novel's status as post–*Dracula* vampire text, I will not be viewing the novel through a postcolonial lens, with its focus on social and political ills. Rather, I will focus on the novel's engagement with textual monstrosity.

Oyeyemi includes a wealth of monstrous figures in the novel, including witches, vampires, soucouyants, and ghosts. Throughout this essay, I use the term "monstrous" to refer to the threatening, supernatural Other that defies boundaries and threatens stability. I will not discriminate between the forms that the Other may take. In *White Is for Witching*, many monsters appear, and Oyeyemi does not concern herself with delineating the types. What I focus on, instead, is the slippage between the multifaceted monsters *in* Oyeyemi's text and the multifaceted monstrosity *of* Oyeyemi's text.

Before I investigate the specifics of the novel, it might be wise, given the book's recent publication date and its complexity, to provide a survey of the novel's architecture. *White Is for Witching* focuses on Miranda Silver, a teenager who lives with her father, mother, and twin brother, Eliot—with whom she appears to have an unnaturally close relationship—in a bed and breakfast in Dover. Following the death of Miranda's mother, Lily, Miranda suffers increasing psychological distress, including her temporary institutionalization for a nervous breakdown and pica, an eating disorder in which the sufferer consumes non-food items, such as (in Miranda's case) chalk and plastic. As Miranda's condition worsens, she becomes aware of a force called the goodlady, emanating from the house. Initially, Miranda thinks of the goodlady as a protective figure, but she becomes progressively more concerned that the goodlady is a vampire/witch/ghost and that this creature is responsible for the deaths of several Kosovan immigrants in the area. She also feels that she, herself, is becoming a vessel for the goodlady and that she (Miranda) may be responsible for some of the deaths. She further realizes that the spirits of her female ancestors for three generations back are imprisoned within the house, which emerges as the chief agent of evil in the novel, using the goodlady incarnation to effect its racist and xenophobic agenda.

In the second part of the novel, Miranda escapes the confines of 29 Barton Road and goes to Cambridge, where she falls in love with a Nigerian girl, Ore, who has been adopted by a white English family. Their time together offers a counter to the evils of Dover, but Miranda feels the house calling to her, and begins to think of preying upon Ore. Sent home after failing the term, Miranda hosts a visit from Ore. The house attempts to force Miranda to kill Ore, but Ore is saved by the intervention of the good magic of the Silver's Yoruba housekeeper, Sade. Ore escapes the house, and Miranda vows to fight Barton Road and the goodlady. What happens to Miranda is left ambiguous, but it appears that she loses her battle and becomes another Silver woman both imprisoned by and haunting 29 Barton Road, continuing its monstrous legacy.

Paranormal Paratexts

White Is for Witching opens with an epigraph, the first four lines from Gwendolyn Brooks' "my dreams, my works, must wait till after hell" (1963). The poem begins by establishing the speaker's ability to "hold" and "store" food supplies (1) in containers firmly shut by her "will" (2). As the poem develops, the speaker announces that she is securing the food against a decidedly Gothic eventuality: her return from Hell. This juxtaposition of the quotidian domestic and the supernatural monstrous is, of course, a typically Gothic motif.

In addition, the lines embody the Gothic concern with the relationship of the container to the contained.[1] The speaker's seeming confidence in her "will"—highlighted by her employment of the personal pronoun and verbs of action and agency to describe her control of the food—is undercut by one of those very verbs. When the speaker "bid's the containers remain closed until her return, she may well be intending to command that they do so (4).

However, while this is certainly one of the definitions for "bid," *The Oxford English Dictionary* lists far more definitions that relate to imploration: "to ask pressingly, beg, entreat, pray" (v. 7). Thus these lines also allude to the Gothic motif of the collapse of the container/contained binary, and to the Postmodern motif of the collapse of the subject/object, controller/controlled, author/text binaries. The speaker can only implore the contained to remain so, can only plead with the objects to remain objectified, and can only beg that the narrative voice remains in control of what it narrates.

However, what is most interesting about Oyeyemi's epigraph is what it leaves out, the very next lines of Brooks's poem: "I am very hungry. I am incomplete/And none can tell when I may dine again"(5–6). These lines relate most overtly to the content of the novel, which focuses on Miranda Silver's battle with pica and with her growing desire to feed, vampirically, on humans. While Oyeyemi leaves the details fuzzy, it appears that Miranda's pica, a trait she shares with her female ancestors, is a symptom of the Silver women's potential for madness and monstrosity. A remote ancestor was "thought an animal" because her "appetite was only for herself," her own flesh and blood (Oyeyemi 24). Miranda's more immediate ancestors, her great-grandmother, Anna, grandmother, Jennifer, and mother, Lily, also eat non-food items. Grandmother Anna, however, takes this strange disordered eating to a new monstrous extreme by becoming, after her death, "the goodlady," a racist, xenophobic, vampire-like creature who haunts her own home and who uses Miranda's body to prey on Dover's immigrant population.

In short, as critics like King and Satkunananthan have noted, the novel is about the Gothic motif of consumption. The elusiveness of Oyeyemi's epigraph becomes allusiveness, then, as the interested reader is motivated to track down the rest of the poem and analyze it for meaning. What is present in the text, then, is the spectral trace of what is absent, those marginalized lines that are really the central ones.

Since paratexts, such as epigraphs, are always in a liminal, ghostly relationship to the main body of the texts, Oyeyemi's opening has extra resonance.

In *Literary Ghosts from the Victorians to Modernism,* Luke Thurston theorizes the epigraph as textual ghost. It is

> an enigmatic apparition at the doorway ... of a host text. An epigraph ... seems both part of the text and ... at odds with it: lodged in the "extimate" interval between the title of a work and its "first" line.... Its precise relationship to the ensuing text remains largely enigmatic.... The epigraph should therefore be accorded a primary *visual* status: it is not an ordinary textual element to be interpreted via the narrative grid of signifiers but, instead, a kind of textual spectre.... An epigraphic text can therefore never be subject to the signifying closure determining a discrete narrative statement but must break off hauntingly, elliptically: an intertextual ghost voice [31].

When we combine what Thurston here defines as the essentially ghostly nature of epigraph, in general, with Oyeyemi's particular manipulation of hers, the effect is decidedly spectral. Not only does her epigraph haunt the indeterminate space between the text and silence but, as we have seen, she has chosen to have the most clearly germane part of it, that which can most easily be "interpreted via the narrative grid of signifiers," occur in the even more spectral gesture toward the absent lines. Those lines that follow the epigraph, which flicker just out of sight, refer to unfinishedness by addressing the persona's hunger and feelings of fragmentation. The epigraph, as edited by Oyeyemi, then, performs its own incompleteness. Both in terms of the content of the absent lines and the very fact of their absence, the epigraph testifies to that which is gone and yet haunts the present. It both articulates and exemplifies its spectral status. Thus, Oyeyemi's epigraph, her novel's "beginning," is already marked with the monstrous, with the ghost-effect.

Further, the epigraph's allusion to the need to attain completion by feeding an unsatisfied hunger is, as I have indicated, a need shared by the goodlady and its current vampiric incarnation, Miranda Silver. In this way, then, Oyeyemi immediately parallels the novel itself to the monsters within, a Gothic and Postmodern collapse of the container/contained motif embodied in an epigraph that both contentually and formally asserts and subverts the notions of such a binary.

Once past the spectral epigraph, the reader expects to encounter the body of the text but, instead, is confronted with a line whose origin, significance, and purpose, remain equally incorporeal. The novel "begins" with a question, centered and bolded on the page, "where is miranda?" (1). The position and font style of this line are suggestive of a chapter heading, the organizational and thematic sorting of a controlling author. However, it is difficult to connect the line to such an author due to its casual, conversational tone, its absence of capitalization, and—mostly—its failure of omnipotence. It is jarring, disorienting, and present without clear origin or purpose—spectral, in effect. Intensifying this sense of disjuncture from the author is that the line does not encapsulate this section of the novel, metaphorize it, or any of the typical functions of chapter titles. Rather, it acts as an interrogative prompt that the novel's three first-person narrators go on to answer, as if they are aware of it. The odd responsiveness of the characters to what appears to be an authorial heading again challenges the line between the novel as container and the characters and plot as contained. In addition, it points out the very porous borders of this novel, where the text seems always excessive and uncanny, overrunning the boundaries that are meant to define and confine it.

After the three first-person narrators' various and varying answers to the spectral question, we get a left-justified, italicized line, *"try again,"* followed by that attempt, another heading-like line, similarly placed and bolded, "is miranda alive?" (3). That, too, is answered by the three first-person narrators, their answers conflicting and indeterminate, leading to another heading, this one again italicized and left-justified, and, now, seemingly frustrated—*"try a different way"*—followed by a new question in the usual "heading" font, "what happened to lily silver?" (4). This, also, receives various mystifying answers by the three narrators.

As I indicated above, the fact that these headings are presented as questions dutifully answered by the character-narrators makes it difficult to see them as meant to be read, within the tale, as products of the author, at least of the author as typically defined: external to the text, omnipotent, and invisible to her characters. So, too, does the fact that when the answers don't produce whatever the questioner hopes for (clarity?), the questioner announces a change in strategy and attempts to get answers "a different way."

This variation in approach is formally mimicked by the variation in position and font style and by the change from the interrogative to the imperative. How is one to read these questions and commands, then? That they are not chapter or section titles is made clear by the characters' awareness of and response to them. That they are not part of the body of the text is made clear by the fact they originate in the liminal space "before" and "between" the "real" text; they are not offered by any of the first-person narrators who attempt answers, nor the novel's fourth narrator, an unremarkable third-person variety of narrator who cannot be the impatient interrogator. Devoid of clear function, liminal, unclear in origin, the questions share in the epigraph's paratextual paranormality, continuing the sense of the novel, itself, as monstrous. Here, it appears to have uncanny agency that cannot be ascribed to author, narrator or character. It is a voice without a body, a presence without presence.

Adding to the feeling that this "beginning" is only provisionally and problematically one is the fact that the question-and-answer section is succeeded by a blank page, and what appears to be an actual authorial section indicator, the Roman numeral I, followed by the all-caps word "CURIOUSER" (11). And, indeed, this section will encompass half of the novel and be succeeded by a section designated "II. AND CURIOUSER" (141). The format and function of these headings seem, as I have said, considerably less ambiguous than any of the other paratexts we have examined. However, if even the epigraph, clearly positioned as such, had spectral qualities due to its form and content, so, too, do these divisors.

Once again, Oyeyemi employs allusion, stretching the boundaries of the text to encompass another, just as she did with Brooks's poem. The other that is encompassed here is *Alice's Adventures in Wonderland* (1865), a text that is about the stretching of boundaries, charting, as it does, its title character's manifold alterations in dimension. Her changes in size are almost always caused by the consumption of food or drink, thus linking these divisors to one of the *Witching's* Gothic themes.

In addition, it is important to note that, once again, what is left out of the section dividers resonates with the text. What follows Carroll's famous line is "She was so much surprised, that for the moment she forgot how to speak good English" (8). Alice's interjection is grammatically incorrect because of her errant formation of the comparative. The rules for constructing the English comparative have to do less with logic than with felicity of expression. That is, words of one syllable are made comparative with the addition of "er," thus "larger."

Words of two syllables are sometimes allowed the use of the "er" ending if the word ends in y, or if it is a short-sounding adjective: "happier," but also "simpler." Words of three syllables must take the modifier "more," so Alice's line should properly read "more curious." The different rules, then, are based on the length of the word and how ungainly it would sound with the supplement of an additional syllable. When Alice first utters the word, "curious," she uses it to describe the sensation of having her body shrink to tiny size (6). When she utters the phrase, "curiouser and curiouser," shortly thereafter, she is responding to the feeling of having her body expand to gigantic size (8). Carroll, in other words, matches the short adjective to the act of shrinking and the grammatically incorrect ungainly adjective to Alice's parallel gargantuanism. For the character, this formation is not "good English," but read extra-textually, as the author's literary manipulation of the form of the word to parallel the content of the character's experience, it is decidedly "good."

Returning to Oyeyemi's choice of these section dividers, the effect of the stark boundaries suggested by bold type, numbered order, and surrounding blank pages—along with their association with an omnipotent, controlling, containing author—is subverted by the spectral nature of the headings. They are, themselves, "curious," gesturing outside the boundaries they seem designed to delineate, and serving as signs that point in the direction of absent referents, the ghostly traces that haunt the novel. In this case, those traces relate to Alice's consumption, its monstrous effects (her ever-changing body size), and the way in which Alice's language parallels the effects of her consumption. Carroll's text becomes, here, whatever Alice eats. By alluding to this process, Oyeyemi's novel becomes a kind of double for Carroll's story and the dynamic included in the allusion's context. If *White is for Witching* is about disordered, monstrous eating, this allusion suggests the way in which it, too, will become what it contains, an uncanny version of that which it incorporates.

29 Barton Road

Everything that I have just discussed must be seen as preamble, that which exists before the "real" beginning of the novel, since it exists, spatially, before the novel's denominated first section. However, it also demands to be read as an epilogue since the material in it can only be understood when read *after* the completion of the novel. Readers must re-read the opening after turning the final page in order to place that question-and-answer section where it chronologically belongs. In addition, the "preamble" material originates later in time than the spatial end of the novel. This is the case because the novel's spatial end concludes with Eliot, Miranda's twin, trying to interpret the sounds emanating from the attic of 29 Barton Road as indicative of Miranda's presence in the house and promise to return:

> "Miri. Are you coming back?"
> Step, step, halt.
> I asked, "When?"
> Three creaks. She stepped three times.
> What is the meaning of it? Three creaks, three weeks? [245].

The preamble, however, sees Eliot acknowledging that he last saw Miranda "five months ago," the day of her disappearance (3). This confusion of beginnings and endings, false starts that are real endings, and so on, makes Oyeyemi's novel's architecture misleading—its overt structure covering a covert one beneath.

This is important because it makes the novel a formal double for the monster at the heart of the story, 29 Barton Road. Anna Good Silver responds to the death of her husband in World War II by uttering a curse against the Other: "I hate them … Blackies, Germans" (118). Anna is a witch, and her fear of the other somehow awakens her house into agency. It becomes the means of fulfilling her desire to exterminate the Other. As Barton says, "she gave me my task" (118). However, in a dynamic that Oyeyemi never quite makes clear, the monster Anna Good awakens soon exceeds her control. The result of the house becoming the primary agent of evil in the novel is the transformation of Anna Good into "the goodlady," a vampiric figure who kills immigrants. The house continues Anna Good's mission, after her death, using Miranda's living body as the vehicle for Anna's predatory goodlady. Thus, it is the house, not the witch/eventual vampire/eventual ghost Anna, who is the primary monster, a fact Barton makes clear: "Anna Good you are long gone now, except when I resurrect you to play in my puppet show, but you forgive since when I make you appear it is not really you, and besides you know that my reasons are sound.… Indeed you are a mother of mine, you gave me a kind of life, mine, the kind of alive that I am" (24). Barton Road is, thus, setting, villain, and, most fascinatingly, one of the novel's three first-person narrators. Haunted houses that become characters or, at least, have more agency than mere settings are nothing new—from Jackson's Hill House to King's Overlook Hotel. However, it falls to the Gothic postmodern to test the line between setting, character, narrator, and narrative structure. In this way, Oyeyemi's text is more like *House of Leaves* (2000) than it is *The Shining* (1977).

Just as Anna Good's fear and hatred give the house a voice so, too, does Oyeyemi's narrative structure. The novel's form mimics the Gothic motif of the slippage between container and contained. As in "Fall of the

House of Usher" (1839) (a text which I would place firmly—despite its publication date—within the genre of Gothic postmodernism), the setting has agency—indeed more agency than any of the living or dead human inhabitants. And in another resonance with Poe's story, the boundaries of this confusion extend beyond the plot, to the literature itself. Just as the ending of "Usher" suggests the collapse of not just setting/house/agent/character, but also of Poe's story itself, so too Oyeyemi's container becomes a double for the fiction that contains it. We can see this, in the broadest terms, analogically: the novel as container of all that is within it—character, plot, narrative structure, etc.—is doubled with Barton, which contains all of those things within itself.

More specifically, the doubling between *Witching* and 29 Barton Road is indicated by their parallel architecture. Barton Road, like *House of Leaves*'s Navidson home, contains more space within it than its floor plan allows, including secret internal spaces that it can entrap people in, thus neatly combining the Gothic motifs of containment and consumption. For instance, when Miranda's grandmother, Jennifer, threatens to leave the house and run away with her foreign boyfriend, the xenophobic house responds by trapping her within its secret spaces: "I unlocked a door in her bedroom that she had not seen before" (84). Similarly, when Miranda resists the house's racist, homophobic, xenophobic desire for her to kill Ore, the house decides to "take her [Miranda] away" (194), and suggests in the preamble/conclusion that it has internalized her, like her grandmother: "Miranda is at *home* … she is stretched out inside a wall" (3). Miranda's mother, Lily, also haunts the house, though we are less clear if the house compels her posthumous residence there (it is not the agent of her death) or if she chooses to return there to watch over Miranda.

In addition to the secret spaces within walls, the house also has "extra floors" filled with "looking people" who are part of the house's repertoire of ghouls (57). As one character who tries to warn Miranda emphatically puts it, "*The house is bigger than you know*" (57). These extra floors are accessible by the lift, which the house uses to transport its victims to its monstrous spaces. The ability of the lift to travel between the real and spectral spaces of the house is paralleled by a spatial choice Oyeyemi makes in her writing about it:

But she heard someone talking to Luc downstairs, she heard the clatter of cutlery, she heard the whirr of
> the lift

broke down in the night. No one knew what time. The timing became important when Azwer and Ezma couldn't find their older daughter in the morning [35].

In this passage, Oyeyemi uses the phrase "the lift" to link two different passages, occurring hours apart. The effect of this startling device is to visually and formally mimic the house's monstrous architecture, as Oyeyemi's "the lift" bridges the space between two times in the novel, exactly as the elevator itself travels in the interstices between the real and the monstrous. At the same time that it suggests the ability to link the real and the spectral, "the lift," floating in the middle of the page, is suggestive of being lost in the interstices, like an elevator caught between floors. And, indeed, when the Kurdish employees' child, Deme, is found, she is trapped in the elevator which has "gr[ound] to a halt between floors" (53). Later, Deme will explain her mysterious disappearance to Miranda in the lines I quoted above, where she warns Miranda about the "extra floors" the lift travels to, and the figures who dwell there. These monsters can trap characters between the real and the supernatural, just as Oyeyemi's prose, here, turns text into paratext.

The Postmodern Gothic monster that is Barton Road is not just self-aware. It is also aware of its status as the container for the plot and for the act of reading that plot: "I am here, reading with you. I am reading this over your shoulder. I make your home home, I'm the Braille on your wallpaper that only your fingers can read—I tell you where you are. Don't turn to look at me. I am only tangible when you don't look" (73–74). This metafictive moment has several levels. First, the house *within* the story becomes the house *outside* it, as Barton Road exceeds its novelistic bounds to claim identity with the readers' individual surroundings, thus rendering the house of the reader haunted. In addition, it suggests a parallel between the act of reading and the architecture of the haunted house in the imagery of legible wallpaper. Third, it suggests that it, too, is a reader, again marking the novel readers' activity with the house's monstrosity.[2]

While Barton Road is the most postmodern narrator, it is not the only one whose boundary-exceeding status renders the novel monstrous. While each of the four narrators merits discussion, in the interests of space I will look at only one more, the one who seems the most distinct from Barton.

Ore Lind

On the surface, Ore is the antithetical narrator to Barton Road. She is the Nigerian child, adopted by white English parents, whom Miranda meets and dates at Cambridge. Their potentially liberatory relationship is eventually menaced by Miranda's growing madness and/or possession and concomitant desire to kill Ore. Miranda is aware of and horrified by her desire, warning herself to "*manage your consumption…. Ore is not food. I think I am a monster,*" her very comment one of the many self-conscious, reflective comments on the Gothic made by characters (191–192). But while knowledge of the conventions might seem like it would offer a tutorial in how to escape conforming to them, Miranda's insight is no more effective at preventing her descent into monstrosity than is Mary Shelley's Creature's. The girl who once confidently stated that she would never get stuck in the House of Usher because she would have been off "like a shot" when she saw it (94) cannot escape the pull of her own haunted house, telling Ore, "I'm to go home. The house wants me" (176). Indeed, it appears that the literariness of her Gothic condition, the textuality of her situation, worsens rather than eases Miranda's condition. Just as the Creature's sense of his own monstrosity "only increases with knowledge" (123), so, too, Miranda's well-stocked Gothic bookshelf—"Grimm's *Fairy Tales*, Petrault, Andersen, LeFanu, Wilkie Collins, E.T.A. Hoffman"—seems only to entangle her in previous representations rather than allowing her egress from them (160). When Ore sees a photograph of Miranda, she describes Miranda as looking like "one of those Gothic victims" (162) that might appear in the books Ore has noticed on the shelves.

Nor is Ore's self-awareness any more liberatory, for it is she who is the most immediate Gothic victim, a fact that she realizes, vowing to "look for wounds" left on her body by Miranda (185). But Ore's knowledge that she may be being fed on by Miranda or, at least, endangered by her, does not prevent her from visiting Miranda at Barton Road during the school break. As Miranda's father trenchantly replies after Miranda's boast about Usher, "easy to see the solution when you're not in the story, isn't it?" (94). Once you *are* in the story, however—once trapped in the haunted house of fiction—there is no ease of egress for either Ore or Miranda.

Barton's initial joy at getting her back is soon challenged by the discovery of Miranda's interracial, same-sex relationship. Miranda's grandmother and great-grandmother, along with 29 Barton Road, determine that the "ivory wand" that was the nearly perfected Miranda (192) has picked up an unremovable "taint" (194) from her relationship with Ore. Barton decides, therefore, "I will not allow her [Miranda] to live" (4). But before it acts to "take her away," Barton attempts to use Miranda as the goodlady to kill the visiting Ore (194). Ore is saved, however, by her heroic battle against the goodlady, and by the timely intervention of Sade. Ore is last heard from fleeing home in a train, her final line the very closural "That's all I know. Now I have said all that I know" (232).

However, this tidy explication of Ore as character-narrator, and the neat closure of her tale are misleading. This is, in part because of the chronological/spatial confusion that I mentioned earlier in the essay. Spatially, Ore's last lines involve her closural sounding statement but, chronologically, it is clear that her opening lines, lines which are also the opening lines of the novel's preamble, are actually her final identified contributions to the novel. Thus the beginning is mixed with the ending, openings with closings, and questions with answers.

The fact that Ore gets the (spatial) first line of the novel is suggestive, and works, immediately, to destabilize her apparently clear status as character-narrator. Why should Ore get the pride of place that is opening the novel instead of Miranda's twin brother, the haunted house, or the third-person narrator? One answer to this question lies in the possibility that what authorizes Ore to begin (and end) the tale is that she may be its fictional "author." Her/the novel's opening lines, in answer to the query about Miranda's whereabouts, appear to be in the form of a free verse poem—not the form the other narrators' answers will take. The poem/answer includes literary, crafted-feeling metaphors, such as Ore's description of Miranda as "a star planted seed-deep" underneath 29 Barton Road (1). It also appears on the page with spacing suggestive of poetic line breaks:

> …I miss the taste of her I
> see her in my sleep [1].

That Ore might craft a poetic response to the initial query is fitting. She is, after all, a raconteur. Her mother provides her with a book of Caribbean folk tales written "for storytellers" (147), and she will go on to repetitively recite her favorite of these tales: the soucouyant who sheds her skin to take the form of a ball of flame and feed on the souls of humans. In addition, she declares, "I wanted to write about her. I still do. What do I want to write? Just a book, probably, another tooth for the U[ndergraduate] L[ibrary]'s mouth. Something that explores the meaning of the old woman whose only interaction with other people was consumption" (155).

It is, thus, possible that the only avowed writer among the characters, and the first of the characters to get a line is, in fact, the fictional author of everything that follows. *White is for Witching*, in that case, would be Ore's effort to make good on her desire to write about the soucouyant—either by imagining the perspectives and voices of the other participants in Miranda's life or inventing the entire thing. In either case, we must now scrutinize the authenticity of the novel's only purely sympathetic narrator-character. Ore as likeable, potential victim, who recognizes her danger and manages to escape it, suddenly becomes not the stable moral center of the novel but merely another shape-shifting breaker of boundaries in a text whose monstrosity is defined by such transgressions. Indeed, if being "not in the story" is the only way to "see the solution," as Miranda's father has previously suggested, the very fact of Ore's survival suggests her status somehow exterior to the novel—perhaps in the role of author (94).

Ore's narration, including her ambiguous status as character/narrator/author, is the site for meaningful parallels with *Dracula* (1897), parallels which accentuate the monstrosity of Ore's act of narration and, thus, of the novel as a whole. Ore's relationship with Miranda, begins as a result of encountering her in the library where Ore is spending a "listless half hour flipping through critical essays on *Dracula*" (155), her dismissive attitude another self-conscious nod toward Oyeyemi's self-consciously belated Gothic revision.

The resonance of Oyeyemi's references, overt and covert, to Stoker's work are myriad. First, it continues the allusive nature of Oyeyemi's text, its Gothic tendency to consume the Other, which is consistent with, rather than opposed to, the monstrous practice of 29 Barton Road and its goodlady. That it is Ore who makes overt the beholdingness inherent to any vampire novel after *Dracula* is suggestive. It is she who makes the reader confront *Witching* as a textual response to the definitive vampire (and a definitive Gothic) text and to confront the critical and literary legacy that *Dracula* has spawned, the massive amount of scholarship, literature, film, and other popular culture that continuously feeds off the body of Stoker's text. She is less than overwhelmed by the critical response, suggesting that *Dracula*, for all its impact, offers a less than nourishing diet, a sort of disordered eating, for those who come after. And yet, for all her cynicism about the afterlife of this text, all Ore can think to do is contribute her own vampiric tale to the library, adding nothing but another "tooth" to the library's "mouth" (155), another digestion aid to break *Dracula* down into finer and finer remnants, picking the bones clean.

Ore's desire to write her own version of the vampire tale marks her overtly as an authorial figure in the wake of *Dracula*. More interestingly, it ties Ore as author-figure and vampire's lover, to *Witching*'s real author, Oyeyemi, who acknowledged in an interview with Ben Machell in *The London Times* that *Witching* came about because she "wanted to write a vampire story…. I spent a lot of time in bed with *Dracula*" (n.pag). It is possible to see *White is for Witching*, then, as another tooth for the library's mouth, another consuming, belated, parasite on the Stoker host, reliant on, ancillary to, yet preying on the ur-text. Barton Road conceives of immigrants as the "Other," a foreign body that relies, leech-like, on the dominant culture, and yet Barton does not investigate the irony of its own punitive consumption of immigrants, its internalization of everything it wishes to externalize. This is, of course, the central examination of Stoker's novel—the extent to which the "primitive" foreigner consumed by colonial forces in a similarly unreflective act might turn the tables and make the west its victim. In each trajectory of colonization, the monster is made by its assumption of primacy in regard to the Other, but it is ironically made *up* of that Other. So, too, does Ore—and by extension Oyeyemi whom she doubles—nonetheless embody a problematic position in regard to her status as consumer/creator of vampire literature. Oyeyemi's desire to write a vampire novel after reading *Dracula* both asserts primacy (that she can do something new, say something different than did Stoker or his many revisers) and places herself in a necessarily belated, defensive posture in regard to that text.

Ore also parallels *Dracula*'s lead female character, Mina. Both characters are the most sympathetic, sane, and likeable in their respective novels, and they are both potential victims who miraculously escape the worst. They are also both in ambiguous and vexed relationships with the texts they inhabit. Just like Ore, Mina's apparent status as character/narrator becomes progressively more unclear. *Dracula*, like *Witching*, opens with a paratext, a headnote notifying the reader that "all the records chosen are exactly contemporary, given from the standpoints and within the range of knowledge of those who made them" (Stoker 6). However, as the language of choice here suggests, and later parts of the book confirm, the narratives are (at least) picked, arranged, and edited by one of the character-narrators, Mina Harker. As her husband reflects, "it is due to her ... that the whole story is put together in such a way that every point tells" (264). Given that Dracula goes on to burn nearly every original document, leaving only Mina's compiled, typewritten version, the characters concede, at the novel's end, that the manuscript looks like "a mass of typewriting," without "one authentic document" to give it credence (402). In other words, the presence of Mina's clean, compiled, chronological, typed text, in the absence of corroborative originals on which it was based, lends Mina's text a fictional appearance: she could have authored the entire thing herself. As Jonathan Harker's final lines make clear, the presence of Mina's edited text and the absence of authentic first-hand texts renders their experiences unverifiable: "We could hardly ask anyone ... to accept these as proofs of so wild a story" (402). The characters' experience with vampires, thus, slips from the "simple fact" promised in the head note to what appears to be fiction (6).

This appearance of fictionality matters in *Dracula*. Van Helsing has previously explained that in the skeptical late–Victorian period when "men believe not even what they see, the doubting of wise men would be his [Dracula's] greatest strength" (342). Now the very text that was to record the unthinkable, to present evidence for the unbelievable, is tainted by that which it sought to expel—the very mythic, fictional nature of vampire lore. If Dracula is not, in fact, eliminated at the end of Stoker's novel (which the many textual oddities involved with his supposed execution make a real possibility), the contamination of Mina's text by fiction, the suggestion that she may be the document's sole author, facilitates the monster's survival.[3]

In the same way, Mina's doubling of Ore's tendencies suggest that she, too, is crafting, not (or not just) experiencing the events the novel records. In both cases, the first-person narration, which should guarantee a feeling of immediacy and authenticity, undoes itself, suggesting an unstable, protean text infected by the monstrosity it sought to contain. Ore, who seemed positioned as the antithesis of the monster house may, in fact, be its shape-shifting double, creator and voice. That readers cannot trust this voice any more than they can trust Mina's is a necessary corollary. It is easy to reject Barton's voice, to resist the overt monster, but what about the other character-narrators? Barton makes clear what I have attempted to argue for above—that Ore's narration becomes infected by the very monstrosity it is overtly positioned against. The very ambiguity of her status feeds the protean, expanding, indeterminate body of the text.

Ore's ultimate narrative act is to kill off Miranda, just as the overt trajectory of Mina's document is to record Dracula's defeat. It is Ore who, in the novel's opening lines, consigns Miranda to the grave, answering the opening query about if Miranda is alive with "Probably not" (3). Ore's desire for closure is most interesting when read as a narrative, authorial impulse. Earlier Ore has noticed that stories about the soucouyant seem obsessed with finality: "the story of her is much more to do with how she is ended than how she began.... It's as if she's so wrong that even in the mind of the storyteller she must be killed immediately" (210). It is impossible not to retroactively read Ore's declaration that Miranda is "in the ground beneath her mother's house" (1) as just such a narrative impulse. Yet, in the same way that *Dracula*'s ending traces the overly tidy disposal of the monster, foregrounding ambiguity instead of certainty, Ore's comments about Miranda do the same. After all, it is not clear if Ore is presenting Miranda as dead and buried or if she is suggesting her posthumous inhabitation of the house in continuation with the fate of her female ancestors. In such a way, the story offers not closure, but indeterminacy, not a happy ending but no ending. The monster is not contained, defined, expelled in either Oyeyemi or Stoker's texts: rather the text becomes a monstrous double, mutating, shape-shifting, self-aware, challenging fixed centers of reality and stable identities, exceeding boundaries, defying labels. The monstrous Gothic house of Oyeyemi's fiction is not, at the end, "just" setting/character/and narrator; it is the form of the novel itself, as we see *White Is for Witching* become the monstrous house of Gothic fiction.

Exit

In a 2009 podcast with *The Guardian*, Oyeyemi responded to questions about the novel's intertextuality in a peculiar way: "I think the story's ... very knowing.... As I was writing it, it very much knew about itself, especially with the element of the [haunted] house. It knew about other stories that had come before it, that were like it" (Armistead). What is interesting here is both how Gothic and how postmodern Oyeyemi's conception of the novel is. Like many a haunted house, cursed item and reanimated corpse before it, *Witching*'s inanimate manuscript has agency and knows the literary tradition of which it is part. More importantly, the novel knows *itself*; it is both the subject and object of its epistemological appetite, consuming itself as object of its own knowledge. It is important to note, too, that the effect of this "knowing" novel is to destabilize the notion of a controlling author. Indeed, while the manuscript's knowledge is referred to three times, Oyeyemi herself is reduced to only "thinking," and even more, to a servile thinking defined by trying to figure out what the manuscript *knows* about itself and other Gothic texts.

Indeed, Oyeyemi has consistently indicated confusion about her own text. For instance, in a 2012 interview with Patricia Armion, Oyeyemi says:

> Nobody knows the answer to ... the question of where Miranda is.... Even I who have written it ... I'm not sure what happened to her. At some point ... I thought: she's definitely fighting against this, this is her way of exiting the story, that's what her disappearance is, she refuses to be the next line, the next in line. But sometimes I felt as if she just couldn't fight the voices anymore [n.pag].

Ultimately, *White Is for Witching* exceeds the control of its large complement of narrators, its characters, and even its author. As Oyeyemi suggests, the only way to escape the monster in the plot is to escape the monstrous plot, to decline "to be the next line." As Miranda puts it, "Please to tell me a story about a girl who gets away.... Please have her get out and run off the page altogether" (165).

Notes

1. I am thinking, particularly, of "The Fall of the House of Usher," where the "equivocal appellation of the 'House of Usher' ... seemed to include, in the minds of the peasantry who used it, both the family and the family mansion" (Poe 16). Of course the slippage between the container and contained, in Poe's story, comes to have massive thematic and formal implications, so that the ending of the tale sees the collapse of the "'HOUSE OF USHER,'" the capitalization and quotation marks suggestive of not only the house and family, but Poe's tale itself (29). "Usher" will be referenced in multiple ways in Oyeyemi's tale, from the twin incest motif that characterizes Miranda and Eliot's relationship, to Miranda's vow that if she found herself in the House of Usher, she would have the good sense to run and fetch a priest. Her father's reply, "easy to see the solution when you're not in the story, isn't it?" continues the metatextual, intertextual nature of the novel, along with its association of narrative with monstrosity (94).

2. This sequence may also be another of Oyeyemi's allusions to other ghost stories. It is reminiscent of the scene in Dickens's *A Christmas Carol*, where the third-person narrator describes the ghost of Christmas Past as close to Scrooge "as I am now to you, and I am standing in the spirit at your elbow" (18). Dickens's story also features a short paratext, a preface that calls *Carol* a "ghostly little book" which its author hopes will "haunt [readers'] ... house's pleasantly" (ix).

3. These textual oddities are, perhaps, too well known to require enumeration, but include the ambiguity about whether the Crew of Light uses one of the approved methods for vampire extermination, the unexpected ease with which Dracula "dies," the less than clearly auspicious timing of the Crew's attack, and so on.

Works Cited

Armion, Patricia. "An Interview with Helen Oyeyemi." *Assises Internationales du Roman* 2012. Transcript. La Clé de Langues. May 31, 2012. Web. May 10, 2014.
Armistead, Claire. "Book of the Week: *White is for Witching* by Helen Oyeyemi." *The Guardian Books Podcast*. The Guardian. June 19, 2009. Web. May 10, 2014.
"Beg." v. 7. *Oxford English Dictionary Online*. 2014. Web. May 11, 2014.
Beville, Maria. *Gothic-Postmodernism: Voicing the Terrors of Postmodernity*. Amsterdam: Rodopi, 2009. Print.
Brooks, Gwendolyn. "my dreams, my works, must wait till after hell." *Selected Poem*. New York: Harper and Row, 23–24. Print.
Carroll, Lewis. *Alice's Adventures in Wonderland. Alice's Adventures in Wonderland* and *Through the Looking Glass*. New York: Bantam, 1981. 1–109. Print.
Cousins, Helen. "Helen Oyeyemi and the Yoruba Gothic: *White Is for Witching*." *The Journal of Commonwealth Literature* 47.1 (2012): 47–58. Print.
Dickens, Charles. *A Christmas Carol*. Mineola, NY: Dover Thrift, 1991. Print.
Fleenor, Juliann E., ed. Introduction. *The Female Gothic*. Montreal: Eden Press, 1983. 3–28. Print.
King, Amy K. "The Spectral Queerness of White Supremacy: Helen Oyeyemi's *White is for Witching*." *The Ghostly and the Ghosted in Literature and Film: Spectral Identities*. Ed. Lisa Kröger and Melanie Anderson. Newark: University of Delaware, 2013. 59–74. Print.
Machell, Ben. "Helen Oyeyemi: *The Times* Interview." *The London Times*. May 23, 2009. Web. May 4, 2014.
Oyeyemi, Helen. *White Is for Witching*. London: Picador, 2009. Print.

Poe, Edgar Allan. "The Fall of the House of Usher." *"The Gold Bug" and Other Tales*. Ed. Stanley Applebaum. Mineola, NY: Dover Thrift, 1991. 14–29. Print.
Satkunananthan, Anita Harris. "Textual Transgressions and Consuming the Self in the Fiction of Helen Oyeyemi and Chimamanda Ngozi Adichie." *Hecate* 37.2 (2011): 41–69. Print.
Shelley, Mary. *Frankenstein*. Ed. Maurice Hindle. New York: Penguin, 2003. Print.
Spooner, Catherine. *Contemporary Gothic*. London: Reaktion Books, 2006. Print.
Stoker, Bram. *Dracula*. Ed. Maurice Hindle. New York: Penguin, 2003. Print.
Thurston, Luke. *Literary Ghosts from the Victorians to Modernism: The Haunting Interval*. Routledge Studies in Twentieth-Century Literature. New York: Routledge, 2012. Print.

"*Madness and monstrosity*"
Notions of the Gothic and Sublime in Comics Adaptations of H. P. Lovecraft

Rebecca Janicker

Preoccupied with the tenacious grip of history and the evocative power of setting, and characterized by an atmosphere of dread, the fiction of H. P. Lovecraft can readily be placed in the Gothic tradition. His anxious depictions of antiquated and wilderness spaces—frequently disturbed by awesome events and monstrous entities—encompass elements of physical, as well as psychological, horror. In this regard, Lovecraft draws on both the thematic and the stylistic properties associated with the Gothic. Building on these foundations, he also introduced a distinctive aura of cosmic wonder that permeated his own fiction and influenced the horror genre as a whole. This sense of mystery, of incredible forces lurking just beyond the scope of daily life, and of the transformative potential inherent in encounters of this kind, is epitomized by the breathtaking power known as the *sublime*. Yet Lovecraft's fiction, laced as it is with themes of repugnance and destabilization, threatens annihilation and madness rather than promising progress through enlightenment.

Perhaps in response to these bleak and devastating visions, a plethora of both faithful adaptations and innovative re-imaginings has materialized since the initial emergence of Lovecraft's atmospheric tales. The process of conveying literature in other media forms presents many challenges, yet this has not stymied those authors who, to a greater or lesser degree, have taken inspiration from his work. Elaine L. Graham notes that the "discourse of monstrosity," bound up as it is with destabilizing encounters with the non-human, is driven by the compulsion to *display* (12). Indeed, the desire to display these Lovecraftian marvels in some form has long been in evidence. In this chapter, I will focus on recent adaptations of Lovecraft's work for comics. Bearing in mind the medium's capacity to blend words with images, I maintain that comics provide a rich arena for enacting tales of the Gothic and the sublime. Taking examples from SelfMadeHero's *Lovecraft Anthology: Volume I* (2011) and *Volume II* (2012), as well as *At the Mountains of Madness* (2010), I demonstrate that these comics—in giving visual expression to Lovecraft's astounding narratives—both encapsulate his portrayals of monstrosity and exploit the intrinsic power of comics in order to reinvigorate the sense of shock and madness engendered by these literary brushes with the sublime. In doing so, I will highlight ways in which comics can make a singular contribution to Lovecraftian Gothic.[1]

Lovecraft: The Visual, the Gothic and the Sublime

Taking inspiration from the fresh perspectives yielded—both figuratively and quite literally—by his forays into science and the arts, Lovecraft came to cultivate the idiosyncratic worldview conveyed in his fiction.[2] Though drawn mainly to express himself in creative outlets of a blatantly *literary* nature— such as letter-writing, poetry and prose—he was captivated by the visual arts from a young age. In a missive from 1916, he cites an edition of *Paradise Lost* illustrated by Gustave Doré as a likely cause of the fearsome creatures he termed "night-gaunts," which in "fretting & impelling [him] with their detestable tridents" (Lovecraft, "To Reinhardt Kleiner [sic]" 35), frequently disturbed his childhood slumber and eventually found their way into his tales. The lurid creations of the likes of Doré, Henry Fuseli, and Francisco Goya held considerable sway over Lovecraft's imagination. One of the most iconic of his fictional backdrops, the vast and ancient Antarctic city of *At the Mountains of Madness* (1931), was inspired, at least in part, by Nikolai Roerich's paintings of the Himalayas (Joshi, *A Dreamer and a Visionary* 300). Besides singling out works by these renowned artists, Lovecraft was also stirred by the output of lesser-known figures, including Sidney H. Sime, illustrator for the fantasy author Lord Dunsany, as well as the nineteenth-century English painter John Martin. A letter from 1928 conveys his particular affinity for the "spirit of awful and tenebrous sublimity" with which Martin endowed his depictions of "great desolate pillared halls; unholy abysses & blasphemous torrents; terraced titan cities in far, half-celestial backgrounds whereon shines the light of no familiar sky of men's knowing" (Lovecraft, "To Vincent Starrett" 219).

For Lovecraft, art thus offered a stimulant for the imagination, especially given its potential for invoking previously-unimagined beings and landscapes beyond the accepted sphere of everyday human experience. In a similar vein, he was also inspired by architecture. Though repulsed by his experience of the city at close quarters, a visit to New York City in the early 1920s saw him mesmerized by the romantic symbolism of the Manhattan skyline:

> I nearly swooned with aesthetic exaltation when I beheld the panorama—the evening scene with innumerable lights in the skyscrapers, shimmering reflections and bobbing ship lights on the water, and at the extreme left and right, the flaming Statue of Liberty and the scintillant arc of the Brooklyn Bridge, respectively. But even this was not exactly the climax. That came when we went out on the flat roof ... and saw the thing in all its unlimited and unglassed magnificence [Lovecraft, "To Mrs F. C. Clark" 352].

In the same way that art has the power to inspire strong responses in the viewer, architecture is capable of eliciting a sensation of wonder. Found often at the heart of Lovecraft's fictions, overwhelming and transformative experiences such as those detailed above are typical of the state known as the sublime.

An important influence on eighteenth-century thought in general and on the Gothic in particular, Edmund Burke's *A Philosophical Enquiry into the Origin of our Ideas of the Sublime and Beautiful* (1757) characterizes the sublime as "the strongest emotion which the mind is capable of feeling" (39). Following Burke, Emily Brady discerns that the state of sublimity consists of such intense emotions as fear, terror and awe (24), likely stemming from sources that epitomize extremes of size and power (25–26). For example, epic scenery, wild beasts, and raging elements may all give rise to feelings of overwhelming dread. Gothic fiction, with its portrayals of potent supernatural forces played out against wild vistas and mountainous terrains, reacted against prevailing Enlightenment values in presenting a stylistic and thematic "excess that could not be processed by a rational mind" (Botting 39). Such ideas can readily be extended into more contemporary settings. Likening a range of mountains to a cluster of skyscrapers, Brady remarks, "some works of architecture do possess the scale necessary for sublimity" (142) in "surpassing everything around them and evoking a feeling of something beyond oneself" (144).

Transcendence is a pivotal concept to these discussions of sublimity and Paul Crowther ascertains that Immanuel Kant "construes the sublime as occasioned by powers which transcend the self" (15). In a similar vein, Brady recognizes that the Romantic poets utilized experiences of sublimity in order to stimulate the reader's imagination by "inspiring metaphysical thoughts about one's place in the universe" (104). This emphasis on encountering something more powerful than the individual can be connected to the philosophy Lovecraft came to espouse. As a result of his astronomical studies, he became "thoroughly impressed with man's impermanence and insignificance" and thus formulated those "pessimistic cosmic views" which permeated his fiction (Lovecraft, "To Edwin Baird" 302). Such conclusions, along with the observation that "an infinite reservoir of mystery still engulfs most of the outer cosmos" (Lovecraft, *Supernatural Horror in Literature* 14), form the basis of the so-called *cosmicism* seen by many critics as integral to Lovecraftian horror. In view of this preoccupation with outer space, it comes as no surprise that Lovecraft is also often linked to science fiction, a genre that Scott Bukatman casts as "immediately and deeply bound to the tropologies of the sublime" (257).

By conveying visualizations of, and brushes with, such awe-inspiring mysteries, Lovecraft can be seen to index the sublime within his fiction. In addition to his cosmic worldview, Lovecraft is perhaps best known as the originator of the Cthulhu Mythos: "a corpus of fictitious narratives which share as their common background a system of invented lore" (Carter xvii). This lore pertains to a pantheon of "gods" akin to Cthulhu—monstrous extraterrestrial entities which precede, transcend, and threaten to engulf human civilization—and the Mythos comprises tales that detail encounters with these beings. These colossal creatures suggest sublimity by virtue of both their size and might. For instance, the physical appearance of the eponymous monster in "The Call of Cthulhu" (1926)—tantalizingly cast as a "Thing [that] cannot be described" (167)—is conveyed through a metaphor denoting its incalculable bulk: "A mountain walked or stumbled" (167). The sight of this creature inspires acute feelings of horror, even instigating insanity in some, and transcendence is evoked by the conclusion that Cthulhu represents a source of "cosmic potency" (168) that could one day expunge life on earth: "Loathsomeness waits and dreams in the deep, and decay spreads over the tottering cities of men" (169). With its madness-inducing visions of awe-inspiring monstrosity, this tale clearly proffers a literary encounter with the sublime.

Besides their inclusion of monsters, many of Lovecraft's tales take place in settings notable for their wildness, remoteness, and general hostility to humanity. From the depths of rural New England in tales like "The Picture in the House" (1920), to the remotest regions of the Pacific in "Dagon" (1917), and the farthest reaches of the Australian outback in "The Shadow Out of Time" (1935), many a Lovecraftian protagonist has found himself (whether by accident or design) in far-flung, inhospitable locales that soon prove to harbor unsuspected horrors. Arguably the clearest articulation of the power of setting can be found in those "terrible mountains of the forbidden land" (336) portrayed in the aforementioned *At the Mountains of Madness*. Deep within the Antarctic wilderness, the protagonists come up against a "limitless, tempest-scarred plateau" on which they espy "the almost endless labyrinth of colossal, regular, and geometrically eurhythmic stone masses" that causes them to "cr[y] out in mixed awe, wonder, terror, and disbelief in [their] own senses" (283). As with "The Call of Cthulhu," this novella works to impart sublime visions that challenge the perceptions of both protagonist and reader with both their extravagance and their undertones of cosmic horror.

Following the observations made above about Lovecraft's early sources of inspiration, it is also worth noting the centrality of art to his fiction and the way in which art often paves the way for the sublime. Works of art play a vital role in many of his tales, for example, the perturbing illustrations of cannibalism in "The Picture in the House" and the ghastly paintings on display in "Pickman's Model" (1926). The power that art exerts over the imaginative faculties is also routinely exploited, as with the archaic ivory bust in "The Temple" (1920) and the exotic tiara in "The Shadow Over Innsmouth" (1931). In Lovecraft's world art is ever-present, whether working as a stimulant, a harbinger of doom, or a conduit for accessing previously-unimagined realities beyond the sphere of known human experience. Like the evocative settings and grotesque creatures, art is used to foster a sense of engagement with potent and destabilizing forces.

Bradley A. Will argues that Lovecraft employs the Kantian sublime to establish a "sense of awe and wonder which makes his stories so powerful" (20). Yet Vivian Ralickas, in focusing on "the centrality of the human subject" as a critical component of the sublime, maintains that Lovecraft's cosmicist, and thus *anti-humanist*, stance is entirely at odds with sublimity (367). She makes the case that "In the morally sterile world of Lovecraft's tales, the knowledge characters gain unveils the fallacy of their humanistic notions of subjectivity, permanently barring them from experiencing the Burkean and Kantian sublimes" (387). Sublimity is thus essentially concerned with the human subject's reaction to a transformative, uplifting experience that verifies that subject's position of "supremacy over nature" (364). In contrast, Lovecraft depicts events that not only establish the complete insignificance of humanity within the wider universe, but also, in so doing, privilege the phenomena over the response of the protagonist. However, despite the incongruity Ralickas identifies, I suggest that Lovecraft draws on the sublime in the same way that he draws on the Gothic. In other words, he subverts them both in order to develop, and thus delineate, his own brand of horror fiction. As Will recognizes, much of the content and ambience of Lovecraft's tales depends upon the impressions and mental states associated with sublimity. Inevitably, then, through the kinds of fictional strategies identified above, Lovecraft undoubtedly makes use of the sublime even if aspects of this theory might ultimately be said to conflict with his own philosophy.

Challenges of Adaptation

Having established ways in which Lovecraft's original fictions connect to sublimity, I will now turn attention to exploring how these tales find expression in other types of media. His fictional domain, beset as it is by interdimensional activities and the monstrous creatures roused as a result, has been vividly evoked through his own idiosyncratic, strikingly extravagant prose. Designated by Stephen King as "the twentieth-century horror story's dark and baroque prince" (44), Lovecraft wrote fiction characterized by lengthy descriptive passages, strongly detailed and gripping, that escalates to a fever pitch of intensity with the move towards its narrative climax. Architectural features, historical anecdotes, geographical characteristics, regional detailing, and a profusion of adjectives all contribute to a textual excess that helps shape his distinctive brand of horror. Recalling Botting's remarks about the relationship between the Gothic and the sublime, it can be seen that the excessive style of the language helps shore up a sense of the excessive nature of the sublime phenomena this language is used to convey.

It is thus important to consider the implications of adapting this prose for new and fundamentally different media forms.[3] The numerous cinematic adaptations of Lovecraft's work in the decades since his death stand as testament to the deep-seated impulse for adaptation and also to its concomitant challenges.[4] In his Preface to *Lurker in the Lobby: A Guide to the Cinema of H. P. Lovecraft*, S. T. Joshi makes the following observations about attempts to adapt Lovecraft for cinema: "Many have asserted that Lovecraft's tales are 'unadaptable' to film or any other medium; and in a sense that is true, if one assumes that such an adaptation should mechanically seek to duplicate the effect of the written word on the screen. Such an undertaking is futile from the start" (7). Joshi thus highlights the belief that unquestioningly faithful adaptations of Lovecraft's work are nigh-on impossible to accomplish. Why should this be the case? Julian Petley's chapter "The Unfilmable? H. P. Lovecraft and the Cinema" seeks to elucidate by identifying the following challenges to adaptation inherent within these fictions:

> short on "characters" (especially female ones) and "action" as conventionally understood, no sex (except occasionally—and only implied—in the back-story, and then between degraded humans and unspeakable monstrosities), heavy on description, sometimes only a few pages in length, underpinned by a complex and not always coherent mythos, and informed by a philosophy of the bleakest pessimism, their cinematic potential is not immediately obvious. Even ardent Lovecraft aficionados agree that his work is not easy to adapt [43].

Though Joshi and Petley both indicate the difficulties of *literally* realizing Lovecraft's unique visions in new media forms, their assessments also signal the importance often attached to capturing something of the *mood*—what Will describes above as a "sense of awe and wonder" (20)—produced by reading his fiction.

Mood is certainly crucial to the Gothic as a genre and a significant feature of Lovecraft's suffocating tales of cosmic dread. Following Botting, it can be seen that a key component of conjuring up and sustaining a typically Gothic mood is the deployment of excess. Writing on comics and the Gothic, Julia Round notes that "gothic narratives often rely upon notions of excess" (76) through their recourse to style, structure or theme. She contends that

> comics offer an *excess of style* as words, images, emanata, and other icons are presented as idiosyncratic hand-drawn devices.... Competing perspectives are offered (both extra- and intradiegetic speakers and dis/embodied visuals) and swift plunges through diegetic layers (for example into flashback or fantasy) further contribute to the excess of the page [76].

In this way, Round forges a link between the Gothic genre and the medium of comics courtesy of their shared predilection for such conventions as convoluted narrative strategies and extremes of subject matter, as well as for the use of ornate, perhaps over-wrought, assemblages of words and images. Integral, then, to both the Gothic and to comics, the invocation of mood is also central to Lovecraft's fiction, bound up as it is with the portrayal of extraordinary events and monstrous beings.

Despite the adaptation challenges identified here, the fact remains that Lovecraft's tales are driven by anxious escalations towards awe-inspiring, even paradigm-shifting moments, and this means that an emphasis on *description* is paramount. Michel Houellebecq echoes Petley's claim that this fiction is strongly descriptive in remarking that Lovecraft eschews characterization entirely, asking no more of his gentleman-scholar protagonists than that they bear witness to the astonishing events played out in the tales (68). Essentially, for Houellebecq, "Lovecraft's characters function as silent, motionless, utterly powerless, paralyzed observers" (69). Because the tales are first and foremost concerned with these astounding moments of display, their primary goal is to depict observable phenomena, phenomena that are capable of expression in written or in visual form. The sights that these protagonists are obliged to perceive—monsters, immense, rugged landscapes, and awesome architectural forms—are *events*, *things* and *creatures* that, with regard to their nature and their effect upon those who behold them, encapsulate the kind of excess discerned by critics such as Round and can be said to constitute experiences of the sublime. While adapting them has certainly proved to be challenging in terms of realizing specific details, the stress Lovecraft places on *describing* them in the first place means that his tales hold a strong sense of visual appeal that makes them seem ripe for adaptation into a visual medium.

Given the obstacles to cinematic representation posed by Lovecraft's fiction, yet mindful of its potential for visual treatment, I suggest that comics—defined by a matchless union of words and images intrinsic to the form—offer an appropriate medium through which to appreciate Lovecraft's visions of Gothic sublimity. In both *Understanding Comics* (1993) and *Reinventing Comics* (2000), Scott McCloud calls attention to the power of this medium to stir the imagination. Similarly, Will Eisner, in his seminal study *Comics & Sequential Art*, explains that the "format of the comic book presents a montage of both word and image, and the reader is thus required to exercise both visual and verbal interpretive skills" (8). Further, it seems that comics lend themselves especially well to horror, as Round argues that the interaction between their formal properties, e.g., artistic style and what she terms "visual/verbal play," gives rise to a "sense of gothic excess" (77). Comics thus constitute a forum in which readers can engage with images of horror, monstrosity, and sublimity while still drawing on their own imaginative abilities. Following McCloud's claim that in comics "the reader's imagination makes still pictures come alive" (*Reinventing Comics* 1), and bearing in the mind the capacity for retention of the original prose,[5] a case can be made for comics as an example of a visual medium that is conducive to an appreciation of Lovecraft's remarkable visions as well as to the intense emotional and psychological states to which they give rise.

Comics and Sublimity

From their earliest years, comics have readily provided a home for narratives of violence, monstrosity, and various types of horror. Putting the challenges of adaptation aside, it can be seen that the form enjoys an exceptional power to inspire the mind's eye that lends it well to genres bound up with atmosphere and mood such as the Gothic. In the sections that follow, I will turn attention to three examples of SelfMadeHero's recent adaptations of original Lovecraft tales for comics, revealing how they facilitate, even *demand*, a degree of creative input even as they offer up an abundance of provocative imagery.

"Dagon" (1917)

Only a few pages in length, the claustrophobic "Dagon" is the tale of a supercargo who, having evaded incarceration by the German troops that commandeered his vessel, spends several days at the mercy of the elements—adrift "upon the heaving vastnesses of unbroken blue" (1)—before finally becoming marooned in the remotest part of the Pacific. In terms reminiscent of the unsettling effect of the sublime, Lovecraft sets the scene for the unprecedented horror to come by describing the "sinister quality" and "barren immensity" (2) of the "slimy expanse of hellish black mire" (1) in which this man finds himself immured. The protagonist conjectures that this fantastic environment must be the result of volcanic activity that had brought part of the ocean floor to the surface, thus "exposing regions which for innumerable millions of years had lain hidden under unfathomable watery depths" (2). Here, the extreme wildness of the setting—not only is it situated far from known, civilized space, but it is also cast as fundamentally *primitive*—and the isolation of the narrator conspire to evoke an air of vulnerability. Likewise, the graphic adaptation quickly infuses its content with an atmosphere of menace through the use of *chiaroscuro*. A succession of panels that position the tiny figure of the protagonist against shadowy vistas of rugged, moonlit crags further augments his helplessness within the context of this sublime landscape.

On exploring this unprepossessing terrain, Lovecraft's narrator comes across the awesome spectacle of a "gigantic piece of stone" adorned with carvings of figures "supposed to depict men ... disporting like fishes in the waters of some marine grotto, or paying homage at some monolithic shrine" (4). A brief sequence of panels conveys the appearance of this sculpture through a mixture of captions and pictures while also generating an air of suspense about more tangible horrors to come. McCloud suggests that the most common category of combining words and images in comics is the "interdependent," whereby "words and pictures go *hand in hand* to convey an idea that neither could convey *alone*" (*Understanding Comics* 155), such as a panel picturing someone pointing to an image of something and asking, "What's this?" This technique is in evidence here as details of the monolith give way to a tantalizing glimpse of something *biological*. No longer purely figurative, the sublimity of the backdrop abruptly yields to the sublimity of the monster that inhabits it. The panel prior to that which reveals the repugnant Dagon of the title shows a close-up of a webbed, clawed hand accompanied by a caption stating, "Then, suddenly, I saw it" (Lockwood and Duke 5). The sight of this appendage whets the appetite even as the wording helps the reader infer the significance of the fragmentary image to the story as a whole.

Indeed, the discovery of the statue foreshadows a horrifying vision of monstrosity: "Vast, Polyphemus-like, and loathsome, it darted like a stupendous monster of nightmares to the monolith, about which it flung its gigantic scaly arms, the while it bowed its hideous head and gave vent to certain measured sounds" (Lovecraft, "Dagon" 5). The protagonist of the tale and the comic both testify to the overpowering impact of this sight by reflecting, "I think I went mad then" (Lovecraft, "Dagon" 5 and Lockwood and Duke 4). In depicting this beast, although to some extent prescribing the nature of its physical appearance, the graphic version of the tale nevertheless exploits the power of comics as an art-form. Commenting on the form's propensity for stylistic excess, Round explains that comics can "immerse us in the story by giving us the literal point of view of a character [and] show us a scene from a physically impossible viewpoint" (86). Here the monster is shown simultaneously from very different perspectives—from a distance that reveals its scale, as well as from a far closer position that shows its visage in a disconcerting level of detail—in a montage that enhances the sublime horror of the narrator's predicament.

Framing techniques also foster a sense of engagement with themes of sublimity. For Eisner, the choice of frame has the power to "heighten the reader's involvement with the narrative" (46). The page on which this behemoth makes its appearance in the comic dispenses with panels entirely. Various images of the creature looming over the stunned protagonist intermingle with a panorama of stars, planets, and other astral bodies that illumines the night skies enshrouding the latter. McCloud discerns that "borderless" panels of this type can take on an intriguing "timeless quality" (*Understanding Comics* 102). The protagonist's placement at the foot of this same scene—in bed at the San Francisco hospital where he finds himself after fleeing the island—suggests, in pictorial form, that these overwhelming sights, with all their connotations of cosmic awe, linger with him long after his return to civilization. Indeed, both this version and the original tale are framed by a hopeless sense that this man will soon take his own life out of fear of ever glimpsing this grotesque being again. It can be seen, then, that formal properties ingrained within comics work to convey the thematic concerns of Lovecraft's original tales.

At the Mountains of Madness (1931)

Like "Dagon," *At the Mountains of Madness* (1931) exploits the Gothic promise of an unimaginably remote setting in order to tell a tale replete with outré horrors, though it is far more ambitious in terms of its narrative scope and its implications for humanity. The plot divulges a geology expedition made to Antarctica by Miskatonic University. From the outset, Lovecraft seeks to ensconce the reader in a mindset apropos of the sublime by relating the crew's "thrill of excitement at beholding a vast, lofty, and snow-clad mountain chain ... an outpost of the great unknown continent and its cryptic world of frozen death" (249). Another way of blending words and images in comics takes the form of "word specific combinations," when pictures simply serve to illustrate the text (*Understanding Comics* 153). Abridging the original prose helps to preserve the letter of Lovecraft's fiction whilst still permitting new interpretations of his stimulating subject matter through art. Examples of "word specific" panels are rife in this graphic novelization, as they are in the text-heavy *Lovecraft Anthologies*. Considering the importance of Lovecraft's prose to creating mood, it is noteworthy that the adaptation process here has sought to adhere closely to the source material. Comprehensive text-boxes, strongly reminiscent of the original novella in describing a "cryptic realm of ice and death" (Culbard 7) and a "vast and lofty snow-clad outpost of the great unknown" (8), are thus illustrated by an image of ships approaching the forbidding Antarctic Circle, followed by a stark, awe-inspiring vista of snowy peaks that covers half the height of the page and extends across a double-page-spread.

This sense of vulnerability to Nature's might is heightened when Professor Lake heads up a sub-expedition to the northwest of the main base. A hitherto unsuspected threat is introduced as a result. When all communications cease, a rescue party led by the narrator, Professor Dyer, flies out to Lake's camp only to be shocked by evidence of recent carnage involving both the human and canine members of the splinter group. This adaptation utilizes a Spartan *ligne claire* artistic style that excels at conveying a Lovecraftian "sense of restraint" (Murray and Corstorphine 182). In such a context, the panel showing the dismembered bodies of a man and a dog laid out side-by-side on a table inside one of the tents is shocking in its goriness—brought out further by the use of a deep, red color—and unsettling in its approximation of the dissections carried out earlier by Lake's faction on the strange specimens they found near their camp. Desperate to make some sense of this, and recalling Lake's early wireless transmissions about a nearby mountain range "surpassing anything in imagination" (Culbard 26), Dyer—along with graduate student Danforth—seeks to witness this geographical marvel for himself. On their arrival at the foot of these mountains, the technique of bleeding—"when a panel runs off the edge of the page" (*Understanding Comics* 103)—expresses a moment of sublimity akin to those found in nineteenth-century art, as with paintings by the likes of Théodore Géricault and Caspar David Friedrich in which human figures are dwarfed by their placement in landscapes of might and grandeur.

As the pair descends into the ruins of the huge, prehistoric city they dis-

Danforth and Dyer overshadowed by the sublime Antarctic landscape in *At the Mountain of Madness*.

cover on their journey, bleeding is used once again to illustrate the enormity of this cityscape and intensify the protagonists' amazement. Delving into the deepest recesses of the metropolis, they find a series of murals that lays bare its history—it was built by a civilization of extraterrestrials that created human life essentially by accident. Disturbed from their centuries-long slumber by Lake, members of this race were responsible for the tragedy at the camp. Whereas the scale and the wildness of the mountains are certainly overwhelming, the sensation of the sublime here seems to be largely engendered by the city. Brady indicates that certain types of architecture are capable of provoking sublimity and Lovecraft was certainly receptive to the capacity of the cityscape to rouse the imagination. These towering, alien edifices, symbolic as they are of the ultimate insignificance of humanity, exemplify the quality of cosmic wonder so characteristic of Lovecraft's fiction.

Beyond the marvelous city itself, however, Lovecraft also incorporates monstrous beings to amplify the mood of this tale, and the graphic novel aims to render these visually. Here, the comic may well fall prey to the usual charges leveled at adaptations of Lovecraft's inventions—the frightful "viscous masses" (Lovecraft, *At the Mountains of Madness* 300) known as shoggoths seem exceptionally hard to translate into visual media—though bleeding at least helps to convey something of the shock and repulsion felt by Dyer and Danforth as one of these shapeless, many-eyed creatures almost fills a page that shows the men fleeing from it through the depths of the ancient city. Once more, the sight of such a monster is linked to emotional and psychological extremes akin to madness as Dyer repeatedly testifies that his young companion has been irrevocably traumatized by their shared experience of the sublime.

"Pickman's Model" (1926)

The thrust of the nightmarish "Pickman's Model" concerns the narrator's involvement with Richard Upton Pickman, an artist spurned by the Boston Art Club for his morbid choice of subject matter. In keeping with the Gothic tradition, setting is as crucial to this tale as it is to those previously discussed. The difference here, however, is that the monstrosity is to be found within one of America's biggest and most historic cities and is thus especially disconcerting in its proximity to humanity. Horror is specifically associated with the oldest parts of the city, extolled by Pickman as sites "overflowing with wonder and terror and escapes from the commonplace" (Delano, Pugh and Haward 6). As Pickman's sole confidante, the storyteller accompanies the artist to his quarters in colonial North End, where he is subjected to a private viewing of the "madness and monstrosity" (7) that Pickman seeks to capture in his art. Copious in number and prodigious of talent, these canvases prove so perturbing partly because of their content and partly because they run the gamut from scenes of long-gone horrors to entirely contemporary pictures of torment and devastation. The ghoulish tour culminates with the "colossal, nameless blasphemy" (9) that Pickman, with fiendish glee, unveils on an easel when they plumb the depths of his subterranean studio.

"Pickman's Model" is an interesting choice for a comics adaptation. Though it is concerned chiefly with outlining the nature and effects of inherently *visual* material in the form of paintings, it is obvious that the original tale aims to excite the imagination without recourse to illustration. As is so often the case, Lovecraft is at pains to titillate as much as possible by explaining that Pickman's art is "quite beyond the power of words to classify" (Lovecraft, "Pickman's Model" 83). Yet, even with its wealth of illustrative imagery, this adaptation permits active engagement from the reader and instills impressions of sublimity. Arguing that the "*heart* of comics lies in the space *between* the panels" (*Reinventing Comics* 1), McCloud ascribes much of the stimulating power of the medium to its capacity for *closure*. This refers to the process of observing only parts but seeing a whole, like interpreting the series of still images on a film strip as one long tale of continuous motion. McCloud elaborates thus:

> All in all, [comics] is an *exclusively visual representation. Within* these panels, we can only convey information *visually*. But *between* panels, none of our senses are required at all. Which is why *all* of our senses are engaged! Several times on every page the reader is *released*—like a *trapeze artist*—into the open air of *imagination* ... then *caught* by the outstretched arms of the *ever-present next panel*! Caught *quickly* so as not to let the reader *fall* into *confusion* or *boredom*. But is it possible that closure can be so managed in some cases—that the reader might learn to *fly*? [*Understanding Comics* 89–90; ellipses McCloud's].

In this way, the presence of *gaps*, such as those that link the panels, enables readers to fashion a personal and creative response, even in the presence of prescribed imagery. Closure here interacts with other methods employed by comics to express the sublimity of viewing Pickman's art.

As in *At the Mountains of Madness*, the revelatory moment of "Pickman's Model," centering on the loathsome figure, is enhanced when the panels of the preceding pages give way to a full-page spectacle in which bleeding puts across the shock and awe prompted by Pickman's compelling portrait of monstrosity. No distinct picture of the monster is actually provided; instead, we are shown the narrator, in profile, as he gazes at the picture on the easel. Round avers that comics often deploy "non-realistic seeing ... for example to convey emotion or demonstrate state of mind" (85) and such a technique is in evidence here. This scene, in withholding a clear representation of the beast in its entirety, enjoins the reader to extrapolate his or her own vision of the monster from a cacophony of fragmented images of huge, glaring eyes and jaws brimming with immense, cruelly-curved teeth.

The shift from calm, orderly panels to a frenzied assault on the senses makes manifest, in pictorial form, the narrator's progression from a rational world to one suddenly thrown into chaos and terror. Flanked by small panels offering extreme close-ups of the narrator's horrified response, this scene—in conjunction with staccato bursts of terse captions that serve to heighten the sense of panic—draws on the power of closure to both communicate the protagonist's reaction to this encounter with sublimity and to kindle a similarly-destabilizing impression of awe in the reader. Even the artwork in the more accessible part of the house is singled out for its "madness and monstrosity," but this is a revelation—the quintessence of sublimity in its facility to induce such repugnance and fright—which "might well have driven an excitable man to madness" (Lovecraft, "Pickman's Model" 87). Despite the potentially contentious use of imagery, as opposed to mere prose, to communicate the horror of this scenario, this adaptation draws on the unique power of comics to create a gripping version of this tale.

Conclusion

Inspired by the novel insights gained from forays into science and the arts, as well as by travels to fascinating new places, H. P. Lovecraft drew on a variety of visual sources that came to shape and pervade his distinctive fictional realm. Many of these sources, bound up as they are with scale and infinity, and with feelings of terror and awe in the face of sheer majesty, are characteristic of that set of circumstances known as the sublime. Lovecraft's thematic stress on the existence of spheres beyond known human experience, in conjunction with his narrative emphasis on monstrous creatures, wild settings, and destabilizing art, confirms that sublimity can be distinguished as an intrinsic feature of his mindset and one that found frequent expression in his fiction. Cinema has often struggled to encapsulate these literary creations with real fidelity, yet they are inherently *descriptive* and have given rise to countless, often heavily visual, interpretations and reinterpretations of his fiction notwithstanding. Comics, as a visual medium concerned with stimulating the imagination as much as it is with mere display, provides a natural home for Lovecraft's vividly-rendered visions of madness and monstrosity. In examining case studies of faithful adaptations, this essay reveals ways in

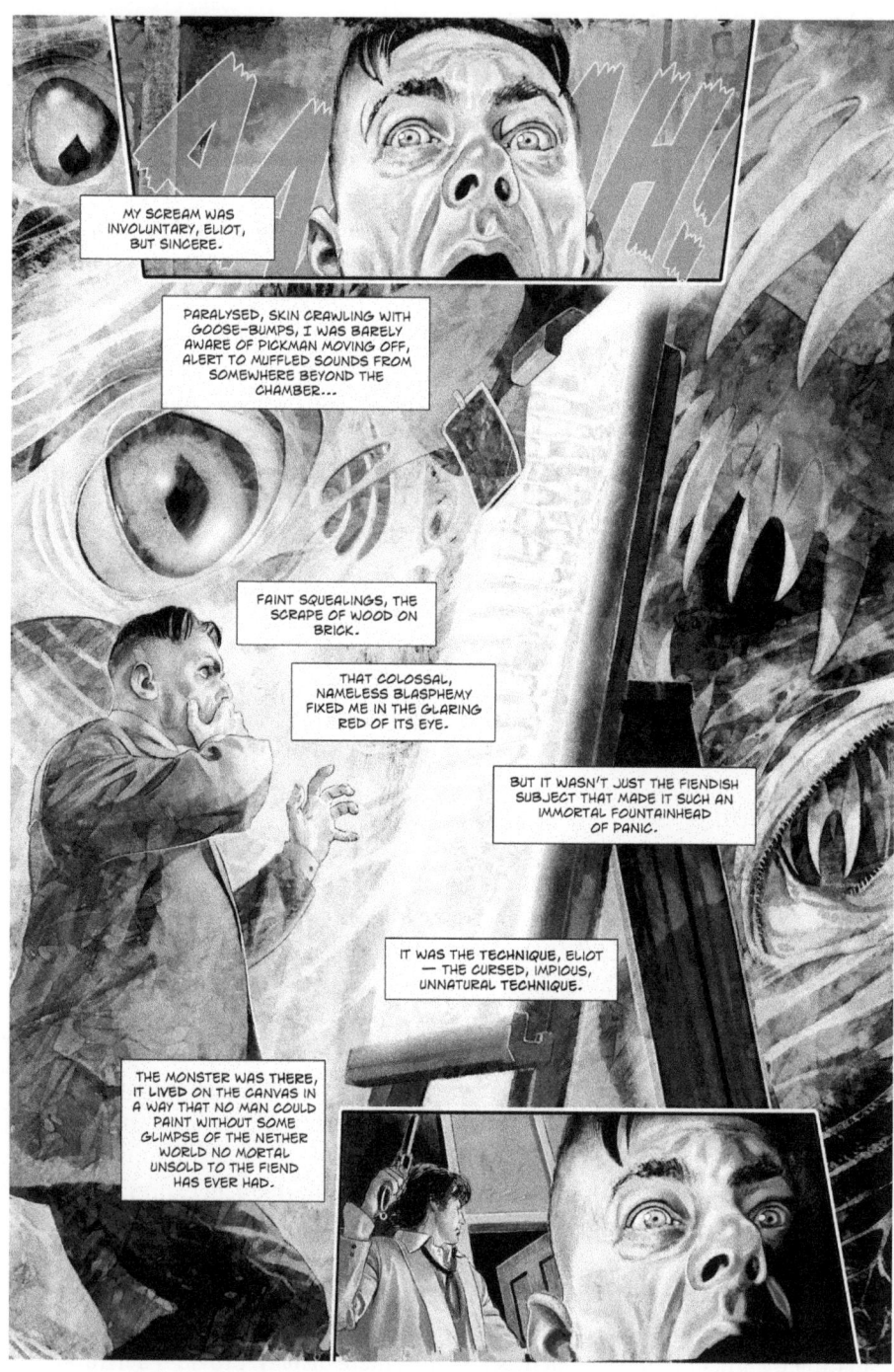

The eponymous horror escapes the confines of the page in "Pickman's Model."

which formal properties of comics nurture a creative response and thus help breathe new life into Lovecraft's Gothic tales of sublimity.

Notes

1. At the time of writing, scholarship on Lovecraft and comics is still relatively scarce. "Co(s)mic Horror" by Chris Murray and Kevin Corstorphine in *New Critical Essays on H. P. Lovecraft* (2013), edited by David Simmons, offers a critical overview of those comics that might be considered more or less Lovecraftian from the 1940s right through to the twenty-first century. Matthew J. A. Green examines re-imaginings of Lovecraft's work for comics in "A Darker Magic: Heterocosms and Bricolage in Moore's Recent Reworkings of Lovecraft" in his own edited collection *Alan Moore and the Gothic Tradition* (2013). It should be noted that both of these essays are very recent, and there are signs that this is an area of burgeoning critical interest. For instance, forthcoming publications edited by Jeffrey A. Weinstock and Carl H. Sederholm—entitled *The Age of Lovecraft: Cosmic Horror, Posthumanism, and Popular Culture*, plus an accompanying special issue of *Journal of the Fantastic in the Arts*—both contain pieces on Lovecraft and comics. My own essay "Visions of Monstrosity: Adapting Lovecraft for the Comics Arts" is due for publication in the latter.

2. For example, astronomy was to exert an especially profound effect on Lovecraft's understanding of the universe and the place of the human race within it. He devoted much time to gazing through telescopes at the solar system, and a letter of 1924 reveals that his first encounter, via his astronomical studies, with "the myriad suns and worlds of infinite space," in revealing the smallness of Earth in relation to the vastness of the universe, was one of the "most poignant sensations of [his] existence" (Lovecraft, "To Edwin Baird" 302).

3. As Brian McFarlane indicates, the field of adaptation studies has long been cognizant of the issue of fidelity to source material (8–9). Building on this debate, Linda Costanzo Cahir explains that adapting literature for cinema is essentially a process of translation, one that involves "moving the language of literature—made up of words—into the language of film" (14), and thus stresses the *complexity* of prioritizing fidelity (15). Scholars of adaptation have come to critique the fidelity model (Hutcheon 16), yet the urge to give life to compelling fictional universes, perhaps especially those with the longevity of Lovecraft's creations, with something approximating true fidelity does seem to persist.

4. Murray and Corstorphine extend cautionary arguments about failed attempts to express literary texts in visual media to comics with their claim that "visual media, such as film and comics, often cannot resist the temptation ... to show the creature, and in doing so, break the mood by presenting creatures that are unconvincing at best, and ridiculous at worst" (172).

5. Although he swiftly dismisses the potential of both comics and films to do justice to Lovecraft's works, Don G. Smith uses his catalogue of Lovecraftian texts in popular culture to acknowledge and commend the fact that comics adaptations (though his survey concludes with a publication from 2003) often quote Lovecraft directly. See *H. P. Lovecraft in Popular Culture: The Works and Their Adaptations in Film, Television, Comics, Music and Games*, 137–138.

Works Cited

Botting, Fred. *Gothic*. London: Routledge, 1996. Print.
Brady, Emily. *The Sublime in Modern Philosophy: Aesthetics, Ethics, and Nature*. New York: Cambridge University Press, 2013. Print.

Bukatman, Scott. "The Artificial Infinite: On Special Effects and the Sublime." *Alien Zone II: The Spaces of Science Fiction Cinema*. Ed. Annette Kuhn. London: Verso, 1999. 249–275. Print.
Burke, Edmund. *A Philosophical Enquiry into the Origin of our Ideas of the Sublime and Beautiful*. London: Routledge and Kegan Paul, 1958. Print.
Cahir, Linda Costanzo. *Literature into Film: Theory and Practical Approaches*. Jefferson, NC: McFarland, 2006. Print.
Carter, Lin. *Lovecraft: A Look Behind the Cthulhu Mythos*. Mercer Island, WA: Starmont House, 1992. Print.
Crowther, Paul. *The Kantian Sublime: From Morality to Art*. Oxford: Clarendon Press/Oxford University Press, 1991. Print.
Culbard, I. N. J. *At the Mountains of Madness: A Graphic Novel*. London: SelfMadeHero, 2010. Print.
Delano, Jamie, Steve Pugh, and Jon Haward. "Pickman's Model." *The Lovecraft Anthology: Volume II*. Ed. Dan Lockwood. London: SelfMadeHero, 2012. Print.
Eisner, Will. *Comics and Sequential Art*. Tamarac, FL: Poorhouse Press, 1985. Print.
Graham, Elaine L. *Representations of the Post/Human: Monsters, Aliens and Others in Popular Culture*. New Brunswick: Rutgers University Press, 2002. Print.
Houellebecq, Michel. *H. P. Lovecraft: Against the World, Against Life*. Trans. Dorna Khazeni. London: Weidenfeld & Nicolson, 2006. Print.
Hutcheon, Linda. *A Theory of Adaptation*. New York: Routledge, 2006. Print.
Joshi, S. T. *A Dreamer and a Visionary: H. P. Lovecraft in his Time*. Liverpool: Liverpool University Press, 2001. Print.
_____. "Preface." *Lurker in the Lobby: A Guide to the Cinema of H. P. Lovecraft*. Eds. Andrew Migliore and John Strysik. Portland: Night Shade Books, 2006. 5–8. Print.
King, Stephen. *Danse Macabre*. London: Warner Books, 1993. Print.
Lockwood, Dan, and Alice Duke. "Dagon." *The Lovecraft Anthology: Volume I*. Ed. Dan Lockwood. London: SelfMadeHero, 2011. Print.
Lovecraft, H. P. *At the Mountains of Madness*. *"The Thing on the Doorstep" and Other Weird Stories*. Ed. S. T. Joshi. London: Penguin, 2001. 246–340. Print.
_____. "The Call of Cthulhu." *"The Call of Cthulhu" and Other Weird Stories*. Ed. S. T. Joshi. London: Penguin, 2002. 139–169. Print.
_____. "Dagon." *"The Call of Cthulhu" and Other Weird Stories*. Ed. S. T. Joshi. London: Penguin, 2002. 1–6. Print.
_____. "To Edwin Baird." 3 February 1924. *H. P. Lovecraft Selected Letters I: 1911–1924*. Eds. August Derleth and Donald Wandrei. Sauk City, WI: Arkham House, 1965. 294–304. Print.
_____. "To Mrs F. C. Clark." 29–30 September 1924. *H. P. Lovecraft Selected Letters I: 1911–1924*. Eds. August Derleth and Donald Wandrei. Sauk City, WI: Arkham House, 1965. 345–354. Print.
_____. "Pickman's Model." *"The Thing on the Doorstep" and Other Weird Stories*. Ed. S. T. Joshi. London: Penguin, 2001. 78–89. Print.
_____. "To Reinhardt Kleiner [sic]."16 November 1916. *H. P. Lovecraft Selected Letters I: 1911–1924*. Eds. August Derleth and Donald Wandrei. Sauk City, WI: Arkham House, 1965. 29–42. Print.
_____. *Supernatural Horror in Literature*. New York: Dover, 1973. Print.
_____. "To Vincent Starrett." 10 January 1928. *H. P. Lovecraft Selected Letters II: 1925–1929*. Eds. August Derleth and Donald Wandrei. Sauk City, WI: Arkham House, 1968. 218–222. Print.
McCloud, Scott. *Reinventing Comics: How Imagination and Technology Are Revolutionizing an Art Form*. New York: William Morrow/HarperCollins, 2000. Print.

_____. *Understanding Comics: The Invisible Art.* Northampton, MA: Kitchen Sink Press, 1993. Print.
McFarlane, Brian. *Novel to Film: An Introduction to the Theory of Adaptation.* Oxford: Clarendon Press, 1996. Print.
Murray, Chris, and Kevin Corstorphine. "Co(s)mic Horror." *New Critical Essays on H.P. Lovecraft.* Ed. David Simmons. New York: Palgrave Macmillan, 2013. 157–191. Print.
Petley, Julian. "The Unfilmable? H. P. Lovecraft and the Cinema." *Monstrous Adaptations: Generic and Thematic Mutations in Horror Film.* Eds. Richard J. Hand and Jay McRoy. Manchester: Manchester University Press, 2007. 35–47. Print.
Ralickas, Vivian. "'Cosmic Horror' and the Question of the Sublime in Lovecraft." *Journal of the Fantastic in the Arts* 18.3 (2007): 364–398. Print.
Round, Julia. *Gothic in Comics and Graphic Novels: A Critical Approach.* Jefferson, NC: McFarland, 2014. Print.
Smith, Don G. *H. P. Lovecraft in Popular Culture: The Works and Their Adaptations in Film, Television, Comics, Music and Games.* Jefferson, NC: McFarland, 2006. Print.
Will, Bradley A. "H. P. Lovecraft and the Semiotic Kantian Sublime." *Extrapolation* 43.1 (2002): 7–21. Print.

The Monster of Massification
A Serbian Film

L. Andrew Cooper

> "I can't unsee what I saw.... In many ways *Serbian Film* is like going to war.... You don't want to see *Serbian Film*. You just think you do"
> —Tex Massacre, *Bloody Disgusting*, March 18, 2010

On November 27, 2010, London newspaper *The Guardian* called Srdjan Spasojevic's *A Serbian Film* (2010) the U.K.'s "most censored film in 16 years" (Shoard 15). Until just before the "uncut" U.S. DVD release in May 2012, the English-language Internet Movie Database made the film's information accessible via cast and crew names or the Serbian-language title but not the English-language title (Gingold 8, personally verified). The tale of Angel Sala, the director of Spain's Sitges Film Festival who screened the film and subsequently faced prison for violating child pornography laws (Gingold, Carey, et al.) now travels with the film, as does the tale of the "US distributor [who] fainted as he tried to leave a screening ... hit his head on the door and ended up needing stitches," leaving a "British sales agent ... hurriedly trying to clear up the pool of blood" (Macnab). These tales of censorship, harassment, and violence experienced by exhibitors and audiences become addenda to the *Serbian Film* narrative, which concerns Milos, a retired Serbian porn star, called back to work by Vukmir, a wealthy psychologist-turned-filmmaker who claims to make artistic pornography for export. As Milos learns, Vukmir's films actually involve mixtures of sexual violation and murder. Vukmir's movies hurt people, and the tales of Angel Sala and the wounded U.S. distributor extend the point: *A Serbian Film* hurts people, too. As reviewer Tex Massacre at leading horror website *Bloody Disgusting* proclaims, the film is "like going to war" (Fig. 1). The film hurts and changes viewers who cannot

Figure 1. Milos, the film's central character, gets stamped for censorship. To represent attitudes toward the film (not necessarily the author's opinion), this image appears alongside Alec Kubas-Meyer's March 26, 2012, review at Flixist.com.

"unsee" it and are therefore likely wrong about *wanting* to see it. Indeed, my personal viewings, Kubas-Meyer's comment that he "could probably have done a shot-for-shot remake of at least 50 percent of the film from [his] movie-induced PTSD flashbacks," and other anecdotal evidence online agree with Tex Massacre: the film triggers reactions akin to trauma.

The film's infamy centers not only on the question in one newspaper article's title, "Is this the nastiest film ever made?" (Macnab), but also on the question, are people right to be afraid of it? Critics and governments have reacted as if *A Serbian Film* poses a threat because of its taboo-breaking extremity and have issued outraged calls for censorship. This reaction suggests that the movie is a monster to be contained; like many monsters, the movie hurts people, leading them into legal danger, self-harm, and troubled psyches. In the argument that follows, I use *A Serbian Film* to interrogate how a film text can transition from being *about* (representing) monstrosity to *becoming* monstrosity and to address the social and political significance of the mediated object's apparent transformative agency.

Ultimately, a hermeneutic approach reveals that the film's diegetic monstrosity is consistent with the Gothic tradition. The Serbian national Other that holds a mirror up to the globalizing Western self implicates shifts in global political and economic structures behind a relatively superficial critique of Serbian society. However, such narrative doubling—parcel to the plot of a man descending into a monstrosity opposed by the normative social self, which mirrors the very deviation it opposes—is neither new to Gothic horror nor likely to foment the outrage that *A Serbian Film*'s short life has raised, and the analysis that reveals such doubling also involves an unbalanced tendency to emphasize a monstrosity that it names Serbian.

The film's innovative monstrosity is simpler: it derives from affect. As Tex Massacre notes, "you don't want to see" it. While no film can anticipate and control the affective responses of all audience members, and thus audience members could, as censors have worried, feel sexually stimulated by its images of necro- and pedophilia, the composition and sequencing of these scenes in *A Serbian Film*, unlike their presentation in the (fictional) film Vukmir is shooting, do not emphasize the erotic. The difference between Vukmir's (fictional) film and Spasojevic's (actual) film stems from the titillation emphasized by the former and the disgust encouraged by the latter. The absence of *want* that viewers are likely to experience with *A Serbian Film* leaves little refuge from disgust. For most, watching this horror film is a horrible experience. The experience's apparent source, the distinctly *Serbian* film unleashed on unwary masses, therefore appears villainous. I contend the opposite: *A Serbian Film* returns horror to horror and conveys that experience through a politically subversive act of image-driven, taboo-shattering violence, shifting horror spectatorship's central affect from pleasurable fear to unpleasant violation, relocating villainy from a Serbian essence onto global mass media as a collective monster. Massifying (or disseminating to global masses through mediation) an affirmative connection between extreme taboo violation and pleasure, as Vukmir does, might confirm *A Serbian Film*'s villainy, but Spasojevic's film's scant pleasures deny it. Beyond representing monstrous violence, *A Serbian Film* performs violation, and the violation pushes spectators toward limits of thought where new logics emerge, such as a logic that turns experiencing *A Serbian Film*'s violation into an ethical act. *A Serbian Film*, then, has the potential to bring about sociopolitical and intellectual transformations through its interactions with audiences. However unpleasant, these transformations could serve a higher ethical end.

The Controversy: The Monstrous Movie Attacks!

Before addressing *A Serbian Film*'s push toward the new, I must note that the type of outrage surrounding the film is anything but novel. In a 1797 review of Matthew Lewis's *The Monk*, Samuel Coleridge faults the gruesome novel—which, like *A Serbian Film*, features incestuous rape and violence against children—for being too well-written, as quality adds "subtlety to a poison by the elegance of its preparation" (qtd. in Cooper, *Gothic* 50). In other words, the text is more dangerous to audiences for being well-made. Approaching, but not quite reaching Coleridge's rhetoric, A.O. Scott of *The New York Times* on May 13, 2011, remarks that "this spectacle ... is filmed, not without skill, in slick and lurid widescreen composition," using a litotic double negative and pairing "slick" with "lurid" to make any hint of compliment backhanded. Under the title "Torture or Porn? No Need to Choose," this article gives what skill it acknowledges a negative spin. Parky at the Pictures of *The Oxford Times*, January 27, 2011, gets closer to Coleridge by declaring the film "a more than capably crafted piece of torture porn," while concluding "it always feels more like a cynical exercise in exploitation than a serious political tract." For these critics, whatever *A Serbian Film*'s high quality may be worth, it isn't artistic redemption or political analysis.

The Gothic horror tradition—defined broadly to include a range from the eighteenth-century novel to the current global horror film—is coextensive with a history of "media panics" or historical moments when people have turned toward cultural texts or movements as blameworthy *causes* for normatively undesirable social phenomena. As most critics who have given *A Serbian Film* more than a passing notice acknowledge, Spasojevic's traumatizing imagery did not appear out of a film-world vacuum. Contextualized with works by Europeans Alexandre Aja, Tom Six, Gaspard Noé, Pascal Laugier, Lars von Trier, Michael Haneke, and (differently) Americans James Wan and Eli Roth, *A Serbian Film* may be one of the ghastliest offspring of the so-called "New Extremism" that has been courting controversy under that or a similar label for more than a decade. The "New" in "New Extremism" is misleading, however, and the critics who make extreme sadism these films' defining commonality are often clever enough etymologists to tie the trend—once again, back to the eighteenth century—to the Marquis de Sade. Tirdad Derakhshani offers a representative summary in his ultra-brief review of *A Serbian Film* for *The Philadelphia Inquirer* on October 15, 2010: "The political fable is about a male porn star who is paid a fortune to perform in a film he soon finds out involves more *actual* violence than anything the Marquis de Sade could have dreamed up." To contend that the atrocities of *A Serbian Film*, or any atrocity without modern technological enhancement, exceeds de Sade's imaginative grasp suggests a limited reading of de Sade (who uses thousands of pages cataloguing maximally hideous permutations of rape and murder), but Derakhshani's point is nevertheless insightful.

Tex Massacre gets to this point directly by making the first (post-disclaimer) word of his *Bloody Disgusting* review "*Salo*" (1975), Pier Paolo Pasolini's loose adaptation of de Sade's *120 Days of Sodom* (1785). Critical connections to both de Sade and Pasolini help contextualize *A Serbian Film* within film history first because they indicate Italian investment in extreme aesthetics through the 1970s and 80s, not just in *Salo*, but throughout the works of cult giants such as Dario Argento and Lucio Fulci. This phenomena is fairly consistent up through the emergence of "New Extremism," particularly if factoring in the aesthetic dialogue between Italy and Japan visible in 1990s masterpieces by Takashi Miike, Hisayasu Sato, and others, not to mention the early films of New Zealander Peter Jackson in the late 80s and early 90s. More accurate than "New Extremism," then, might be to examine a trend, with *Salo* as a *rough* starting point (note predecessors H.G. Lewis, et al.) for deeper cinematic investment in extreme aesthetics—Aesthetic Extremism, if we need capitals—in which film and other media use extreme imagery and affects to resituate morbid dimensions of nineteenth-century Aestheticism in a post–World War II, globalized context.

What makes *Salo* and *A Serbian Film* salient nodes in this more-or-less uninterrupted history of Aesthetic Extremism that recalls and reworks eighteenth-century de Sadean aesthetics is not that they embrace combinations of blood, gore, and sex—all films in the tradition do, with mainstream successes relying less on sex—but that they embrace another important dimension of de Sade: driving the repetitive use of blood, gore, and sex so far that the violence of both the imagery *and* the repetition serve critical political ends. And neither *Salo* nor *A Serbian Film* is subtle about *somehow* being political. *Salo* resets de Sade's story, which harnesses the Revolutionary energies in the disintegrating France of de Sade's time, at a villa run by Italian Fascists under Mussolini's reign. In *A Serbian Film*, Vukmir's monologues about the Serbian people (more on the monologues soon) and Milos's wife's job at the Hague (she once remarks, "Vukmir sounds like a name of one of our guys at the Hague Tribunal"), leave little doubt, if the film's title weren't clear, that the film aims at Serbian political identity.

I don't suggest that other recent extreme horror films haven't used de Sadean aesthetics to produce political ends. While I'm neither a Marxist nor a psychoanalyst, I find Fredric Jameson's premise in *The Political Unconscious* (1981) too persuasive for the idea of an apolitical film to make sense. Therefore, pace Oscar Wilde, producing aesthetics also produces politics. So *Salo* and *A Serbian Film* are in good company when they combine Aesthetic Extremism with politics, but they stand in a much smaller group because the *overtness* of political significance they associate with violent imagery gives them a specific kind of *philosophical* extremity that combines with their aesthetic-political extremity, and that specific philosophical extremity, also to be found through prose in de Sade, sets these films apart from many other brilliant extreme films of recent decades.

Pasolini and de Sade—about each of whom exists a significant body of work—are not my focus, so I will discuss them briefly, uniting them through a source Pasolini cites within *Salo*: Roland Barthes's *Sade/Fourier/Loyola* (published 1971, translated into English 1976). In this work Barthes identifies two basic "rules" that govern a "grammar" of "erotic code" emerging from de Sade's work: the second is "reciprocity," which establishes that ("with the exception of torture") the roles of violator and violated are interchangeable, and the first, and most relevant rule for *Salo* and *A Serbian Film*, is "exhaustiveness" (29–30). Despite the sprawl of de Sade's novels, they employ a fairly efficient linguistic/philosophical process that explores combinations of erotic subjects, actions, and objects until virtually all combinations—all sentences available within a closed socio-linguistic system—are exhausted. Thus in *Salo*, the narrative progresses through taboos such as kidnapping, rape, and homosexuality, working up through combinations toward coprophagia and ultimately torture and murder (Fig. 2). Similarly, *A Serbian Film* catalogs taboos, leaving few unbroken, including rape, necrophilia, pedophilia, incest, murder, and various combinations. Although neither film has the narrative

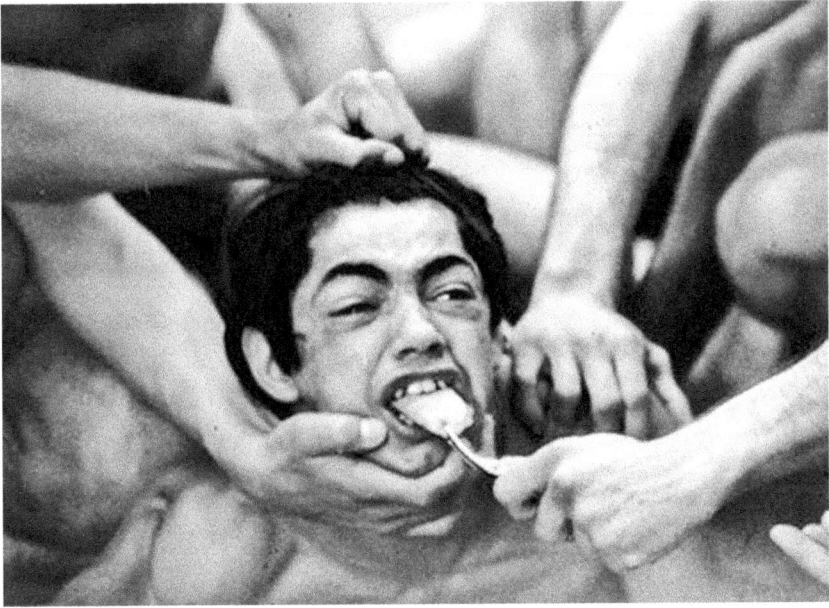

Figure 2. An (in)famous image from Pasolini's *Salo* (1975), in which the torture of a boy is the culmination of an exhaustive system of philosophically-driven political violation. The removal of the tongue suggests exhaustion of *language*, verbal and visual.

space-time that de Sade has to achieve actual exhaustion, the same principle gives structure to *Salo* and *A Serbian Film* as the expanded *Justine* (1791) or the *120 Days of Sodom*. The principle of exhaustion creates the condition of philosophical extremity that I have described: it is a systematic elimination of possibilities for signification other than death or nothingness.

This philosophical dimension might suggest allegorical significance as clearly as the overt political commentary, but in a December 13, 2010 review published in *The Guardian*, David Cox surmises, "*A Serbian Film* might well be telling us that only someone a bit daft would try to make an allegorical film" because not every moment suggests a correspondence between the literal level and figurative political reference. This reviewer takes the most catastrophic view of *A Serbian Film*'s irredeemable extremity: *because every frame can't be decoded as a political reference, the film ruins the entire medium's potential for allegory*. However, the "purest" allegorical texts have long had multiple interpretive senses according to even the most orthodox methods of medieval exegesis (Jameson 29–32). Expecting *Salo, Serbian Film*, or *any* text, much less one using a strategy that evacuates signification itself, to make mono-semantic sense in order to qualify as a work of art or a "serious political tract" places a burden on it that may lack historical precedent.

More compelling than the absurdity of expecting mono-semantic signification from a film, however, are the questions those expectations raise. In each pro-censorship review I've analyzed lies a correlation between a confrontation with *A Serbian Film* and a confrontation with the limits of film as a medium. How far can or should the medium go? Could Spasojevic, like the director-character Vukmir, transform viewers, as Vukmir transforms Milos, into murderous necrophiliac pedophiles? Can graphic images of what Milos becomes actually achieve mono-semantic allegorical significance? Are texts driven by the principle of exhaustion capable of meaning or redemption?

The Cultural Symptom Defense

The question of whether such a film can be meaningful arises repeatedly in critical responses, and the answer usually hinges on whether the film's political agenda—often articulated by the director—appears legible within the film. Thus, the film's cultural status as ban-worthy "filth" or well-crafted political art has largely relied on a hermeneutic defense: the film's detractors find nothing worth interpreting, and the film's supporters insist on reading *through* the devastating imagery. For simplicity, I will follow common usage and conflate "fable," "allegory," and "metaphor" to reflect, loosely, the *figura-*

tive: a favorite strategy of the film's defenders is to interpret its violent images as figures for the political violence of recent Serbian history, the police-state reign and genocidal campaigns of Slobodan Milosevic, NATO bombings, and periods of lawlessness when street violence and rape seemed, to some, quotidian.

Embracing the role of *auteur* rather than pornographer, Spasojevic provides one of this strategy's best articulations:

> We used pornography as the major metaphor ... because people in our region, after all those years of wars and mass manipulation and political corruption and moral collapse, we were brought to a point where we had to consider our lives as pure exploitation. We were intellectually, creatively, and psychologically raped every day from the moment we were born. This is pornography as a metaphor for real life [Brady].

Spasojevic refers to the content of *A Serbian Film*—the manipulation of Milos into situations that include the rape and murder (order optional) of girls and boys, women and men, of *any* ages—and provides direct metaphoric correspondences, a hermeneutic guide to read past the surface and locate the figurative substance found wanting by some critics.

Taking Spasojevic's advice and reading *A Serbian Film* as a metaphor for what "we," the Serbians, *are*, wraps the figurative strategy (the film figures who we are) in the historically dominant hermeneutic paradigm of film studies, particularly horror film studies: psychoanalysis, especially theories of identity, particularly such theories as they associate the formation of the individual self with the social or national self. In other words, the real-life director invites us to join fictional director, Vukmir, in approaching film as psychologists, as Marko, Milos's brother, reveals that prior to entering the world of television and film, Vukmir "worked as a psychologist in orphanages until 1992; then he moved to the Children's Program of the State TV." Indeed, Vukmir comes close to defending his (fictional) film with the same strategy Spasojevic uses to defend his (actual) film, as Vukmir describes his work as "Art! Naked art! Truth! Real people! Real sex!" For both the fictional and nonfictional directors associated with *A Serbian Film*, then, the elevation and justification of their work as art is a relation to reality, a relation achieved through figurative association. A pivotal example is that for both Spasojevic and Vukmir, the latter of whose work in orphanages sharpens the point, the idea of Serbians being figuratively fucked since childhood becomes images (and in Vukmir's film, acts) of fucking children.

This film isn't only *A Serbian Film*, but a film of Serbian-ness, and as such, it offers an identity for analysis. Scholarly analysis, like mainstream critical commentary, has been rare for *A Serbian Film*, but scholar Mark

Featherstone has accepted the offer to submit the film to psychoanalytical hermeneutics in two overlapping publications. In the first, Featherstone and co-author Beth Johnson rightly note that, from the title through the first half of the film's frequent discussions of life in Serbia, the film is "difficult to read as anything but [an explicit critique] of Serbian society" (67). Grounding their psychoanalytic reading, they draw on Slavoj Žižek's idea of "the national thing" as the aspect of Lacanian sociolinguistic identity bound up with the Real, which they succinctly describe as "the ever present hard core of who we really are and what really makes us tick" (65). With this idea in place, they argue that the film is "overloaded with brutal sex, ultraviolence, various forms of abuse and, ultimately, suicide, which reveal the true horror of the Serbian real," and so they "read *A Serbian Film* [and one other film] as traumatic representations of the Serbian national thing unleashed by Milosevic" (67–68).

The second of these publications, with Featherstone as sole author, focuses on "exploring *A Serbian Film* as a representation of post-socialist identity," particularly on "the problem of psycho-sexual identity in Serbia" (129). Perhaps detecting the "problem" of pathologizing the identities of an entire people, this later publication maintains that sadism is central to Serbian national identity but also extends the earlier piece's consideration of a significant counterargument against the idea that the film is *about* Serbian-ness at all. "The critical view," Featherstone writes, citing Tomislav Longinovic's *Vampire Nation* (2011), "of *A Serbian Film* as a horror film about the sadism of Serbian identity is, therefore, that it says nothing about the Serbs, but is rather a cynical, orientalist, construction for the western market" (130). While admitting validity in this view, Featherstone instead adopts the idea of "wound culture" from Mark Seltzer's discussion of American serial killers in order to advance his reading of Serbian national identity as traumatized (wounded) and sadistic. That this deeply disturbed identity must also confront an orientalized identity imposed by the globalizing West, or, in Feathersone's evocation of psychoanalyst Julia Kristeva, "come to terms with its own excremental past in the face of a global symbolic system that has cast it as the shit of European civilization" (131), only exacerbates the Serbians' pre-existing sadistic pathology. Thus for Featherstone, "*A Serbian Film* is not necessarily an orientalist text, but rather a social, historical, critique of what we might call 'Serbian-Being-in-the-World.' In this way noting the violent, sadistic, elements of this identity does not necessarily equate to orientalism, but rather may be employed to trace and explain a *cultural* history of violence" (135–36). Orientalism is not *necessarily* involved, and the image of identity is somehow true enough to yield to psychoanalysis that produces an accurate picture of a cultural psyche that has the explanatory force to find rational coherence in a cultural history of violence. Ultimately, Featherstone concludes with "a combination of these two positions, which recognizes both the violence of recent Serbian history and offers a critique of possible violence to come through its representation on the global market" (139). Both the monster, "the ever-present real behind Milos, Vukmir, and the sadistic quasi-state machine" (139), and that which informs and proliferates the monsters through mediation, the global market, are interdependent, mutually-implicating images of one another. The hermeneutic picture is complete.

The validity of Featherstone's reading of *A Serbian Film*'s double-edged critique is in some ways unquestionable. Just as Vukmir's history in psychology tinges his actions with psychological significance that invites analysis, so does the film critique both "the Serbian" and Western globalization. The film offers many overt nods at the critique. Early in the film, dialogue often evokes post–Serbian struggles with national selfhood. It appears casually, as when Milos's brother Marko comments, "Friends? In Serbia? You can't check them enough," a line that later becomes ironic when Marko, a policeman, rapes Milos's wife while Milos, in a drug-induced frenzy, unknowingly rapes his own pre-pubescent son. When Vukmir, capturing the rapes on camera, reveals what Milos and Marko have done (Fig. 3, left), he pronounces, "A real, happy Serbian family!" gleefully almost insisting that the Serbian national thing is, in fact, sadistically inextricable from a compulsion to violate the most sacred taboos.

Similarly direct evidence appears for a critique of Western globalization's projected fantasies of barbarism onto Serbia's excremental position in the European imaginary. The film's opening shot features a sign for "Le club Filth" (Fig. 3, right), a pointed mixture of French and English, marking French- and English-speaking (not Serbian-speaking) populations as the sources of demand that stimulate supply from poorer countries that could use support from development in *any* industry. To drive the point home, the shot turns out to be from a movie starring Milos, a DVD of which Milos's too-young son has discovered and is watching. The DVD's title, which appears on a DVD case *in English*, is *Milosh the Filthy Stud*. The very "Filth" that English-speaking countries would ban and censor was made for them, these English-language names suggest. More pointedly, as Vukmir's assistant Lejla recruits Milos from retirement, she emphasizes that Vukmir makes films "in Serbia ... only filmed here, for the foreign market." Whether or not Vukmir makes films that reveal a Serbian "national thing," Zizek's formulation of a national psyche's relation to the Lacanian Real, Vukmir makes films that reveal a global-market *thing* for the very filth it would repudiate.

This method of critiquing globalized culture through an apparent critique of Serbian culture is not new to Serbian film, according to Dusan I.

Figure 3. (Top) When Vukmir, center, reveals that Milos, left, and Marko, right, have just raped Milos's son and wife, he speaks the subtitled line "A real, happy Serbian family," announcing that the tableau is a figure for how fucked Serbian family identities truly are. (Above) *A Serbian Film*'s opening shot, which turns out to be a shot from the fictional porn film *Milosh the Filthy Stud*, features a sign for "Le club Filth," a mixture of French and English.

Bjelic. Bjelic traces an image of the "wild Balkan man," grounded in an even older tradition, through Serbian cinema of the 1990s:

> He, in contrast to the Eurotechnocrats, embodies the enemy of European civilization. He is, at the same time, truly European in that he represents a new and energized European man who uninhibitedly acts out a system of masculinity.... He expresses with passionate physicality what Eurotechnocrats emotionlessly express in economy and law [107].

Milos, manipulated by Vukmir into exploiting and destroying vulnerable people just as easily as citizens are manipulated by powerful states to exploit and destroy vulnerable populations, is a descendant of this "wild Balkan man": his taboo-breaking behavior pits him against civilization at the same time that he embodies unbridled masculinity. However, although Featherstone cites Bjelic, Bjelic's argument examines the "wild Balkan man" in order to reveal how, "taking the cliché of the 'wild Balkan man' produced by global media through their coverage of the ethnic war and the United Nations sanctions imposed upon Serbia and Montenegro, Serbian cinema succeeded in exploiting the stereotype brilliantly, using Hollywood's own language of cinema to turn the global media against itself" (103). According to this reading, the "wild Balkan man" is not a valid object for psychoanalysis, at least not one that would attain knowledge of the actual Serbian rather than of the global media that invented this fantasy of Balkan primitivism.

Halls of mirrored doubles, reflecting individual and/or social structures, are mainstays of Gothic fiction, upon which Freud based key theories of the human social psyche. That psychoanalytic hermeneutics discover a variation on this pattern in *A Serbian Film*, then, reflects a worthwhile endeavor, but in the end the outcome is unsurprising, and it downplays the film's radicalism. Furthermore, treating the film as a symptom of culture, a bias pervasive in the not-quite-over-psychoanalysis mainstream of cultural studies, tends to emphasize culture-as-patient, i.e., the culture under scrutiny as pathologized object to be investigated. However much the film may critique the West, a hermeneutic approach that makes the text, and by extension the culture that produces it, its patient, makes the text and the culture its primary objects of diagnostic critique. As Christian Metz famously writes in *The Imaginary Signifier*, "the effort towards knowing is necessarily sadistic insofar as it can only grasp its object against the grain" (15). In submitting *A Serbian Film* to a psychoanalysis that concludes it reveals the sadism of the Serbian psyche, the analyst must treat the film—and the psyche—sadistically. Psychoanalysis discovers sadism through sadism.

The No Defense Defense: Skullfucked into New Dimensions

Spasojevic, who claims, "I am no theorist," offers scattershot defenses in the interview already cited:

> This is what it was like to live in our region for the past two decades. It was stupid and brutal. We were in a stupor. This was the only way to recreate that feeling.... I believe the images defame violence. The film is about the destruction

of the family unit.... It is hell. It is not meant to be commercial. It is not meant to be popular. We were not thinking about audiences or film festivals when we made it. It is not an entertainment [Brady].

Unlike the cultural symptom defense that I cited previously, these comments emphasize not the film's potential for figurative political redemption but for the conveyance of affect. Spasojevic's "what it was like" involves not the *like* of simile but like of empathy, the sharing of phenomenological process that Featherstone alludes to, but only critiques, when commenting on "'Serbian-Being-in-the-World.'" The emphasis, as Spasojevic goes on to explain, lies with the *recreation of feeling*, and with that recreation comes no entertainment. The experience of the film, according to the director, should not be pleasurable fear, the affect that most mainstream horror films offer at the box office; it should be hell. As a hell, it needs no defense if, instead of entertaining, it puts viewers through hell.

My aim is not to side with a director who, scattershot, takes many positions that favor his film. However, I do agree that *A Serbian Film*'s innovative contribution to monstrosity is not just that it locates monstrosity on the level of national and global structures but that it inflicts that monstrosity through its exhaustive barrage of hellish affect, becoming monstrous not in the sense that it is villainous—as is Vukmir's (fictional) film that actually involves murder—but in that its performance has the potential to violate, implicate, and transform. I therefore close this section by tracing the film's performance through its controversial second half.

The first half introduces Milos and his family, features philosophical and political reflections about Serbia and pornography, and shows Milos drawn into Vukmir's disturbing world of art-porn. The second half, the onslaught, begins as Milos sits before a screen, much like *A Serbian Film*'s audience, listening to Vukmir's most frenetic political diatribe:

> Would you believe me if I told you that me and this wonderful family [of pornographers], that you are so anxious to leave, are the only warrant of this nation's survival? ... Only we can prove that this nation is alive and useful for anything.... Not pornography, but life itself! That's the life of a victim. Love, art, blood.... The flesh and soul of a victim. Transmitted live to the world who has lost all that and now is paying to watch all that from the comfort of an armchair.... We are victims, Milos. You, me, this whole nation is a victim.... Milos, you're the only one in this film who is not a victim. Allow me, as your shepherd, to show you the power of a real victim.

Vukmir projects a scene from his film. A woman gives birth. A man assists the delivery then rapes the baby (prosthetic, but shown, in close-up, while impaled in the uncut *Serbian Film*). The mother smiles (Fig. 4, left).

Figure 4. (Top) The new mother's reaction to the rape of her baby within Vukmir's film models pleasure, while (Above) Milos's reaction to the baby's rape within Spasojevic's film models disgust.

Milos stumbles from the room, like a U.S. distributor so disoriented that he injured himself exiting *A Serbian Film*. While Vukmir's frenetic introduction about his film's significance and the reaction of the mother within the film to her baby's rape suggest the production of filmic pleasure (they both model joyous reactions to the visual event), Spasojevic's scene's grinding soundtrack, disorienting angles and cuts, and emphasis not on moral outrage or anything rational but the pure disgust and disorientation of Milos (Fig. 4, right) combine to create a mirror image between what Milos is experiencing and what an audience likely experiences at the introduction of what Vukmir calls "newborn porn": shock and horror.

"Newborn porn." Vukmir says it in English. It's an export commodity. It *rhymes*. Catchy, isn't it?

It hit. On October 11, 2013, Oren Peli, architect of the multi-hundred-million dollar *Paranormal Activity* franchise (2007–2014), told *The Hollywood Reporter* that the film is "really, really horrible … I'll give you one example: There's a baby-rape scene" (THR Staff). Parky at the Pictures can't help but quote-and-condemn "the repugnant genre of newborn porn." Most critics, however, follow Peli in using "baby-rape," "baby-defilement," or a phrase other than Vukmir's brand. The distance from the language, forced particularly into English-speaking ears, established either by judging or mocking the quote, suggests time for reflection. Such time has not yet passed while Milos is stumbling from the room and Vukmir is shouting the rhyming phrase after him: the shock of the rape and of its mocking, branded-for-export name have no distance at all. "This is a new genre, Milos. Newborn porn!"

Those words ring and carry a double shock of cognitive dissonance, both in their breaking of a fundamental taboo—the rape of a newborn exploited for scopic pleasure—and in their rendering of that break as linguistically *cute* in their succinct rhyming, compounding the rape by naming it after a quality the act itself violates. Baby-rape called newborn porn short-circuits the intellectual programming of civilization-based logic: it produces a physical, neuronal shock to the body that has transformative potential for thinking, what Gilles Deleuze calls the *nooshock*:

> [W]hen movement becomes automatic [as the mind interacts with the cinematic image] the artistic essence of the image is realized: *producing a shock to thought, communicating vibrations to the cortex, touching the nervous and cerebral system directly … Automatic movement* gives rise to a *spiritual automaton* in us … [which designates] the shared power of what forces thinking and what thinks under the shock, a *nooshock* [156].

The movement-image, which includes images of affect as well as action, always carries the capacity for such shock, so aesthetic extremity is not a necessity for the phenomenon Deleuze describes. Nevertheless, an image prone to provoke an extreme reaction seems equally prone to provoke an extreme nervous vibration, perhaps a vibration resulting in disorientation like that which Milos models as a response to the screen-within-the-screen.

Milos's disorientation, and the likely disposition of most viewers, does indeed come from the power of engaging with the new: execrable as it may be, newborn porn is (one hopes) a "new genre," as Vukmir claims. Thus Vukmir has achieved what Stanley Cavell characterizes as "the task of the modern artist":

> one of creating not a new instance of his art but a new medium in it. One might think of the task as establishing a new automatism. The use of the word seems right to me for both the broad genres or forms in which art organizes itself … and those local events or *topoi* around which a genre precipitates itself [104].

In discovering the newborn within porn, Vukmir has discovered a new automatism, and with it a new form of shock that can act like a neural razor, discovering a new condition of thought inside the old just as the shocking image discovers a new medium within the old. The question overtly confronting so many viewers when they emerge from this film—how far can a medium go?—contains a hint of the newborn's disorienting uncertainty, because within this new genre, automatism, or even medium, in Cavell's view, lies an unknown frontier. Perhaps here, *anything* is thinkable.

After the confrontation with newborn porn, Milos's journey and consciousness become fragmented, as he has unknowingly ingested powerful, agency-stealing drugs while watching Vukmir's film. He returns to himself days later having flashes of disturbing memories. Following various clues, he pieces together what has happened to him (or to his body). Now, with the unlimited potentialities of the newborn, the film enters its exhaustive mode in earnest, using cuts between Milos's recovered memories and his present to reveal escalating horrors that run through a catalog of atrocities. First, he wanders into a room, and the setting triggers memories of what happened there: after informing Milos he has dosed him with the equivalent of cattle Viagra, Vukmir unleashes him to rape a woman. Egging him on with misogynistic comments, Vukmir directs him to decapitate her and continue raping her. He does. The film shows details, including the woman's blood collecting on the floor, and cuts to the same floor in the diegetic present, where Milos, in grip of the memory, vomits. He has experienced the images in his memory as the audience has experienced the images in the film, presently, and again he models response, the affective and bodily response Linda Williams marks as definitive for horror as a "body genre," the bodily demonstration of disgust, vomiting. Temporal cross-cutting performs a complete separation of Vukmir's present being and the past, agency-deprived being, and his present (model) response, vomit, aligns his present self with a horrified audience.

If hearing Vukmir comment on "the magic of rigor mortis" while the agency-deprived Milos engages in necrophilia with a decapitated corpse hasn't yet pushed viewers past their thresholds of disgust, the film still has much further to go. In the next set-piece, present Milos puts together another event not through memory but through watching DV tapes, including one of his past self that begins with his naked, unconscious body. A man approaches his body, talking to the camera as if he knows present Milos sees, and rapes his unconscious body. *A Serbian Film* cuts back and forth between the screen Milos is watching and shots of Milos's reactions, which once again display a mixture of shock and disgust but no outrage, but this time, of course, the editing pattern and the content he watches make clear that, unlike with the baby, he *identifies* with what he sees. While identification in this moment once again seems to invite psychoanalysis, it is less a diagnostic form of psychoanalysis than a phenomenological psychoanalysis, such as Carol Clover's *Men, Women, and Chain Saws* exemplifies by demonstrating that viewers of some horror films are capable of identifying with films both sadistically and masochistically either alternately or simultaneously. Such identifications would create sadistic and masochistic experiences as dimensions of spectatorship. When *A Serbian Film* opens for identification, however, it leaves no point of sadistic entry into the violence: the direct perpetrator of the most violence, Milos, is always a victim, always agency-deprived at the moment of past horrific action, a being separate from the one who passively remembers or observes in the present. The perpetrating Milos of the past is a figure with whom the present one can identify, but only as past Milos figures complete lack of subjectivity, an identity with no interior, a filmic image. His experience of perpetration involves no will or culpability, and it appears in *A Serbian Film* only filtered through the pain of remembering or of delayed, mediated witnessing. Vukmir lies about Milos escaping victimization, but he does his best to make his argument about universal victimization true.

Milos's exhaustive narrative journey of victimizing one-upmanship culminates (arguably) with the event to which I've already alluded: Milos finally remembers that, in his drugged stupor, Vukmir tricked him into raping his son right by his brother Marko, who was raping Milos's wife. When Vukmir reveals the act by pulling hoods off the heads of the rape victims, a final battle results in the deaths of Marko, Vukmir, and Vukmir's crew. One of the crew, a bald man who has always appeared in sunglasses, loses his glasses in the struggle. The man is missing an eye and has a large ocular cavity behind a mound of tissue (Fig. 5). Milos, enraged and drugged, has an enormous erection. With several close-up shots leaving no doubt about what happens, Milos skull-fucks him to death.

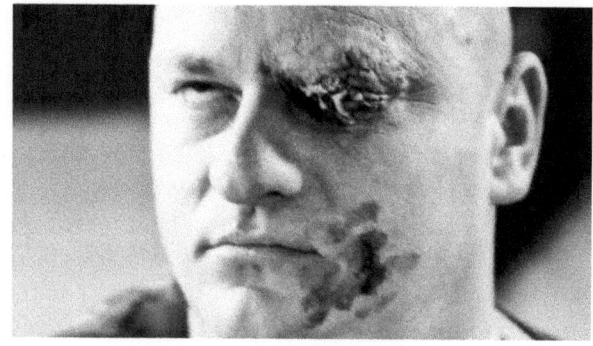

Figure 5. The eye is the entryway to the skull.

While skullfucking is not a new concept, its extreme visualization in such a political context once again pushes against the edges of the medium, threatening to spawn something new. The film has fucked with the limits of genre, and it has fucked with the limits of thought.

It has, in short, fucked with your head.

The Monster of Massification and the Ethics of Masochism

I have claimed that *A Serbian Film* closes off most avenues of sadistic gratification (except maybe the skullfucking itself, which is a cathartic revenge) by making Milos a victim even as he perpetrates the most heinous acts, but I have neglected a major avenue of sadistic experience in not considering Vukmir as a candidate for monstrous identification. As the mastermind manipulating Milos and directing the snuff porn, he is the Gothic villain of the piece, is he not?

No. Vukmir has a Byronic quality, a bombastic, romantic self-presentation that prompts the more pragmatic Milos to describe him as "some kind of artist-philosopher." But when push comes to shove, the Gothic monster *does* something. Vukmir tells others to do horrible things, but in the end, that's all he does: talk. Unlike his friend in sunglasses, who gets a momentous send-off, his death is pathetic, as even having his head easily bashed in can't stop his prattling about the higher cinematic significance of the real-life slaughter

Figure 6. Vukmir is too pathetic to be a monster. Dying, he says, "That's it, Milos. That's the cinema," still incapable of stopping his theoretical prattling despite the carnage around him.

surrounding him (Fig. 6). Hitler talked, too, but his monstrosity stems from his charismatic, synecdochal relation to the Nazi Party. Intensely private, rather than charismatically public and almost dandyish in self-presentation, Vukmir is neither Hitler nor Milosevic, and he kills no one we see. By himself he is insufficient to be a monstrous figure for sadistic identification, as he needs a vast apparatus, both human and technological, to turn his talk, his *direction*, into violence. Maybe the "it," rather than the national thing, again does not require hermeneutic decoding: it is, as Vukmir claims, the cinema. To riff on a saw, when it hurts people, the medium is the monster. In creating the demand for experiences of Serbian hell, global mass media that would displace monstrosity onto Serbia *and revel in it*, not a sadistic Serbian unconscious, stand out as a collective monster.

The film's denouement underscores Vukmir's irrelevance and the monstrosity of mass media. Demoralized and traumatized, Milos takes his wife and son home, where they huddle together in bed, and Milos, firing one shot, commits family suicide. But that is not the end. After a fade to black, light comes up on their home and bodies. A three-man crew enters. The Western-dominated global mass media's demand for images of Serbian atrocity is powerful enough not to make Vukmir immortal but to make the apparatus that has converted his systematically exhaustive butchery into economic and cultural capital continue operating independently from the lives and deaths of individuals. Neither Milos's murder of Vukmir nor his suicide escapes systemic exploitation; even in death, he and his family

Figure 7. A crew arrives to prove that the global mass media exploitation that begins at birth need not end at death. The director, center, speaks *A Serbian Film*'s final line, "Start with the little one," while the actor, left, unzips his pants, and the cinematographer, right, sets up *A Serbian Film*'s final shot: the huddled corpses of Milos and his wife Marija, with their son Petar between them.

will continue to be raped on camera (Fig. 7). The monster of massification that exploits without regard to human boundaries is a monster of globalization as well, and the source of the experience of hell that *A Serbian Film* offers is this monster. If the film is an assaultive political weapon, global mass media are the assaulter, and if the film's aim is to reorient people politically, the affects resulting from assault generally do not involve positive associations with the assaulter. The film conveys that the monster of massification is that which has turned Serbia into "the shit of European civilization."

The difference between Vukmir's (fictional) film and Spasojevic's (actual) film is precisely the smile on the face of the new mother in Fig. 4: Vukmir, as a cog in the global mass media machine, revels in shit, while Spasojevic puts shit on display and frames it with disgust. To experience the film as hell rather than entertainment, while unpleasant in the moment, is to receive the experience of hell that opens up new dimensions of thinking that can, with release and time, result in productive pleasures as well. The thinking opened runs through the violence of the recent Serbian past while offering self-reflexive challenges to preconceptions current in global mass media. Whether or not *A Serbian Film* matches the actual experience of a Serbian citizen, experiencing the film challenges constructions of Serbianness that much of the world may not be aware of. By denying sadistic identification with imagery that many people can only describe as sadistic, the film also opens the paradoxical possibility that, instead of becoming its hermeneutic analysts, sadistically, viewers can and should *submit* to its sadistic imagery—masochistically—in order to receive something productive from the assault. The assault, to borrow the title from another assaultive film by Takashi Miike, provides an imprint, and masochistic acceptance of it could create empathic connections with exploited identities, connections rooted in new thinking and capable of healing ancient wounds. To get shocked into sense, our minds need a good fucking now and then.

Works Cited

"Also Showing." *The Daily Telegraph* (London) 10 Dec. 2010: FEATURES, p. 35. *Lexis-Nexis*. Web. 10 Mar. 2014.

Arata, Stephen D. "The Occidental Tourist: *Dracula* and the Anxiety of Reverse Colonization." *Victorian Studies* 33.4 (Summer 1990): 621–645. *JSTOR*. Web. 16 May 2014.

Barthes, Roland. *Sade / Fourier / Loyola*. Trans. Richard Miller. New York: Hill and Wang, 1976. Print.

Bjelic, Dusan I. "Global Aesthetics and the Serbian Cinema of the 1990s." *East European Cinemas*. Ed. Aniko Imre. New York: Routledge, 2005. 103–119. Print.

Brady, Tara. "'It is hell. It is not an entertainment.'" *The Irish Times* 9 Dec. 2010: Features p. 17. Lexis-Nexis. Web. 10 Mar. 2014.

Carey, Adam. "Political parable or perversion?; CINEMA 'I found it a particularly disgusting piece of work.'" *The Age* (Melbourne, Australia) 2 July 2011: INSIGHT, p. 20. Lexis-Nexis. Web. 10 Mar. 2014.

Cavell, Stanley. *The World Viewed, Enlarged Edition*. Cambridge: Harvard University Press, 1979. Print.

Clover, Carol. *Men, Women, and Chain Saws*. Princeton: Princeton University Press, 1992. Print.

Cooper, L. Andrew. *Dario Argento*. Urbana: University of Illinois Press, 2012. Print.

_____. *Gothic Realities*. Jefferson, NC: McFarland, 2010. Print.

Cox, David. "*A Serbian Film*: When allegory gets nasty." *Guardian Unlimited* 13 Dec. 2010. Lexis-Nexis. Web. 10 Mar. 2014.

Deleuze, Gilles. *Cinema 2: The Time-Image*. Trans. Hugh Tomlinson and Robert Galeta. Minneapolis: University of Minnesota Press, 2010. Print.

Derakhshani, Tirdad. "'Graveyard' Series: Films on the edge." *The Philadelphia Inquirer* 15 Oct. 2010: FEATURES WEEKEND, p. W20. Lexis-Nexis. Web. 10 Mar. 2014.

Featherstone, Mark. "*Coito Ergo Sum*: Serbian sadism and global capitalism in *A Serbian Film*." *Horror Studies* 4.1: 127–144. JSTOR. Web. 10 Mar. 2014.

Featherstone, Mark, and Beth Johnson. "'Ovo Je Srbija': The Horror of the National Thing in *A Serbian Film*." *Journal for Cultural Research* 16.1 (Jan. 2010): 63–79. JSTOR. Web. 10 Mar. 2014.

Gingold, Michael. "'A Serbian Film': The Controversy Continues." *Fangoria* 308 (Nov. 2011): 8. Print.

The Internet Movie Database. IMDb.com.

Jameson, Fredric. *The Political Unconscious: Narrative as a Socially Symbolic Act*. Ithaca: Cornell University Press, 1982. Print.

Kubas-Meyer, Alec. "Cinema Disturbia: *A Serbian Film* (2010)." *Flixist: Blogging Movies Daily* 26 Mar. 2012. Web. 16 May 2014.

Longinovic, Tomislav Z. *Vampire Nation: Violence as Cultural Imaginary*. Durham: Duke University Press, 2011. E-book.

Massacre, Tex. "A Serbian Film (limited)." Review. *Bloody Disgusting* 18 Mar. 2010. Web. 16 May 2014.

Macnab, Geoffrey. "Is this the nastiest film ever made?; With its mix of pornography and ultra-violence, *A Serbian Film* is genuinely disturbing, but offers more than just shock value, says Geoffrey Macnab." *Arts & Book Review* 19 Nov. 2010: FILMS p. 12. Lexis-Nexis. Web. 10 Mar. 2014.

Metz, Christian. *The Imaginary Signifier: Psychoanalysis and the Cinema*. Bloomington: Indiana University Press, 1977. Print.

Miike, Takashi, dir. *Imprint*. Showtime / Anchor Bay, 26 Sept. 2006. DVD.

Parky at the Pictures. "(DVD 27/1/2011)." *The Oxford Times* 27 Jan. 2011. Lexis-Nexis. Web. 10 Mar. 2014.

_____. "(DVD 12/12/2013)." *The Oxford Times* 12 Dec. 2013. Lexis-Nexis. Web. 10 Mar. 2014.

Pasolini, Pier Paolo, dir. *Salo, or the 120 Days of Sodom*. Criterion Collection, 26 Aug. 2008. DVD.

Scott, A. O. "The Listings." *The New York Times (Late Edition)* 20 May 2011: C-15. Lexis-Nexis. Web. 10 Mar. 2014.

_____. "Torture or Porn? No Need to Choose." *The New York Times (Late Edition)* 13 May 2011: C-11. Lexis-Nexis. Web. 10 Mar. 2014.

Shoard, Catherine. "Serbian thriller is most censored film in 16 years." *The Guardian*

(London) 27 Nov. 2010: GUARDIAN HOME PAGES p. 15. *Lexis-Nexis*. Web. 12 May 2014.

Spasojevic, Srdjan. *A Serbian Film UNCUT*. Invincible Pictures, 22 May 2012. DVD.

THR Staff. "'*Walking Dead*'s' Robert Kirkman, Rob Zombie Reveal the Grossest Thing They've Ever Seen Onscreen." *TheHollywoodReporter.com* 11 Oct. 2013. *Lexis-Nexis*. Web. 10 Mar. 2014.

Williams, Linda. "Film Bodies: Gender, Genre, and Excess." *Film Quarterly* 44.4 (Summer 1991): 2–13. *JSTOR*. Web. 16 May 2014.

"Bears that dance, bears that don't"
Aggression, Civilization and the Gothic Bear

JULIE WILHELM *and* STEVEN J. ZANI

> "[A]s war becomes dishonored and its nobility called into question those honorable men who recognize the sanctity of blood will become excluded from the dance, which is the warrior's right, and thereby will the dance become a false dance and the dancers false dancers. And yet there will be one there always who is a true dancer.... There is room on the stage for one beast and one alone. All others are destined for a night that is eternal and without name. One by one they will step down into the darkness before the footlamps. Bears that dance, bears that dont"
> —Cormac McCarthy, *Blood Meridian*.

Most contemporary audiences understand the idea of the bear primarily in its monstrous aspect. Bears represent the wild and untamable, occupying only the borders of American and European civilization. Numerous stories characterize bears as the animalistic-other: documentaries of actual bear attacks such as Werner Herzog's *Grizzly Man* (2005), Stephen Colbert's parodic reference to them as "godless communists," the bears of the Disney-Pixar film *Brave* (2012) (where the urgent need to undo the mother's transformation into a bear drives the plot forward), John Irving's *Setting Free the Bears* (1968) with its eruptions of violence, and many more. But bears are not simply monstrous or violent. With figures such as Beowulf (bee-wolf, i.e., the hero whose totem is a bear) and many others, bears have long occupied a cultural space that is strangely both animal and human at the same time. The French legends and folktales of Jean de l'Ours, the half-man, half-bear who defeats the devil and lives happily ever after, cut to the heart of the issue: bears occupy the borderline between humans and animals. Bears are fascinating because they, along with many other animals in literature and culture, enable us to address the limitations of the human and by extension give a narrative to questions about human identity.

Why, then, would bears be more relevant to an understanding of the Gothic than any number of other appropriate creatures—for example, the bats, ravens, spiders, and wolves that make up the traditional iconic Gothic landscape and that similarly occupy the borderlands between humans and animals? We will argue that the bear has particular relevance to Gothic literature and to our understanding of the Gothic because bears allow us to frame the question of the Gothic in ways that other animals do not. That is, the bear has a history and status in animal literature that other animals do not, and moreover—as we will demonstrate—original Gothic authors and those who follow them employ the bear in very particular ways. The bear, as something that is both regal and authoritative on the one hand, yet unsettling and disruptive on the other, occupies a Gothic register unlike any other animal.

In this essay, we will demonstrate that Gothic bears represent not only an uncivilized foil to humanity but also human incivility, aggression, and imbalance in a way that troubles the means through which human beings understand and constitute themselves. Terrifying bears like Mor'du' of Disney-Pixar's *Brave* behave in a way that captures the aggression that Jacques Lacan describes as typical of young children: "One need but listen to the stories and games made up by two to five year olds, alone or together, to know that pulling off heads and cutting open bellies are spontaneous themes of their imagination, which the experience of a busted-up doll merely fulfills" (*Ecrits* 105; 85). Lacan attributes certain aggressive human behavior to "a vital dehiscence that is constitutive of man" (*Ecrits* 116; 94), arguing that "man's relationship to nature is altered by a certain dehiscence at the very heart of the organism, a primordial Discord betrayed by the signs of malaise and motor uncoordination of the neonatal months" (*Ecrits* 97; 78). "Dehiscence," in both its botanical sense of the bursting open of seed vessels and its medical usage of the rupturing of a sutured wound, denotes a breakdown of boundaries at a site that is, whether naturally or as a result of past trauma, already vulnerable. Though we will speak about this site primarily in Gothic rather than Lacanian terms, we assert that the Gothic bear's aggression represents a dehiscence that embodies the discord that is always-already at the center of the human self. While much of culture and language works to provide comfort, to suture these fragments or distract from the fragmentary state, the Gothic bear instead evokes fear not only through its capacity to rip open human bodies and tear apart fantasies of wholeness and organic unity—a natural threat that bears as well as many other animals in literature pose—but also through its representation of something more centered than humans. Though in various cinematic and literary portrayals Gothic bears are larger and heftier (and in theory more awkward) than humans, they nonetheless often maintain a balance and gracefulness, exemplified by the dancing bear, which exposes various human imbalances.

Understanding this interplay of balance and imbalance is key to understanding the Gothic bear and the question of the Gothic in general, though the consequences of that statement contain another revelation about the nature of human writing itself—namely, that we must also realize that reading an essay about Gothic literature is not the same thing as reading Gothic literature itself. Walter Benjamin's arguments about translation shed light on this distinction. In his article "The Task of the Translator," Benjamin gives an account of translation that runs counter to traditionally accepted notions, stating, "a transmitting function cannot transmit anything but information—hence, something inessential" (69). Instead of imparting information or conveying the same content as the original, the act of translation, he argues, should do something else: seek out the "pure language" that is only hinted at by the original text. For Benjamin, a translation does not deliver content or information, but rather it delivers something else accomplished by the text, something that is otherwise ineffable or impossible to detect. Another way to make the point is that translation should address what is accomplished *by* the text as much as what is *in* the text. For Benjamin, the process of translation is useful because it opens up a question of the limitations of language. In sum, he argues, "It is the task of the translator to release in his own language that pure language which is under the spell of another, to liberate the language imprisoned in a work in his re-creation of that work" (80). The problem of translation—how to "say" the same thing in a different language—becomes a manifest question of the meaning behind the texts themselves. Again, for Benjamin the shift is that translation allows the reader or translator to think about the language itself being employed, rather than only what is being said within it. We will argue here that the bear in Gothic literature serves the same function. In the Romantic period the Gothic destabilized meaning and created or revealed the ever-shifting centers of culture, thought, and language at the time. The bear facilitated this destabilization during the Romantic period, and we argue that it continues to do so in a number of contemporary texts. In its literary appearances, the Gothic bear does not give its reader information, providing a comforting truth or stable message; it serves another purpose entirely, a Gothic purpose, one that delivers anything but stability.

"On the Marionette Theater" and the Fencing Bear

What can we address, then? Or rather, how can we explain the extent to which representations of bears achieve an essential/inessential purpose that provides a touchstone into thinking about the Gothic? We will begin with a singular example from the original Gothic period before addressing the bear in its more modern appearances. In the early nineteenth century, Heinrich von Kleist published "On the Marionette Theater" (1810), a dialogue about dancing puppets and the nature of humanity that ultimately uses the bear as the vehicle for its primary message. The narrator encounters an old friend, Mr. C, who "had recently been hired as the principal dancer of that city's opera and was already all the rage" (264). The narrator is surprised to learn that the dancer also relishes spending his time working with marionettes, about which Mr. C asserts "in no uncertain terms that a dancer inclined to improve his technique could learn a thing or two from them" (264). The narrator continues to ask probing questions, and through their dialogue Mr. C makes the argument that the movement of the center of gravity, in such theater, works in a straight line, and the art form therefore relates something profound about dance: "[T]his same line ... was nothing less than the pathway of the dancer's soul; and [Mr. C] doubted that it could be produced in any other fashion than that the machinist adopted the center of gravity of the marionette, in other words, that he danced" (266). Explaining the point further, Mr. C asserts that the beauty of the work depends upon the lack of humanity involved: "if a mechanic could build him a marionette according to the stipulations he envisioned ... he would have it perform a dance which neither he himself nor any other skilled dancer of the day ... could execute" (267). The grace of the marionette derives not only from its lack of humanity, but its *non-thinking* process, for Mr. C asserts that people with artificial limbs occupy a similar category, and they can use them to dance with a "calm, ease, and comeliness that makes every thinking person stand in awe" (267). The grace available to these dancers is particularly alien to those who think about the process, which suggests that thinking itself carries with it an anxiety and discomfort. The idea is recognizable enough as a Romantic trope—John Keats writes, in *Ode to a Nightingale* (1819), "Where but to think is to be filled with sorrow," an idea found in countless other melancholic texts of the period—but Kleist's essay uses thinking and non-thinking to address a question of grace. Mr. C studies this grace, evident in the artificial world of marionette theater, to improve his own technique.

To elaborate upon his point about the gracefulness of non-thinking, Mr. C suddenly begins talking about a past encounter with a fencing bear, and here is where the work becomes, we argue, specifically representative of the Gothic. He explains to the narrator that he once stayed at the country estate of a nobleman, one with several sons enthused by the sport of fencing. After Mr. C defeated the eldest, he was told that nonetheless he would meet his master because the nobleman owned a bear that had no match in swordplay. That bear could not be defeated since it refused to respond to distractions or deceptions. The account reveals a bear that occupies a state of grace akin to that of the marionettes:

> I lunged with my rapier; the bear made a very slight movement with his paw and parried my thrust. I tried with feints to trick him; the bear did not budge. And once again I lunged with a nimble stroke that would have pierced without fail any human breast; but the bear made a very slight motion with his paw and parried the thrust.... The bear's perfect calm helped rob me of my own composure, I varied thrusts and feints, sweat dripped from my brow: for naught! Not only did the bear, like the foremost fencer in the world, parry all my thrusts; but, unlike any human counterpart would have done, not a single time did he go for my feints: Looking at me eye to eye, as if he could read my soul, he stood stock still, paw raised and ready, and if my thrusts were ruses, he did not even budge [272].

The description has much in common with the earlier descriptions of marionettes. The bear operates with perfect calm while the man does not, and the text pointedly asserts how the bear's abilities are unlike that of "any human." The bear can apparently "read [his opponent's] soul," which is described in other parts of the essay as the site of affect.

Mr. C—perhaps speaking for Kleist in this instance as he addresses the concerns of the unnamed narrator[1]—distinguishes people from marionettes and fencing bears in terms of the advantage marionettes and bears have, which is curiously not that they have a quality above and beyond that of humanity. He says of marionettes: "The advantage? First of all a negative one, my dear friend; and that is that it would never behave with affect. For affect, as you know, is produced when the soul (*vis motrix*) can be found at some other point than the center of gravity of movement."[2] What does the bear have that the man does not? One way to answer that question is to ask it again in the negative, in reference to Mr. C's comment regarding marionettes: what has happened to the man so that he has something which the bear does not? The answer to the question is that both marionettes and bears do not have a soul that is unbalanced, a soul that exposes itself, sweat dripping from its embodied brow, in affect and deception.[3] In short, Kleist's essay argues that human beings, as opposed to marionettes and bears, are unbalanced, both literally in terms of their physical bodies and also figuratively in their personality and humanity. When people interact with others, it is with attitude and affectation, which results in misrepresentation and hence a loss of the grace, a loss that comes from no longer being entirely genuine.[4]

Mr. C claims that "[o]nly a god" (269) could be as graceful as a puppet, and his reference to gods is telling. To challenge Mr. C's point, one might contend that there seems to be no end to myths and legends about gods behaving poorly in many circumstances; gods, in any number of classical texts, make mistakes, commit crimes of passion, act with rage and jealousy, and perform other actions we would not consider graceful or beautiful. While this may be true, even in these actions the gods—at least the Western, classical gods that are more likely the subject of Mr. C's observations—nonetheless exhibit the centered-ness to which Mr. C aspires in the essay. They always behave with a kind of natural, unaffected direction in all their actions, even cruel and narcissistic ones.[5] The essay asserts that this lack of balance, revealed in the affectations and attitudes that people adopt, demonstrates something more profound as well; it is what separates humanity from perfection. Kleist's reference to gods is buttressed by several references to the Garden of Eden, and the assertion is made that humans, now that they have left the Garden and occupy a postlapsarian state, no longer have the same consciousness, the same knowledge that they would otherwise have.

With Kleist's text and its revelations, we begin to see that the bear represents something beginning importantly here in "On the Marionette Theater" of 1810, when the Gothic first erupted as a dominant literary form—something that we will argue is an essential element of Gothic literature. On the one hand, the bear represents a grace that is terrifying because it exposes the instability and internal struggle of humanity. But the bear also represents something that humanity does not have graceful mastery over or the ability to understand. The bear creates a lack of grace in those who try to understand it, a perpetual discomfort and frustration.

Brave *and the Banished Bear*

The first time a bear appears in Disney-Pixar's *Brave*, it is shocking and terrifying—a huge, menacing, unexpected eruption into the peaceful birthday gathering of the opening scene. This bear, Mor'du, has a presence in the film that explodes a predictable family conflict, the affectionate competition between Fergus (the father) and Elinor (the mother), as they both attempt to mold their daughter into versions of themselves and as their daughter performs the predictable role of carefree child. In this prologue, Fergus gives his daughter a bow for her birthday, to which Elinor quietly, femininely objects when their daughter is out of earshot ("A bow, Fergus? She's a lady!"). They follow this disagreement with another one about rationality versus magic: Merida returns from retrieving her arrow to report seeing a mystical creature that, as legend has it, would to lead one to her fate, at which point Fergus sides with rationality, discounting the legend, while Elinor and Merida affirm their belief in magic. Throughout the course of *Brave,* Merida learns to navigate Western social binaries to create her own identity and fate—to be her own person, a lady archer adventurist. The human conflicts in the prologue focus audience attention on the social long enough to make the menacing bear's sudden appearance, growling as he rears up on his hind legs, dwarfing the clansmen, as a shockingly unexpected conclusion to the scene. In Mor'du's attack on human culture, which leaves the audience wondering not who wins the battle but rather if any of the men survives the attack, the bear represents the threat of the third term that overwhelms any familial and social conflicts with its vast unknowability.

This encounter with something that cannot be understood, despite its immediacy and presence, is the primary trauma of the scene. The men expend themselves in their struggle to defeat Mor'du' with Fergus losing a leg in the attack. Because the prologue abruptly ends after the bear's eruption onto the scene, the audience will learn secondhand that Mor'du' took Fergus' leg in the encounter, which suggests that the scene is too horrific to be pictured in the children's movie or perhaps too horrific to be pictured altogether. But clearly the damage Mor'du' does to the clansmen is more than physical. To come to terms with this traumatic encounter, King Fergus defines himself and his clan against the animal antagonist. He tells stories about Mor'du', sings songs about him, and helps to create a cultural identity in opposition to the bear. Signifying that Mor'du' is the absence/void at the center of the family dynamic and even the kingdom, an empty spot hangs in the castle where Mor'du's head will go once he is killed. The story of Mor'du's attack unites the various clans of the kingdom, which otherwise seem to be at odds with each other, and it facilitates solidarity among the children, who roll their eyes in unison when their father retells the story of the bear attack. In contrast, Mor'du' remains centered and unfazed in scenes following his attack. In contradistinction to the human characters, who struggle to construct their own identities and "authentic" fates throughout the movie and often appear buffoonish or chaotic, Mor'du' appears in the film as something already made, in full presence, like Kleist's bear, always carrying a perfect balance and clarity of purpose.

Beyond the prologue, bears continue to represent the unknowable and the undefeatable for humankind in *Brave,* which becomes the central theme of the narrative. For instance, the witch of *Brave*, the only other significant cultural monster in the film, is so closely associated with bears that the one morphs into the other. The witch has a cabin in the woods populated with carved, wooden bears, and the bear is the face of evil in *Brave* long after the witch has disappeared from her house and the movie. In short, while the witch as a cultural figure has a long and interesting tradition, one which pervades many different narratives and has been addressed by many critics, her function here is essentially only an extension of the monstrosity of the bear. Elsewhere the witch is an immensely prolific and influential figure. For example, in Russian folklore the witch Baba Yaga is ubiquitous, and "there is also good reason to believe that she is related to the ancient Germanic Perchta, who gave rise to the famous Frau Holle of the Brothers Grimm's and northern Germanic tales" (Zipes 70). That form of the witch can be seen in many tales, including the wicked fairy godmother in *Sleeping Beauty* (unnamed in the original tale but later given the name "Maleficent" in Disney's *Sleeping Beauty* [1959], as well as in the more recent film *Maleficent* [2014]), the witch from Grimm's Hansel and Gretel (with multiple film versions), and even the three witches in the woods who appear in Lloyd Alexander's *Prydain Chronicles* (1964–68) (reminiscent of other British/Celtic figures and clearly representative of the Three Fates of the Western tradition since the classical period). Instead of drawing on that rich tradition, not of just witches, but specifically of witches occupying cabins in the woods, *Brave* assigns a relatively unimportant role to the witch. When Merida asks the witch to make her a curse to change her mother, the witch turns her mother into a bear; the function of the witch is only to facilitate the mother's bearish transformation.

The film's use of the bear demonstrates our point that bears have continued to function as a marker for something particularly related to Gothic concerns. After all, this narrative could potentially have ignored bears completely and relied on the witch as the primary villain, just as she is employed in multiple Disney films that have preceded this one as well as the countless fairy and folk tales that are the source of the genre. Though film critics have called this film "less inspired than usual for Pixar" (Sachs), "safely forgettable" (Whitty), and "easy to predict" (Kendrick), the use of the bear differentiates it from its predecessors in a way which indicates that it is not simply walking its paces.[6] Here, instead, we find that the bear changes the narrative significantly and represents Gothic dehiscence.

Brave's sudden transition from the witch to the bear, like Kleist's unexpected transition from the marionettes to the fencing bear, reveals a concern with loss and recovery. In *Brave*, this concern is demonstrated as Queen Elinor becomes a focus in the narrative. Before she is transformed, the excessively civilizing Queen is the bear's opposite. *Brave* highlights the clumsiness of her humanity in her inability to function gracefully after she becomes a bear, even in natural settings typically hospitable to bears. The film presents a montage, set to music, of failure and unbalance as Elinor unsuccessfully attempts to eat, catch fish, and swim as a bear. She cannot control herself or her impulses; she devours other animals and seems capable of attacking her own daughter. These images underscore the point that at this stage in the narrative she does not have true grace, either as a bear or a person. As the humanity of Kleist's dancers has unbalanced them so they cannot have the grace of a marionette, the Queen's transformation into an inefficient bear reveals the lack of grace she had all along and exposes the hidden unbalance carried by the entire family. To regain her humanity, Elinor must learn to be truly nurturing and adaptable again. Tellingly, this entails not rejecting or eliminating what the bear represents, but instead recognizing and assimilating it.

As with Kleist, in *Brave* the human question or quest involves a return to a past history, a past trauma, to find a way to recover it. A large tapestry of the family, which Elinor created and which Merida tears during a heated disagreement with her mother, clearly represents the characters' relationships with each other and themselves given its narrative centrality. Read through Kleist, the torn tapestry embodies the conflict and struggle unbalancing humanity. Elinor's process of learning to become a bear and Merida's support through the process takes both mother and daughter on a journey of recovery, rather than discovery, back to the site of the trauma so they can undo the witch's spell. Merida mends the torn tapestry and drapes it over Elinor, who at this point is still a bear. At the climax of *Brave*, Merida, her community, and the film's audience are made to focus at length on the image of the bear covered in a repaired tapestry as they all await Elinor's restoration to her human state. Viewed alongside other Gothic narratives of the bear, this image and the movie's emphasis on it represent humanity's loss of centeredness and integrity and the path to recovery that the Gothic bear invokes.

Brave is an example of how the bear continues to be a relevant symbol in the Gothic tradition as it has been reinvented and reinscribed to be an important aspect of contemporary literature and culture. That does not mean, however, that every bear is a Gothic bear, or that the appearance of a bear in a text means that an element of the Gothic is being evoked. Quite the contrary, since bears can be, and surely are, used for many different purposes in a text, many representations of bears do not accomplish a Gothic objective. For example, Smokey the Bear, a perennial symbol used by the National Park Service to warn children of the dangers of forest fires, might very well be a bear, and in fact he addresses in some oblique, tamed fashion the chaotic yet scientifically predictable horror that is a forest fire, yet the figure of good ol' Smokey nonetheless does not invoke any element of Gothic terror or horror in his viewers. Only in the most comforting of ways is one confronted with a dehiscence and/or anticipated restoration when Smokey appears onscreen, perhaps in the call for action ("Only you can prevent forest fires!") that he touts.

Grizzly Man *and the Bifurcated Bear*

In this fashion, asking what distinguishes the Gothic bear from other bears allows us to better understand precisely what Gothic literature might be. Let us look briefly, then, at a contemporary bear narrative that we assert should be characterized as Gothic, despite the fact that as a documentary it contains no fantastic, ostensibly Gothic elements: the Werner Herzog film *Grizzly Man*. The narrative of *Grizzly Man* centers on the activities of Timothy Treadwell, who spent thirteen summers living near bears in Alaska before being killed by a bear. Much of the documentary is comprised of Treadwell's own footage, taken over several years, as he attempted to commune with the bears and bring a message back from his summers to those unfamiliar with the natural world, a message of its beauty and majesty. Treadwell's footage is compiled and arranged by Herzog, who added framing interviews and discussions with others connected to the tragedy.

In *Grizzly Man*, bears alternate between being described as either comforting or dangerous. Treadwell projects his Romantic[7] understanding onto the bears around him; Herzog takes Treadwell's Romantic videos and frames them with voiceovers and appearances in a way that offers a stark, almost explicitly atheistic account. In this way, Treadwell and Herzog offer a familiar Gothic contrast. As many of the novels and stories of the Gothic era focus on the ambivalence and tension between supernatural elements and mundane human action, this aspect of the film is quite Gothic indeed.[8] In Herzog's construction and presentation of Treadwell's work, Treadwell's vision of bears carries with it a consistently comforting sentiment about the purity and unity that bears can bring to mankind. Treadwell relates, "I come here in peace and love" as he gives the bears reassuring names like "Mr. Chocolate" and "Downy." The references to the bears in kinship and Romantic connection are so pervasive that most reviews and critical approaches to the text focus on that element of the film almost exclusively.[9] It is not that Treadwell is oblivious to the dangers of the bears; he consistently refers to the possibility of his own death: "I may be hurt. I may be killed." But for him, particularly as Herzog's editorial choices present him, the death seems essentially a Romantic one, not unlike the early nineteenth-century sympathies of a Keats or Shelley finding comfort in the negative capability of finally giving oneself over to Nature.

Herzog, while apparently sympathetic to Treadwell's cause, nonetheless continually interjects his opinion of Treadwell's descriptions as an obsessive misperception of reality: "I believe the common character of the universe is not harmony, but chaos, hostility, and murder.... [I]n all the faces of all the bears that Treadwell ever filmed, I discover no kinship, no understanding, no mercy." Herzog's portrayal of Treadwell is in many ways as anthropomorphic as Treadwell's portrayal of the bears, as he continually uses Treadwell to define his own opposing understanding of nature. His voiceovers frame and interrupt Treadwell's account with phrases that highlight this opposition: "I see only the overwhelming indifference of nature. To me, there is no such thing as a secret world of the bears. And this blank stare speaks only of a half-bored interest in food." Herzog implicitly suggests that if one watched Treadwell's raw footage, the documentary would be considerably more Romantic in tone and message, but that fortunately he is there, as documentarian, to give the viewer a more correct understanding. Treadwell, he tells us, would give us a false "secret world" of the bear, but Herzog provides the unromantic reality.

Like many traditional Gothic narratives, the film provides a measure of comfort and stability in both of its perspectives. One either accepts the dominant narrative of the film, rejecting Treadwell's obsessive (and eventually) fatal attachment to the bears and nature, embracing Herzog, or views Herzog as somewhat obsessive himself and celebrates Treadwell as a champion of the bears and a self-proclaimed "warrior" for environmentalism. Some critics of the film have noticed the possibility of a tension between these intertwining accounts and have worked to unravel them by expanding the text to include details outside the reference point of the film itself. Nick Jans' book *The Grizzly Maze* (2005), for example, exposes the film's projection of Treadwell as someone who was carelessly ignorant of bear aggressivity as a construction on the part of Herzog, since people close to Treadwell explained in narratives that never made it into the film, "He didn't get any closer to bears than most wildlife photographers do.... A telephoto lens or lens angle distorts the distance between objects, sometimes creating the illusion of greater proximity" (166). In that sense, Treadwell's position (literally and figuratively) is equally supportable, in direct contrast to that of Herzog: "Grounded as we are in a culture dominated by rational thought, ruled by scientific method, it's easy to write off Timothy Treadwell.... But you only have to drop back a few paltry years to find millions of people, entire cultures, that would not have found his perspective strange" (216). Ultimately *The Grizzly Maze* ends on that note, that "exceptions and unanswerable questions are bound to creep in" (236).

A genuinely Gothic bear narrative, we assert, is one in which the bear is an unavoidable instrument of that opening, of strange perspectives, of uncomforting encounters. Kleist's essay establishes that template; *Brave* begins with just such a rupture, even if the function of the narrative is to repair it; and *Grizzly Man* reveals it similarly in its indecisive interplay between Treadwell and Herzog. All of these texts reenact a scene of rupturing and loss, imbalance and fragmentation, that mirrors Kleist's account of the fall from the Garden of Eden, and they suggest that the essence of the human project is to suture that wound, restore balance, and return to the Garden. There are other bear narratives with different messages that nonetheless repeat these themes, and we would like to end the essay with an analysis of one that fully represents such Gothic concerns, Cormac McCarthy's novel *Blood Meridian, or the Evening Redness in the West* (1985).

Blood Meridian *and the Dancing Bear*

One way to understand the Gothic elements of *Blood Meridian* is to read it as an educational novel, a bildungsroman. The narrative is primarily concerned with the life of "the kid" as he journeys throughout the Southwest, joining a marauding gang of scalp hunters and losing his innocence about the nature of the world. Despite the chaos and violence he encounters, his experiences are genuinely educational. At the novel's end he is called "the man," indicating the kind of emotional maturation that one would expect for the protagonist in a typical bildungsroman.[10] That tradition is thwarted, or at least rewritten, in the kid/man's violent death at the conclusion of the work, which is one of the many reasons critics have found the novel notoriously difficult to read. Critic Dana Philips notes:

> Early reviewers attempting to map this novel's outlandish aesthetic and moral territories resorted to striking but desperate oppositions. To them, the novel seemed a blend of Heironymous Bosch and Sam Peckinpah; of Salvadore Dali, Shakespeare, and the Bible; of Faulkner and Fellini; of Gustave Doré, Louis L'Amour, Dante, and Goya; of cowboys and nothingness; of Texas and Vietnam [434].

Despite these difficulties, the work has achieved a great deal of acclaim in the years since its release. Harold Bloom says of *Blood Meridian*, "I cannot turn away from the novel, now that I know how to read it" (6). Unlike Bloom, we will not presume to tell readers how to read it, but we will say that the Gothic bear makes an important appearance in the final few pages of the work, and using the Gothic as a reading paradigm is a viable touchstone for understanding the impact of the narrative.

The introduction of Gothic elements occurs most profoundly with the appearance of Judge Holden, a strangely threatening and unpredictable character who dominates much of the novel. Holden, described simply as "the judge" for much of the work, is connected to divinity and links *Blood Meridian* on a thematic level to the Kleist essay with which we began our account. When the gang of marauders first encounters the judge, he saves their lives by making them gunpowder using the surrounding rocks to manufacture the necessary mixture of sulfur and other materials. Critic John Sepich, while focusing on the historical precedent of actual events surrounding the travels of Cortez in the new world, reads this account as a Faustian/Satanic narrative (547). For our purposes, the judge's creation of gunpowder in *Blood Meridian* is important because it associates the introduction of knowledge to the world with a concomitant violence or unbalance. The connection is strengthened in an apparently disconnected epilogue, in which a post-hole digger works the land, creating sparks as he scrapes his tool against the earth, "striking the fire out of the rock which God has put there" (337). In this passage, human technology—digging posts to organize and colonize the land—is connected to ideas of the divine, but the narrative is unclear about the consequences or meaning of that connection.

Whether we regard the judge as Satan or Prometheus, he is clearly an unsettling figure in the narrative. The final dialogue in the novel involves the judge and "the man" discussing all that has happened before them in a barroom scene that includes a bear dancing to entertain patrons. After another patron inexplicably shoots the bear, the bear dies dancing in a pool of its own blood, and the judge explains the world by invoking the bear's dance while the man voices disagreement:

> I tell you this, as war becomes dishonored and its nobility called into question those honorable men who recognize the sanctity of blood will become excluded from the dance, which is the warrior's right, and thereby will the dance become a false dance and the dancers false dancers. And yet there be one there always who is a true dancer and can you guess who that might be?
> You aint nothin.
> You speak truer than you know. But I will tell you. Only that man who has offered up himself to the blood of war, who has been to the floor of the pit and seen horror in the round and learned at last that it speaks to his inmost heart, only that man can dance.
> Even a dumb animal can dance.
> The judge set the bottle on the bar. Hear me, man, he said. There is room on

the stage for one beast alone. All others are destined for a night that is eternal and without name. One by one they will step down into the darkness before the footlamps. Bears that dance, bears that dont [331].

What is the bear doing in this narrative? The frame of the Gothic, specifically that of Kleist, his bears, and his perfect marionette dancers, enables us to read the judge in this scene as an extension of the function of the Gothic bear. The judge perceives dishonor and lack of authenticity in the world, the consequences of a fall from grace comparable to those described by Mr. C to the narrator of the Kleist essay—in a sense the judge is comparable to Kleist's bear itself. As all dancers become false dancers, only the person who follows the path to its conclusion will not be excluded from the dance. This person does not move backward but rather forward, traveling "to the floor of the pit," and can therefore find redemption or escape the "night that is eternal." The judge knows the beasts and dances as a bear.

Shortly after the conversation, the narrative implies that the man is found dead in an outhouse after having been killed by the judge in a scene where the details are left to the imagination of the reader, though the men who see the body react apparently in horror by saying, "Good God almighty" (334). The novel ends with the judge dancing nakedly, "huge and pale and hairless, like an enormous infant," proclaiming he will never die (335). Both the nakedness of the dance and the reference to a lack of mortality can again be understood in Kleistian terms as a reference to a return to Eden. However, there is revealing difference between Kleist and McCarthy. For McCarthy, at least as it pertains to the judge, humanity has become excluded from the grace implied in dancing, a dance that is now available only to the beasts and to those who embrace the beastly. McCarthy's return to Eden involves a murderer dancing naked with whores in a bloodstained barroom. While Kleist's essay does not reveal or embrace the horrific consequences that McCarthy's novel does, nonetheless both texts use the image of the bear as a symbol of something that transcends humanity but is essential to the human nonetheless.

Humanity either dances or it does not. At the end of the novel, the judge takes up the dance of the bear, "light and nimble," leading others "in light and in shadow," as the repetition and rhythm of the prose captures the motions of a dance (335). While, in the Kleistian narrative, dancing will lead to grace and takes one down the path to redemption, the dance at the end of McCarthy's narrative offers anything but resolution. There is no clear, Kleistian path to redemption—no sense of where this dancing will take us. There is a beastial grace, but the death of the bear and the judge's mimicry of his role in the barroom setting violently eradicate it. Both texts are Gothic in their unsettling nature, but McCarthy has changed the terms of what that means, and reminds us all the more that we do not yet know the dance.

The bear narratives we have included here vacillate between bears as comforting and horrific as part of a long history that addresses specifically Gothic concerns. When the bear is threatening, it is threatening and unsettling in a way that addresses human identity and its loss, as found in Kleist, McCarthy, and others. When the bear is comforting, such as the maternal bear of *Brave* and Treadwell's affectionately named bears, it is comforting in a way of the Gothic romance, particularly those texts that end with the defeat of instability, the reestablishment of order, and the presence of the universal. In each case, however, the universal can only be understood as a site of trauma and subsequent recovery, a site in which we are excluded from grace until we escape to the world of the bear and understand the lessons it can give.

Notes

1. Some critics detect a distance between Kleist and his characters that makes such arguments untenable. See Victoria Nelson's *The Secret Life of Puppets*, in which she asserts, "Nowhere is the destabilizing action of dialogue more clearly at work than in … Kleist's essay" (61). Nelson's observations about connections between humanity and puppets, found in Kleist and many other Gothic automaton narratives such as Hoffmann's seminal "Sandman" (1816), have obvious significance here, though we do not have the space to address that book's arguments at length.

2. For the majority of this essay, we use a translation from Peter Wortsman, with the exception of this passage, where the translation is our own. The original text reads "Der Vorteil? Zuvörderst ein negativer, mein vortrefflicher Freund, nämlich dieser, daß sie sich niemals *zierte*.—Denn Ziererei erscheint, wie Sie wissen, wenn sich die Seele (vis motrix) in irgend einem andern Punkte befindet, als in dem Schwerpunkt der Bewegung." Wortsman translates variations of "Ziererei" as "attitude" rather than our use of "affect."

3. Readers familiar with Young Adult fantasy may recognize a contemporary correspondence with Philip Pullman's recent novel (and subsequent film) *The Golden Compass* (1996), originally published as *Northern Lights* in the preceding year. In that text, the talking bears of the novels cannot be lied to because they recognize when they are being deceived—the only exception being one bear who wants too strongly to become a man.

4. We read this unbalance in relation to the bear, though there are critics who privilege other aspects of Kleist's work. Elystan Griffiths, for example, attributes the instability of human conduct in Kleist's oeuvre to "the volatile nature of performance" (425). Griffiths writes, "Kleist's characters are forced to perform, but often have little control over the image they project. Thus his fictions outline an unpredictable world where a philosophically rooted unease is matched by an equally terrifying social environment, where the very coherence and continuity of the self are attacked" (436).

5. Stevie Smith, in her *Novel on Yellow Paper* (1936), describes the Greek gods as follows: "I early got an idea of the Olympians as very beautiful, very lovely, cynical and always laughing. And very cruel, cruel in a cold callous and divine way, not with the cruelty of human beings which is of course much crueler. Because human beings can calculate to the last inch just where it is painful and how much, but the gods and god-

desses and that sort of creation really can't be bothered with those ingenuities of cruelty, they just have an idea of what is due to them from mortals, and hand out penalties if they don't get it, without bothering much about the reaction of the victim. Very cruel, very callous, we think the Olympians, but of course it is hardly their fault. They have no heart. They have no heart" (136–137). It is this version of godhood, its lack of a heart to inspire cruelty in Smith's terms or of a soul to be unbalanced in Kleist's, that seems essential here.

6. Interestingly, after criticizing the film for seeming "off-kilter," Colin Covert of the *Star Tribune* deems the "emotional fluency of the bears" the most impressive aspect of *Brave*. Covert's argument that bears achieve a grace beyond the clumsiness of the film gets at the heart of our argument about the function of the Gothic bear.

7. Throughout this essay, we capitalize "Romanticism" and its variants, "Romantic," etc., when it is used as a period-specific term, a noun or adjective referring to the late eighteenth/early nineteenth century, to avoid other connotative meanings of the term in its relation to "romance," or other associations. While there are a number of scholars (Phillipe Lacoue-Labarthe, Jean-Luc Nancy, et al.) who do *not* capitalize the term, conceivably in order to minimize its status and stress the problematic nature of defining it as a formal (non-politicized), clearly established period, in the context of this article we found it useful to retain the capital letter to preserve that distinction.

8. Is Matthew Lewis's eponymous monk being manipulated by Satan or only by other people? Is Ann Radcliffe's Udolpho haunted by ghosts or mere bandits? See books such as Elizabeth's MacAndrew's *The Gothic Tradition in Fiction*, or Marie Mulvey-Roberts' *The Handbook to Gothic Literature*, for two examples of the many critical texts that list common tropes and figures of the tradition.

9. For one of the better comprehensive critical accounts at Naturalism and Romanticism in *Grizzly Man*, see Elizabeth Henry's "The Screaming Silence: Constructions of Nature in Werner Herzog's Grizzly Man." Full citation details can be found in the Works Cited.

10. He is called a "man" only in the final chapter, first by the narrator (321) and later by the judge (330).

Works Cited

Benjamin, Walter. "The Task of the Translator." *Illuminations.* Ed. Hannah Arendt. Trans. Harry Zohn. New York: Harcourt, 1968. 69–82. Print.

Bloom, Harold. "Introduction." *Cormac McCarthy.* Ed. Harold Bloom. New York: Chelsea House, 2009. 1–8. Print.

Brave. Dir. Mark Andrews and Brenda Chapman. Story by Brenda Chapman. Disney/Pixar, 2012. DVD.

Covert, Colin. "Brave is off-kilter." *The Star Tribune.* 22 June 2012. Web. 4 Apr. 2014.

Griffiths, Elystan. "Religion, Power and Instability of Performance in Heinrich Von Kleist's Stories." *German Life And Letters* 64.3 (2011): 421–436. MLA International Bibliography. Web. 2 Apr. 2014.

Grizzly Man. Dir. Werner Herzog. Prod. Erik Nelson. Lions Gate, 2005. DVD.

Henry, Elizabeth. "The Screaming Silence: Constructions of Nature in Werner Herzog's *Grizzly Man.*" *Framing the World: Explorations in Ecocriticism and Film.* Charlottesville: University of Virginia Press, 2010. 170–186. MLA International Bibliography. Web. 15 Apr. 2014.

Jans, Nick. *The Grizzly Maze: Timothy Treadwell's Fatal Obsession with Alaskan Bears.* New York: Dutton, 2005. Print.

Kendrick, Ben. Rev. of *Brave. ScreenRant.* 27 Sept. 2012. Web. 4 Apr. 2014.

Kleist, Heinrich von. "On the Theater of Marionettes." *Selected Prose of Heinrich von Kleist*. Trans. Peter Wortsman. Brooklyn: Archipelago Books, 2010. 264–274. Print.

Lacan, Jacques. *Écrits: The Complete Text*. Paris: Seuil Edition, 1966. Trans. from French by Bruce Fink with Heloise Fink and Russell Grigg. New York: W. W. Norton, 2006.

McCarthy, Cormac. *Blood Meridian, or the Evening Redness in the West*. 1985. New York: The Modern Library, 2001. Print.

Nelson, Victoria. *The Secret Life of Puppets*. Cambridge: Harvard University Press, 2001. Print.

Phillips, Dana. "History and the Ugly Facts of Cormac McCarthy's Blood Meridian." *American Literature* 68.2 (1996): 433–460. MLA International Bibliography. Web. 22 Apr. 2014.

Sachs, Ben. "Brave 3D." Rev. of *Brave*. *The Chicago Reader*. 18 Nov. 2013. Web. 4 Apr. 2014.

Sepich, John Emil. "A 'Bloody Dark Pastryman': Cormac Mccarthy's Recipe for Gunpowder and Historical Fiction in *Blood Meridian*." *Mississippi Quarterly* 46.4 (1993): 547–563. MLA International Bibliography. Web. 22 Apr. 2014.

Smith, Stevie. *Novel on Yellow Paper*. New York: New Directions, 1994. Print.

Whitty, Stephen. "Despite bells and whistles, Pixar films isn't so 'Brave' about its story." *NJ.com*. 22 June 2012. Web. 4 April 2014.

Zipes, Jack. *The Irresistible Fairy Tale*. Princeton: Princeton University Press, 2012. Print.

About the Contributors

Rebecca A. **Brown** holds a PhD in English and teaches at North Seattle College. She has contributed to *Monstrous Children and Childish Monsters* (McFarland, 2015). Her forthcoming publications concern picturebook monsters, vampires in comics, and ghosts in YA-fiction. She credits her interest in the macabre to her father, an antiquarian book dealer, who handed her H.P. Lovecraft, Richard Matheson, and Edgar Allan Poe stories to read at an impressionable age.

Anthony **Camara** completed his doctoral degree in English at UCLA. He is an assistant professor at the University of Calgary. His research focuses on intersections between science and literature in the late nineteenth and early twentieth century, with an emphasis on the popular genres of horror and science fiction. His work has appeared in the refereed journals *Women's Writing*, *Horror Studies*, *Gothic Studies*, and *O-Zone*.

L. Andrew **Cooper**'s scholarship includes *Gothic Realities* (McFarland, 2010) and *Dario Argento* (2012) as well as many articles. His fiction includes the novels *Burning the Middle Ground* (2012) and *Descending Lines* (2013) and the short story collection *Leaping at Thorns* (2014). He co-edited *Imagination Reimagined* (2014), *Reel Dark* (2015), and *Monsters* (2012). He has taught at Princeton, Georgia Tech, and elsewhere; his PhD is from Princeton.

Christopher **Coughlin** is currently completing his MA in English at SUNY Buffalo State College. He is also an academic tutor and plans to pursue his PhD after graduate school. He has read papers at the 2011 African American Literature Symposium at SUNY Buffalo State College and at the Popular Culture Association/American Culture Association National Conferences in Washington, D.C. (2013), Chicago (2014), and New Orleans (2015).

Jameela F. **Dallis**, a PhD candidate in the Department of English and Comparative Literature at the University of North Carolina at Chapel Hill, is William Neal Reynolds Fellow in the Royster Society of Fellows. She is the managing editor of *The Southern Literary Journal*. Her essay "'Life Refusing to End': The Transformative Gothic in Shani Mootoo's *Cereus Blooms at Night*" appears in *Undead Souths: Beyond the Gothic* (2015).

About the Contributors

Mark **De Cicco** is currently pursuing a PhD in nineteenth-century British literature at the George Washington University in Washington, D.C. He received his MA from the University of Amsterdam and his BA from Fordham University in New York. Mark's research interests include late–Victorian Gothic fiction, queer theory, the literature of empire, and identity politics. His dissertation examines the ancient god Pan in Britain in the long nineteenth century.

Sharla **Hutchison** is a professor of English at Fort Hays State University, where she teaches Gothic literature, poetry, and modern fiction. She is also the director of the literary arts concentration for the university's masters of liberal studies program. Recently, she has published articles about the late–Victorian fiction writer Marie Corelli in *English Literature in Transition* and the American poet Marianne Moore in *ISLE*.

Rebecca **Janicker** received her PhD from the University of Nottingham in 2014. She recently published *The Literary Haunted House: Lovecraft, Matheson, King and the Horror in Between* (McFarland, 2015). Her edited collection *Reading 'American Horror Story': Essays on the Television Horror Franchise* is forthcoming. She has published essays on several Gothic writers' fictions. She lectures in film and media studies at the University of Portsmouth in the UK.

Susan **Poznar** is a professor of English at Arkansas Tech University; she has also taught at the University of New Hampshire at Durham, Boston University and North Carolina State University. She has written on diverse authors influenced by Gothic fiction: John Fowles, Margaret Atwood, George du Maurier, Judith Hawkes and J. Meade Faulkner. Her research interests include props and properties of Gothic architecture in nineteenth- and twentieth-century fiction.

Emilie **Taylor-Brown** is a PhD candidate at the University of Warwick, funded by the Wolfson foundation. She is a member of the English and Comparative Literary Studies Department and works in conjunction with the Centre for the History of Medicine. Her research involves the figure of the parasite in the nineteenth and early twentieth centuries and explores the ways in which parasitic disease impacted the cultural understanding of British imperialism.

Bianca **Tredennick** is an associate professor of English at SUNY Oneonta. She teaches nineteenth-century British literature and has published "A Labor of Death and a Labor Against Death: Scott's Cenotaphic Paratexts" (2010) and "Some Collections of Mortality: Dickens, the Paris Morgue and the Material Corpse" (2010). She is the editor of *Victorian Transformations: Genre, Nationalism and Desire in Nineteenth-Century British Literature* (2011).

Julie **Wilhelm** is an assistant professor of arts and humanities at National University, where she teaches American literature and gender and literature. She received her PhD from the University of California, Davis, in 2009. Her research interests include affects, humor, gender studies, and labor studies. She has recently published essays on the intersection of affect and humor in *Legacy* and *Studies in American Humor*.

Steven J. **Zani** is a professor of English at Lamar University where he is a former chair of English and Modern Languages and current director of faculty development. His Gothic-related publications include recent articles in *The Lovecraft Annual* and the *Better Off Dead* (2011) zombie collection; he has also co-written a freshman literature anthology for Penguin, *Inside Literature*.

Index

Numbers in **bold italics** indicate pages with photographs.

Arata, Stephen 13, 27, 35, 46n4
Askew, Alice: *Aylmer Vance: Ghost Seer* 42
Askew, Claude: *Aylmer Vance: Ghost Seer* 42
Auerbach, Nina 2

Barnum, P.T. 113–114
Barthes, Roland 162, 211
Benjamin, Walter 230
Beowulf 228
Botting, Fred 98, 123–125, 163n8, 189, 192–193
Bradbury, Ray: *Something Wicked This Way Comes* 112, 127n11
Brantlinger, Patrick 5, 35
Brave 228–229, 233–236, 239, 242, 243n6
Brooks, Gwendolyn 171, 174
Browne, Sir Thomas 15
Browning, Elizabeth Barrett: *The Battle of Marathon* 54, 66n3; "The Dead Pan" 54, 56; "A Musical Instrument" 54–56
Browning, Tod: *Freaks* 114
Bundy, Ted 130–131

Carroll, Lewis: *Alice's Adventures in Wonderland* 174–175
Carroll, Noël 2, 4
Carter, Angela: *The Bloody Chamber* 92, 99, 108n6; *The Infernal Desire Machines of Doctor Hoffman* 161; "The Lady of the House of Love" 3, 8, 92, 95, 97, 105, 107, 108n2, 108n12
Charcot, Jean-Martin 21
Christianity 52, 54–57, 95, 102–103, 125
Clover, Carol 222
Cohen, Jeffrey Jerome 1, 2, 61, 67, 93, 98, 106, 121, 122
Cold War 8, 72, 76–77, 81, 116, 118, 120, 126n3; *see also Gojira*
Collier, Constance 29

colonialism 1, 7, 13, 18, 23, 24–25, 31, 35, 98, 167, 181–182; *see also* imperialism
Conan Doyle, Arthur: "Lot 249" 34; *The Parasite* 12–26, 26n2
Corelli, Marie: *Ziska* 7, 29–46, 46n5, 244; *see also* Ghost; New Woman

da Pirovano, Maifreda 102; *see also* Christianity; Tarot
Darwin, Charles 17, 20–21, 77, 88
de Balzac, Honoré: *Le Cousin Pons* 15–17
de Gébelin, Antoine Court 94; *see also* Tarot
Delleuze, Gilles 220
de Nerval, Gérard: "El Desdichado" 92, 103–104, 108n10, 108n12, 109n14
Dickinson, Emily 168
drugs 79–80, 82–83, 85–86, 139, 221

Egerton, George (Mary Chavelita Dunne): "A Cross Line" 32, 36, 39; *Keynotes and Discords* 32
Egypt 29–30, 33–40, 45, 46n5, 46n6, 94; *see also* Corelli, Marie

fairy tales: "Hansel and Gretel" 235; *Haunting of Hill House* 156; "Jack and the Beanstalk" 92, 99, 101; "Sleeping Beauty" 92, 100, 104, 105, 235; *White Is for Witching* 179; *see also Alice's Adventures in Wonderland*; *Brave*
feminism 30–32, 45, 46, 120, 153; *see also* Corelli, Marie; Jackson, Shirley
freakery 112–115, 117–120, 122, 126–127n5, 127n9

ghost 29–30, 33, 41–44, 62, 145, 148–150, 152–161, 169, 170, 172–176, 185n2; *see also* Corelli, Marie; Jackson, Shirley; Oyeyemi, Helen
Gojira 69

gothic: castle 104, 137–138, 144–145, 147, 156, 162–163n1; child 150, 153–154; comics 3, 119, 193–194, 196; commodification 1–2, 6, 8, 129–130, 135, 139, 141–143; haunted house 144–147, 150, 156–160, 163n3, 163n8, 169, 176–178, 183–184; postmodernism 7, 8, 98, 168–169, 173, 176, 178, 184; queer 7, 49–52, 53, 55, 58–59, 61–64, 127n9, 150, 151, 157–159; see also lesbianism; transgender

Greek poets 14–15, 52–53

Guglielma (Princess Blažena Vilemína) 102–103; see also Tarot

Gurney, Edmund 41, 42

Haggard, Henry Rider: *Cleopatra* 31; *She* 31; "Smith and the Pharaohs" 47n6; see also Egypt

Halberstam, Judith 1, 2, 44, 47n8, 49–50, 138

Herzog, Werner: *Grizzly Man*, 228, 237–239, 243n9

Hobsbawm, Eric 53, 61

Hodgson, William Hope: *The Casebook of Carnacki* 42; *The House on the Borderland* 70; *The Night Land* 70; "The Voice in the Night" 8, 69–73, 79, 87, 88n9; see also Weird Fiction

Honda, Ishirô: *Matango (Attack of the Mushroom People)* 8, 69–72, 76–80, 82, 84–88, 88n12, 88n14, 88n15

horror: affect 3–4, 123–124, 208, 218, 221; body 3–4, 6, 16, 18, 44, 59–60, 71, 80, 88n7, 95, 113–114, 122–123, 134–137, 139–140, 197, 218–223; Japanese cinema 69, 210, 225; psychoanalysis 2, 155–157, 213–214, 217, 222, 229

Hurley, Kelly 2, 4, 18, 66n5

imperialism 6, 7, 13, 26, 94–95; see also colonialism; Egypt; Said, Edward

Irving, John: *Setting Free the Bears* 228

Jackson, Shirley: *The Bird's Nest* 163n5; *The Haunting of Hill House* 3, 8, 144–162, 162n1

Jameson, Frederic 210, 212; see also Postmodern Gothic

Jans, Nick: *The Grizzly Maze* 238

Joshi, S.T. 160n3, 188, 192; see also Lovecraft, H.P.

King, Stephen: *Danse Macabre* 192; *Gothic* 158; *The Shining* 176

King Tutankhamen 29, 46n5; see also Egypt

Kristeva, Julia 4, 9n2, 104, 109n14, 214

Lacan, Jacques 123, 156–157, 214, 215, 229

Lankester, Ray 21

Laymon, Richard: *The Traveling Vampire Show* 3, 8, 111–116, 118–119, 122, 123, 125, 126n2

Ledger, Sally 32

Le Fanu, Sheridan: *Carmilla* 150, 161

lesbianism 121, 151, 157, 170, 178, 179; see also Queer Gothic

Lewis, Matthew: *The Monk* 126, 208, 243n8

liminality 4, 7, 8, 18, 64, 82, 86–87, 112, 145, 160, 174, 177, 229

Longinovic, Tomislov: *Vampire Nation* 214

Lovecraft, H.P.: adaptation 187–188, 192–197, 203n1, 203n4, 203n5; *At the Mountains of Madness* 187–188, 190, 196, **198**, 199, 200; "The Call of Cthulhu" 190–191; "Dagon" 190, 194–196; letters 189–190, 203n2; narrator 70; "Pickman's Model" 191, 199–**202**; "The Picture in the House" 190–191; "The Shadow Out of Time" 190; "The Shadow Over Innsmouth" 191; "The Temple" 191; see also Weird Fiction

Luckhurst, Roger 35, 38, 40–42, 46n5, 47n7

Machen, Arthur: "The Great God Pan" 49, 55, 59–61, 65, 66n5

Madame Blavatsky (Helena Petrovna Blavatsky): *Isis Unveiled*; 43; *The Key to Theosophy* 43; *The Secret Doctrine* 42; see also spiritualism

Marquis de Sade: *Justine* 212; *120 Days of Sodom* 209, 212; see also pornography

Marsh, Richard: *The Beetle* 7, 12, 16, 18–20, 22–25, 27n13, 34, 125

McCarthy, Cormac: *Blood Meridian* 228, 239–240, 243n10; *Child of God* 3, 8, 129–133, 135–137

Miike, Takashi: *Imprint* 225

Milosevic, Slobodan 213–214, 224

Monnet, Agnieska Soltysik 7

Monogatari, Konjaku: *Tales of Long Ago* 78–79

monster: warning 1, 46, 95, 108n4, 125

Morgan, Jack 6

Nosferatu 3, 98, 100, 108n5

Ovid 55, 57

Oyeyemi, Helen: *White Is for Witching* 5, 8, 168–171, 175, 180–181, 184, 185n2

Pan 3, 7, 49–66, 66n3, 66n4

Pasolini, Pier Paolo: *Salo* 209–**211**, 212

Poe, Edgar Allan: "The Fall of the House of Usher" 144, 147, 176, 177, 179, 185*n*1
Pope Joan 102, 103; *see also* Tarot
pornography 6, 9, 139–140, 206, 208, 215, 216, 218–221; *see also* Marquis de Sade
Punter, David 62, 64, 66*n*5, 145, 162*n*1, 169

Radcliffe, Ann 123, 126, 126*n*2, 145, 243*n*8
Radway, Janice 45
Rohmer, Sax: "In the Valley of the Sorceress" 35
romanticism 2, 52–53, 189, 223, 230–231, 237–238, 243*n*7
Ruskin, John 19

Said, Edward 34; *see also* colonialism; imperialism
SelfMadeHero 188, 194
Senf, Carol 27*n*12, 127*n*10
Sforza, Francesco 94, 101, 102, 108*n*8, 108*n*9; *see also* Tarot
Shelley, Mary: *Frankenstein* (film) 115; *Frankenstein* (novel) 135, 163*n*5; Frankenstein's Creature 2, 3, 114, 133, 135, 179
Showa Japan 69–70, 72–73, 81–83, 85, 87*n*1, 88*n*10
Showalter, Elaine 62
The Silence of the Lambs 142–143
Skal, David 114
skullfucking 222–223
Smokey the Bear 236
The Society for Psychic Research 41; *see also* ghost; spiritualism
Spasojevic, Srdjan: *A Serbian Film* 5, 9, 206, **216**, 218–**219**, 221, **222**, **223**, **224–225**
spiritualism 30, 33, 41, 42, 53, 66*n*1; *see also* The Society for Psychic Research
Spooner, Catherine 1, 168; *see also* Gothic Commodification
Stead, William 42, 47*n*7
Stevenson, Robert Louis: *Strange Case of Dr. Jekyll and Mr. Hyde* 59, 66*n*5, 125
Stoker, Bram: Count Dracula (character) 7, 17–18, 20–21, 24, 27*n*8, 27*n*10, 59, 60, 98, 101, 113–114, 117–118, 146, 183, 185*n*3; *Dracula* (novel) 7, 12–13, 16, 19, 23–25, 27*n*7, 27*n*10, 46, 92, 112, 115, 117, 125, 138, 150, 169, 181–183; *Jewel of the Seven Stars* 35
(The) Sublime 6, 161, 187, 188, 189–191, 194–199, 200–**202**
Swinburne, Algernon: *Atalanta in Calydon* 57; "A Nympholept" 49, 57–59, 66*n*4

Tarot 8, 92–99, 101–107, 108*n*2, 108*n*3, 108*n*7, 108*n*8; "L'Amoreaux" **100**; "La Maison Dieu" **96**; "La Mort" **96**; "La Papesse" **95**
transgender 155–157; *see also* Queer Gothic

Uncanny 3, 16, 51, 64, 147, 153, 174, 175

Vampirella: comics 119; radio play 108*n*1
Verdi, Guiseppe: *Aida* 37–38
Vietnam 7, 126*n*3, 239
Victorian: New Woman 30–32, 40, 44–45, 46*n*3, 62; occult 46; reading 6–7; science 16, 23–24, 64; social degeneration 12, 20–24, 61; time 62–63
Visconti, Maria Bianca 94, 102; *see also* Tarot
Visconti, Matteo 102; *see also* Tarot
Von Kleist, Heinrich: "On the Marionette Theater" 231, 233, 232, 242*n*1, 242*n*4
Vyers, Bertha 29, 46*n*1

Walpole, Horace: *The Castle of Otranto* 108*n*5, 144
Warner, Marina 2
Weird Fiction 7, 8, 50, 65–66, 69–70, 76, 79, 88*n*6, 155; *see also* Hodgson, William Hope; Lovecraft, H.P.
Wilde, Oscar 66*n*5, 210
Wright, Alexa 9*n*1, 111, 117, 126*n*5, 130

Žižek, Slovoj 214, 215

www.ingramcontent.com/pod-product-compliance
Ingram Content Group UK Ltd.
Pitfield, Milton Keynes, MK11 3LW, UK
UKHW041936140426
5217IPUK00014B/510